Preface to the FIRST EDITION

This book is not intended as a thorough study of the cinematographer's contribution to American film; such an endeavor would fill several volumes. Rather, this is more of an overview of American films, stressing the role of the cameraman. The introductory essay attempts to survey this field in a general manner, focusing on various highlights and lingering to take note of outstanding work along the way.

But the core of the book is the interviews themselves, for these five men represent a distinctive cross-section of cameramen over the years. Their comments are based on experience and are surprisingly candid; because of this, they provide rare insight into both their own careers and the world in which they worked.

This book could not have been written without the kindness and generosity of David Chierichetti, who was instrumental in getting this project off the ground, and who participated in the interviews; the late Arthur Miller, whose dedication to the field was an inspiration and whose help to the author will not soon be forgotten; the interviewees themselves, who all were exceedingly kind—Hal Mohr, Hal Rosson, Lucien Ballard, and Conrad Hall; and William K. Everson, Herman G. Weinberg, Tom Jones (Walt Disney Productions), Tom Grey (Universal Pictures), William S. Kenly (Paramount Pictures), Gary. Shapiro (Columbia Pictures), Hal Sherman and Alan Rogers (20th Century Fox), George Stevens, Jon Davison, Lou Valentino, and Jerry Vermilye.

When I embarked upon this project, I knew very little about cinematography. I immersed myself in the subject, and largely through the efforts of the people named above, I learned a great deal. Doing this book has been a revelation for me. I hope that the reader may share in this feeling in the pages ahead.

LEONARD MALTIN

CONTENTS

INTRODUCTION: A Survey of Hollywood Cinematography

Since film itself is only seventy-odd years old, it can be easily understood that film study and criticism are still in an embryonic stage. There is widespread feeling that the 1970s will be the Film Decade and, if so, perhaps we will find ourselves finally coming to terms with various aspects of film which have been either ignored or poorly treated thus far.

It was not until the 1960s that, generally speaking, the director came into his own, outside of the industry itself and the relatively small coterie of film buffs. The "auteur theory," which originated in France, spread to America, endorsed by critic Andrew Sarris. In brief, the theory says that the films of a true auteur (that is to say, a good director) all bear his indelible signature in their style, theme, etc. Suddenly, such long-ignored men as Allan Dwan, Douglas Sirk, Samuel Fuller, and Budd Boetticher found themselves revered alongside such acknowledged masters as John Ford, Alfred Hitchcock, and Howard Hawks. Identifying films by their titles or stars became passé, and phrases like "It's an early de Toth" or "a minor Siegel" came into usage.

The auteur theory had opponents as well as adherents, but the results of its popularity hurt everyone. Many film critics and writers became so immersed in the work of the director that they dismissed the contributions of everyone else connecting with filmmaking. It is no insult to any director to acknowledge the assistance he received from his cast, writer, editor, composer, and staff of technicians. Yet this unjust view of filmmaking continued to dominate film literature for several years.

Now, as we enter the enlightened '70s, however, a welcome breeze of rationality is drifting into film study. Some of the auteur theorists are mellowing and beginning to admit that other people were involved in their favorite films; more time is being devoted to other people behind the scenes. Best of all, recognition is finally coming to the cinematographer.

Surely everyone knows that somebody has been shooting all those pictures we've seen, yet how many people can name two cameramen in the history of motion pictures? Even film buffs have been shamefully neglectful of these men, with fame coming to just a handful—James Wong Howe, Karl Freund, Billy Bitzer.

Yet what more obvious person to admire and study than the man who is actually putting what we see on film? As the novice begins to find out more about cameramen, he realizes just how vital this craftsman is to the making of a film—that there is more to his job than merely looking through a viewfinder and shooting what he sees.

Here we begin to tread on dangerous ground. For in learning about the cameraman it is quite possible to start shutting out *his* associates in discussing a given film. In-deed, the cameraman can become an auteur in our minds, and we can easily make the same mistake with him that many made with the director.

An argument for the cameraman-as-auteur can find strong support, even in the interviews contained in this book. One can read Arthur Miller's comments about working with Henry King, or Lucien Ballard on Henry Hathaway, and conclude that it is really the cameraman who is exercising a personal style in filmmaking, not the director.

But what about Josef von Sternberg, who actually shot some of his own films in collaboration with a cameraman? Or John Ford, who never looked through a viewfinder (according to Miller), but was able to leave his personal mark on every one of his films?

No, it is too easy to make blanket statements about who was more important, and chastise one man because another was responsible for a certain scene or effect in a given film. The answer is clear: filmmaking has always been, and always will be, a collaboration . . . a merging of talents, with each man doing his job to the best of his ability. And in certain cases, one of the team will outshine the others, or one will have to compromise in order to satisfy a colleague.

With this thought in mind, we can now examine the work of great cameramen, focusing on their particular contributions and putting aside, for the time being, the work of their collaborators. But please remember that the others are there and that without them the cameraman might have nothing to photograph.

When the motion picture camera invention was perfected, in the 1890s, it required one man to operate it, to point the lens at whatever he wanted to shoot, and to turn the crank that advanced the film, frame by frame, and expose the strip of celluloid. More likely than not, this same man then took the roll of film into a darkroom and developed it. It is highly probable that the men who first performed this feat were the same men who perfected the camera itself. Thus, they were the first cameramen.

Having invented this machine, however, men like Thomas Edison were eager to move on to other fields, and did not spend their time shooting additional film. That chore was passed on to others, but even for these opera-tors, film was still an invention, a gadget with which to experiment. Early films were primarily devoted to re-cording events (a train passing by, a man and woman kissing, a gentleman sneezing) and experimenting with trick devices.

Not until the turn of the century did stories first appear on film. One of the major figures in this transition in America was Edwin S. Porter, a young man who had held a variety of odd jobs, but whose affinity for machines and electrical equipment led him to the Edison Company. He worked closely with the new projection equipment, and after installing projectors and traveling with a tent show that featured movies as its highlight, he began to photograph his own films. At first he worked free-lance, selling much of his product to the Edison Company, which needed films to supply its various kinetoscope parlors and theaters. In 1899, Porter became a full-time employee of Edison's, turning out an impressive amount of film every week for public consumption.

One of the major influences on Porter was the work of a Frenchman named Georges Méliès. Méliès, a magician and theatrical entrepreneur, was one of the first to be attracted to film's possibilities and around the turn of the century he started making what remain today some of the most imaginative films of all time. His unique understanding of the "tricks" film could accomplish, combined with his imagination and sense of humor, produced a long series of dazzling motion pictures, where the unreal became real before your very eyes.

Porter acknowledged his admiration for Méliès, and for several years concentrated his energies on making his own special-effects films, with varying degrees of success. The aphorism about "nothing new under the sun" is especially valid in the world of film, when one sees how many devices thought to be revolutionary in recent years were actually first implemented in the first decade of the century. Color, sound, 3D, double exposure, split screen, animation . . . all of them were attempted by Porter, Méliès, and other motion picture pioneers.

Porter is also credited with being the first man to use films to tell a story, and this is the turning point in our chronicle. In such films as THE GREAT TRAIN ROBBERY, Porter used the motion picture *not* as a recorder of events but as a communicator, dramatizing a story and telling it in cinematic rather than theatrical terms. A gradual but vitally necessary process was that which separated the motion picture from the theatrical method of presenting a story as on a stage, with the action somehow removed from the audience. Porter helped to *involve* the movie audience by frequent changes of scene, and what is reputedly the first instance of parallel action in a film; that is to say, showing two successive events which, in the story, are happening at the same time. As elementary as this sounds today, it was an important step at the time.

But for all Porter did—and his accomplishments cannot be denied—he never evolved into an artist. The mechanics of filmmaking always meant more to him than anything else. Arthur Miller recalls being told by an associate of Porter's, Hugh Ford, that "if Ed Porter could have decided on one job that he wanted to do, whatever it was, be it writer, director, producer, cameraman, he'd have been the best in that particular job."

Miller continues, "His fault was that he couldn't light in one job. The first picture I ever photographed alone was for him. He had built—see, he took part in building the sets, too—four-inch-high boards off the side of the set, and he had some tar paper, which he had coated with tar, and some water in there. The edge of it ran off the edge of the set. It was a sort of a back yard of a villa. Lights had come in then; we began to use spots on special occasion made by the Kliegl people. I had learned enough to know that to get a reflection in the water I'd have to look at the sun and get it low enough, go on the other side, and I'd get the reflection. Same theory here. So I got a spotlight, put it on an angle to the camera near this pond that he had built, and I got the reflection in this water. He knew I knew my business, as good as it was in those days, which wasn't very good, but he'd come up and ask me, 'Have you got the pressure plate closed? Are you sure you've got this . . . ?' He didn't trust anybody; he had to oversee the whole thing. I was up on a parallel, maybe three feet high, shooting this thing, and he was off perhaps two feet from the angle of the camera. He kept glancing over and he didn't see any reflection in the water. Naturally, from where he was standing he wouldn't; he had to get in line with the camera. So when the scene was over, he said, 'Did you get the reflection in the water?' He had a guy off on the side with a stick, making ripples in the water. I said yes. He said, 'Well, I didn't see it.' I said, 'But you have to see it right from the camera.' He said, 'Well, you go over there and wiggle the stick, let me look through the camera.' So I wiggled the stick, he looked through the camera, and he saw that from this angle you'd see it. Well, we took the scene again, and *he* went over, took the stick, and did the wiggling. The actors just went on performing the way they pleased, with no direction. They just did it. He didn't realize that motion pictures had developed into specialties: directors were developing who did nothing but direct; cameramen did nothing but photograph; some laboratory men had come into the business who did nothing but develop film. Everybody was beginning to specialize. But he couldn't take it—he had to be all over the place."

Around the same time, another ambitious young man *did* decide to specialize. His name was G. W. "Billy" Bitzer, a former electrician who started shooting film in the 1890s; among his early triumphs were footage of William McKinley receiving the Presidential nomination in Canton, Ohio, in 1896, and the Jeffries–Sharkey championship bout in 1899. For the latter occasion, Bitzer installed four hundred arc lamps above the boxing ring! As general know-how man at the Biograph company, Bitzer did a little bit of everything, but his prime interest was in the camera.

When a young actor named D. W. Griffith turned to directing and secured a position at Biograph in 1908, the first one to assist him was Bitzer. Out of this first collaboration grew one of the legendary twosomes in motion picture history. Bitzer remained Griffith's cameraman for the next sixteen years; so close was their relationship and so much was their product a result of genuine teamwork that even today one rarely discusses one man without mentioning the other. Indeed, it is difficult to judge, if one is inclined to do so, exactly who was responsible for what. It is really a moot question. When Griffith came to Biograph, he was an actor, and not an especially good one at that. Bitzer, on the other hand, was already a veteran of the movie world. Yet both men learned and grew artistically during their association. Bitzer later recalled, "All through the following sixteen years that I was at his side he was not above taking advice, yes, even asking for suggestions or ideas. He always said to me, 'Four eyes are better than two.'"

Bitzer and Griffith are credited with such innovations as the close-up, soft focus photography, the iris, the fade-out, and back-lighting. It is possible that they, or Bitzer himself, did devise some of these filmmaking tools, but in dealing

D. W. Griffith looks pleased with the scene he is directing for
THE LOVE FLOWER *(1920). Billy Bitzer is at the camera, Bert*
Sutch is one of the observers.

with an era when every day brought innovations, the
discovery is of secondary importance. What matters is
how Bitzer and Griffith used these tools in their impressive
short films as well as such classic features as THE BIRTH OF
A NATION, INTOLERANCE, and BROKEN BLOSSOMS. They
were never employed as gimmicks but as artistic aids in
telling a story.

Harry Potamkin wrote, in a highly sophisticated analy-
sis of motion picture photography in a 1930 issue of the
Theatre Guild magazine: "The first use of the close-up
[sic] in the movement of a narrative film was made in
THE MENDER OF NETS, in which Mary Pickford acted and
which Griffith directed and Bitzer photographed. . . . We
may note here that in America the close-up has remained
a device for effect. In Europe it has evolved as a structural element and has attained, in THE PASSION OF JOAN
OF ARC, the eminence of a structural principle.

"It was he [Bitzer] who originated the soft focus. . . .
In America, again, we have not gone on with these mod-
ifications of the literal in film photography. It is in Europe
we find their continuation and extension. Cavalcanti films
THE PETITE LILY through gauze to depersonalize the characters, and Man Ray sees his character through a mica
sheet which grains the picture and renders it liquid consti-
tuency.

"The mind of the American film, regarding both content and approach, is literal; and that is why the American

film is still rudimentary, and why no one here has extended or even equalled the compositions of Griffith or logi-
cally developed the innovations of Bitzer." This is one
man's opinion, of course, but it does show the overwhelming respect and admiration which Griffith and Bitzer
earned right from the start.

But these two men were alone in their filmmaking
goals. While they exercised artistry in communicating
ideas and sought visual beauty in their finished product,
the rest of the American film industry was taking a different turn. The general trend was toward entertainment for
the masses, an equally honorable aspiration for any director or producer, but one which brought with it a different
set of rules. Art for art's sake was jettisoned. Good photography, even creative photography, was encouraged—
as long as it was an integral part of the picture and not a
self-indulgent exercise in aesthetics.

Lest anyone think that this made cinematography less
of a challenge, it should be explained that filmmaking was
still in its infancy at this time. Natural light was still the
prime source of illumination; cameras were still cranked
by hand; the orthochromatic film the cameramen used was
far from perfect, being insensitive to blue. These obstacles
were only a few of the many critical problems cameramen
faced just to get a decent picture on the screen. And the
only answer was trial and error; there were no precedents
to follow, no books to consult, no experts to ask. The
great cameramen who emerged during this period (including those who are interviewed in this book) spent every
spare moment experimenting on their own, trying to learn
the many secrets of motion picture photography. Once
assigned to shoot a picture, they were on their own, and
had to know what they were doing.

In the early days, the cameraman also worked in the
laboratory, developing his own film. While extremely hard
work, doubling behind the camera by day and in the
darkroom by night, it was invaluable training. It taught
these men about exposures and filters; what they could
and could not do with the camera, and how to utilize light
to the best advantage. It also showed them what could
and could not be corrected in the developing stage.

On top of other duties (and it must be remembered
that cameramen generally did not have assistants at this
time—they were the one-man cinematography department), many cameramen were responsible for taking still
pictures of every film for advertising and publicity purposes. Still photography was the pathway to motion picture photography for many men, including James Wong
Howe, who got into the film business in 1917. The story
of how he became a cameraman is indicative of the
challenges a cinematographer faced at that time, and a
vivid description of the casual nature of Hollywood moviemaking.

"I was one of four assistants with Cecil B. DeMille,"
Howe recently told a television interviewer. "I was with
him for about three years, then I became what we called a
second cameraman. We didn't have operators in those
days. The second cameraman would set his camera as
close as he could to duplicate the shot of the first
cameraman, and that negative was used to send over to
Europe. It was called a foreign negative. Now we can
duplicate and send a dupe over. So you graduated from
assistant, to second, and from second you went to being
chief photographer, and in 1922 I made my first picture.

Director F. W. Murnau (right), Karl Struss (standing), and Charles Rosher (seated) make a shot of George O'Brien for SUNRISE *(1927).*

It was called DRUMS OF FATE, with Mary Miles Minter. I had photographed a portrait of Miss Minter with my little camera, and she liked it. I enlarged it and gave it to her. She said, 'Oh, I look lovely in this picture; could you make me look like this in the movies?' I said, 'Why, yes.' So two or three months later, I'm called in, and they congratulate me, to go down and get my camera—I'm now Mary Miles Minter's cameraman. And she was one of the *big* stars. They said, 'She wants to talk to you, Jimmy.' I went down, knocked on the door of her dressing room, and she had the picture lying on her dressing table. She said, 'You know why I like these pictures, Jimmy? Because you made my eyes go dark.' She had pale blue eyes, and in those days the film was insensitive to blue, and they washed out. And I didn't realize how I'd made her eyes go dark! I walked, and stood where I took the pictures, and there was a huge piece of black velvet. Something told me, 'Well, it must be a reflection. The eye is like a mirror. If something is dark, it will reflect darker.' So I had a frame made, cut a hole in it and put my lens through, and made all her close-ups that way. It helped her, because it blocked out all the accessories, and the people watching her, and she liked it because it made her eyes go dark. That's how I became a cameraman. After a couple of pictures, Hollywood in those days, each star had his own crowd, they'd have parties, and the news spread around that Miss Minter had imported herself an Oriental cameraman, and he makes her eyes go dark by hiding behind a piece of black velvet. Everybody who had light blue eyes wanted to have me as their cameraman!"

This was the age of the star system, of course, and many stars jealously clung to certain cameramen who made them look good, and knew their business. Charles Rosher, a London-born photographer who moved to America in 1909 and made a name for himself by photographing the famous Pancho Villa newsreels, as well as many Hollywood films, was soon hired by Mary Pickford, literally the number-one star in Hollywood. Rosher remained with her for twelve years, and Pickford's films were widely acknowledged as being the best photographed films in Hollywood. Rosher's knowledge of lighting, along with his experience in still photography and his impeccable taste, made his reputation justified. Undoubtedly his masterwork was SUNRISE (1927), one of the great classic films, directed by F. W. Murnau, and co-photographed by Karl Struss. A moody, sensitively played film with a particular emphasis on the visual, SUNRISE is a German-oriented film (it was Murnau's first in America), but with a lighter touch than most authentic German products. Its elaborate mounting cannot be exaggerated; the very thought that it was done largely on Fox's back lot is staggering. But Rosher was an artist, as was Struss, and together with Murnau they created one of the most hauntingly beautiful films of all time.

Other cameramen were identified with certain stars, and in some cases, with directors, but some of the best cameramen never received recognition and remain ignored to this day. The reason is simple: they believed in functional photography, camerawork that was so good it would go unnoticed. Two of these unsung heroes were Rolland "Rollie" Totheroh, Charlie Chaplin's cameraman, and Elgin Lessley, Buster Keaton's cameraman.

Comedy is an exacting art, no matter what aspect one cares to examine. But in silent-screen comedy, photography was one of the most important factors: it had to be razor-sharp for the audience to catch everything that was happening; framing had to be precise, since the action was liable to depend on something occurring at the extreme top or bottom; the cameraman had to be versatile and inventive in order to capture many crazy stunts on film. The photography had to be perfect in order for the comedies to be funny; sight gags are only good if they look real. Both Totheroh and Lessley had the skill and dedication to accomplish what was required for the comedies they filmed, and their exceptional work should not be forgotten.

Rolland Totheroh was a staff cameraman for Essanay Studios when Chaplin arrived there in 1915. Chaplin was directing his own films by this time, and he liked working with Totheroh; the feeling was mutual, and Totheroh remained Chaplin's cameraman through MONSIEUR VERDOUX, in 1947. In many ways, Chaplin's best films are the dozen two-reel comedies he made for the Mutual company in 1916 and 1917; they include such classics as EASY STREET, THE PAWNSHOP, and THE CURE. Appropriately, the photography of these films is also in many ways superior to that of the later, more elaborate, productions. Chaplin's biographer, Theodore Huff, wrote, "The photography in the Mutuals has remarkable clarity, especially in good prints." Totheroh knew that the secret of good photography in a comedy is to show the action on screen to the best possible advantage. Directorially, he and Chaplin knew exactly what setup would be right for each scene. Looking at a film like EASY STREET, it is impossible to find a shot that doesn't do its job in the best possible way; there are close-ups, medium-shots, and long-shots; the camera dollies forward and backward to show Chaplin, a policeman, patrolling his block; it intercuts a long-shot with a medium-shot in order to catch one of Chaplin's subtle moves when the villain is preparing to beat him up. Totheroh made a valuable contribution to Chaplin's best comedies, and Chaplin knew it; few of his professional associations were as durable as that with Totheroh.

Buster Keaton's brilliant comedies of the 1920s depended on elaborate sight gags, and Keaton, being the artist and perfectionist he was, knew that if the audience

Charlie Chaplin examines the camera in his second film, KID AUTO RACES AT VENICE *(1914); cameraman Frank D. Williams is at the left, director Henry Lehrman at the right*

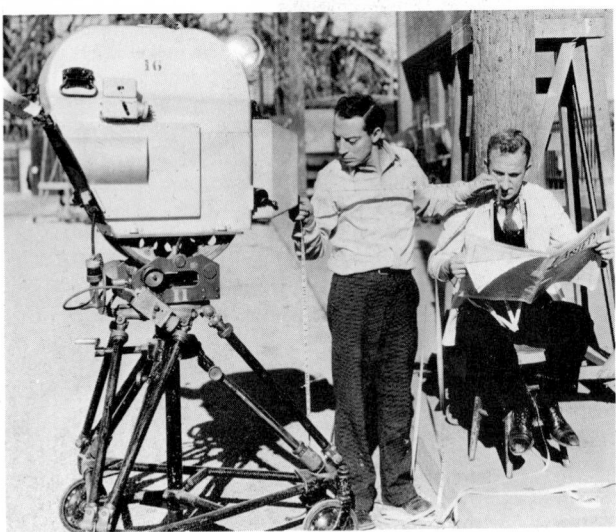

Buster Keaton checks the focal length from lens to Schnozzola, with Jimmy Durante on the MGM lot (ca. 1932).

couldn't see the gags were really happening, they would fall flat. The man who helped him achieve this goal was Elgin Lessley, whom Keaton had met when Lessley was shooting Fatty Arbuckle's comedies several years before. Like Chaplin, Keaton, when he became a star, assembled a production unit to do his comedies; it was composed of some of the top comedy writers, supporting players, and technicians in the business, united by one bond: their dedication to make the best comedies possible. No expense was too great, no task too complex for these men.

In 1921, the unit devised an overwhelming comedy idea which became THE PLAY HOUSE. Its focal scene showed a minstrel show onstage, with nine blackfaced performers doing a song-and-dance routine. They were all to be Buster Keaton (this was the climax of a series of shots showing absolutely everyone in the theater, from the orchestra to the audience, to be Buster—literally scores of Keatons). Keaton told Rudi Blesh, years later, "Actually, it was hardest for Elgin Lessley at the camera. He had to roll the film back eight times, then run it through again. He had to *hand-crank* at *exactly* the same speed *both* ways, *each* time. Try it sometime. If he were off the slightest fraction, no matter how carefully I timed my movements, the composite action could not have synchronized. But Elgin was outstanding among all the studios. He was a human metronome."

Such an endeavor was part of the excitement of making films in the silent era, especially for a man like Keaton. The effort was tremendous, but imagine the satisfaction these men enjoyed when viewing their finished product; indeed, it was something to be proud of. The sheer mechanical genius of Keaton's SHERLOCK, JR. is awesome even today, with photographic devices that have never, but never, been equalled. The film stars Keaton as a movie projectionist who, in a dream, walks into the movie screen and becomes part of the film. But before he blends in with the action on the screen, he remains a separate entity, and is confounded by the fact that although he remains stationary, the backgrounds continually change behind him. Thus, as he dives into a billowing surf at the oceanside the scene changes and Buster lands on a piece

of solid ground—the new background.

Rudi Blesh summed it up quite nicely while discussing another film in his book *Keaton:* "No estimate of OUR HOSPITALITY is complete without mention of Elgin Lessley's camerawork. Its clarity and beauty, altogether exceptional then, are uncommon even by today's standards. Shots such as the views of the locomotive silhouetted on a mountaintop against the towering summer clouds are of particular beauty. Among the many things that keep Keaton's best silent films modern—despite lack of sound, color, and wide screen—Lessley's photography must be included."

If one is seeking justification for the fact that so many cameramen never received recognition, it must be found in an explanation of Hollywood moviemaking at the time. Technical advances were coming to the aid of the cameraman during the 1920s, and photography in general was improving. At the same time, the studios were becoming the giant film factories that were to reign for the next thirty years, built on a foundation of high-quality filmmaking done quickly and efficiently.

The fact of the matter is, that by the 1920s Hollywood had reached a zenith in pictorial quality. Even unimportant B pictures were well photographed, and elaborate, major films had a luster that had never before been seen on the motion picture screen—indeed, it is a quality that Hollywood never really recaptured. Look at a picture like THE BELOVED ROGUE (1927), with John Barrymore, photographed by Joseph August, with art direction by William Cameron Menzies. It is one of the most visually stunning films ever made. Then watch a two-reel comedy like Laurel and Hardy's ANGORA LOVE (1929), photographed by George Stevens. It's just a twenty-minute short, but it is also beautifully filmed, amazingly vivid, with a full range of contrasts—qualities that might have been lacking from many feature films just ten years earlier.

One of the main reasons Hollywood became the moviemaking capital of the world was the technical brilliance which distinguished its films. By the late 1920s, this standard had established itself, and a large number of cameramen were on hand to maintain it.

Meanwhile, something was happening in Europe. In Germany, in particular, a handful of men were creating films that were not only popular and critical successes, but major contributions to the ranks of film classics. The names of these films—THE CABINET OF DR. CALIGARI, THE GOLEM, METROPOLIS, THE LAST LAUGH, VARIETY—remain on the lips of film students today as prime examples of artistry within the cinema medium. And naturally, one of the major contributors to this German Golden Age was the cameraman.

In fact, it was virtually *one* cameraman, Karl Freund, who made his mark on the German cinema at this time by photographing most of these milestone films. For Freund, as for so many others, it was a matter of being in the right place at the right time. Born in 1890, he was working at odd jobs when, at the age of fifteen, he heard of a job opening for an assistant projectionist. He applied for the job, worked up to become a head projectionist, and before long was intrigued enough with the workings of the motion picture to talk his way into being hired as a cameraman.

The demand was great for a young man of his skill and enthusiasm, and Freund was kept busy from that time on. By 1920, he had worked with virtually all of the pioneers

Gustav Fröhlich, Fritz Lang (director), and Karl Freund filming METROPOLIS
(1926).

of German film—most of whom were still feeling their way; such men as Ernst Lubitsch, Emil Jannings, Robert Wiene, F. W. Murnau, Conrad Veidt, Paul Wegener, Carl Mayer, Erich Pommer, and Fritz Lang. With Wegener, he photographed his first classic film, THE GOLEM (1920), in collaboration with Guido Seeber. The tale of a statue which comes to life in a Jewish ghetto of Prague is an impressive work, involving some striking and imaginative trick photography when the figure is first conjured into existence in a mystical ceremony.

Through the early 1920s, Freund photographed Germany's most important films, working with its greatest filmmakers. In 1924 he collaborated with the great director F. W. Murnau on what is widely considered to be one of the greatest films ever made: THE LAST LAUGH. A simple but moving story, told completely in cinematic terms (there are no subtitles), THE LAST LAUGH stars Emil Jannings as an aged but magnificently proud doorman at one of the city's finest hotels. His spotless uniform is his symbol of respect and authority, and he wears it as a suit of armor. A young, callous manager at the hotel decides

to "retire" Jannings and, as a kind gesture, gives him a token job as a washroom attendant. To Jannings it is as if his very life has been taken away. He no longer stands proud and erect but, instead, shuffles along and hides his face in shame. His mind numbed, he cannot even perform his simple washroom duties efficiently. As he changes, so does the attitude of his friends and neighbors, who scorn and laugh at the man they so recently admired.

Mood and atmosphere are everything in THE LAST LAUGH, and the camerawork is largely responsible for their creation. The lighting and photography of the washroom, as well as its physical location in the hotel, make it seem more like a dungeon. The streets outside, once bright and gay for the busy doorman, are now drab and haunting. In one famous scene where Jannings, still a doorman, drinks too much at a party, Freund strapped the camera to his waist, in order to get some shots from the intoxicated Jannings' point of view.

As with every great film, THE LAST LAUGH was the result of a collaboration of artists. The producer was Erich Pommer, who distinguished himself early in his

A production still from METROPOLIS, *with Freund, wearing a white overcoat, barely visible in the upper right-hand corner. The actor at the lower left is Rudolf Klein-Rogge.*

career as a creative administrator, and who cared as much for aesthetic values as he did for the business of making a movie. The director was Murnau, one of the most visually oriented of all directors, who knew the full potential of the film medium. The scenarist was Carl Mayer, whom Freund called "the only 100 percent screenwriter I've ever known." And the star of the film was Emil Jannings, an outstanding actor who amassed a gallery of unforgettable performances over the years.

Like his colleagues, Freund was not a flash-in-the-pan, and THE LAST LAUGH was but one of his notable achievements. He went on to photograph VARIETY (1925), another classic, directed by E. A. Dupont, again a basically simple story of human relations set against the backdrop of a circus. First-person photography, moving camera, dramatic lighting, and meticulous composition were once again used to their full advantage, with such famous scenes as the one where Freund mounted his camera on a trapeze. With director Fritz Lang, Freund helped make METROPOLIS (1926) a filmmaking landmark. This futuristic

film, made on a tremendous scale, involved more special effects than any of Freund's previous endeavors; needless to say, they were carried off beautifully.

After a dazzling decade in Germany, highlighted by many technical achievements, Freund was brought to America, first as a cameraman and then as director. In the former capacity his early talkie work in the 1930s included such notable films as DRACULA, John Ford's AIR MAIL, and the dazzling James Whale melodrama THE KISS BEFORE THE MIRROR. As director, Freund distinguished himself with THE MUMMY, one of the all-time great horror films, and MAD LOVE, a remake of the German classic THE HANDS OF ORLAC which, although largely ignored, ranks alongside the accepted horror classics of the 1930s. In 1936, he returned to cinematography, and was put under contract by MGM, where he photographed CAMILLE, with Greta Garbo, THE GOOD EARTH, a brilliantly detailed production which won Freund an Academy Award, and BLOSSOMS IN THE DUST, a fine example of three-color Technicolor at the height of its powers.

Freund, at the left, filming THE GOOD EARTH (1937), *for which he won an Academy Award. Director Sidney Franklin is seated in front of the camera; the actors are Charley Grapewin and Paul Muni. Note the spotlight positioned outside the window to produce a back-lighting effect.*

After prolific work at MGM, Universal, and Warner Brothers into the early 1950s, Freund was one of the first major cameramen to venture into the field of television. He was director of photography for I LOVE LUCY, and subsequently supervised the filming of all shows at the Desilu studio. His approach to television filming is one of the factors that keeps I LOVE LUCY a fresh experience even in the 1970s.

By 1959 Freund was tired of television work, and he retired from cinematography, although his interest in the art and science of photography was as keen in his final years as it was when he first entered the field. He died in 1970 at the age of eighty; his contribution to the film art cannot be exaggerated.

In Hollywood, cinematography was at its zenith in the 1920s. Typical examples of outstanding work were seen in WHITE GOLD (Lucien Andriot), THE SON OF THE SHEIK (George Barnes), THE PONY EXPRESS (Karl Brown), THE GREAT K & A TRAIN ROBBERY (one of scores of Westerns

shot by Dan Clark), FLESH AND THE DEVIL (William Daniels), WHITE SHADOWS IN THE SOUTH SEAS (Clyde DeVinna), THE THIEF OF BAGDAD (Arthur Edeson), OR-CHIDS AND ERMINE (George Folsey), UNDERWORLD (Bert Glennon), DON JUAN (Byron Haskins), THE KING OF KINGS (J. Peverell Marley), THE MERRY WIDOW (Oliver T. Marsh), WHAT PRICE GLORY (Barney McGill), THE VOLGA BOATMAN (Arthur Miller and J. Peverell Marley) THE WEDDING MARCH (Ben Reynolds and Hal Mohr), SEVENTH HEAVEN (Ernest Palmer), WINGS (Harry Perry), SUNRISE (Charles Rosher and Karl Struss), THE DOCKS OF NEW YORK (Hal Rosson), LA BOHÈME (Hendrik Sartov), THREE BAD MEN (George Schneiderman), THE PATSY (John Seitz), SPARROWS (Karl Struss, Charles Rosher, and Hal Mohr), THE MAN WHO LAUGHS (Gilbert Warrenton), plus untold other films shot by other leading cameramen of the day, such as Edward Cronjager, Lee Garmes, Harry Fish-beck, Ray June, and Alvin Wyckoff.

One reason for this pinnacle of pictorial beauty in Hollywood films was the European boom during the

1920s. Many home-grown filmmakers were put to shame by such imports as Karl Freund's German films, and other examples of European cinema. Hollywood's first reaction was to hire as many of the foreign filmmakers as possible, and indeed, there was a mass exodus to Hollywood in the late 1920s, including the aforementioned Freund, Murnau, Lubitsch, Alexander Korda, etc. But in addition to having these masters in America to produce new pictures, the foreign invasion spurred many domestic filmmakers (often by "request" of studio heads) to improve their own product, imbue it with the continental touch that audiences seemed to be enjoying so much. The competitive spirit asserted itself and was in large part responsible for Hollywood's own pictorial golden age.

Then came sound. It is difficult to envision the mass hysteria that Hollywood experienced when the success of Al Jolson in THE JAZZ SINGER made it clear that if the studios wanted to stay in business, they would have to make talkies. It was almost as if the movies were being reborn from the audience's point of view, for over the next two years, seemingly all previous criteria for judging or enjoying a movie went out the window. All that mattered was sound.

And so it was, for the most part, with cameramen. From the relaxed camaraderie that the best cameramen enjoyed on the set with top directors at the major studios, the "sound stage" became a hotbed of tension, with everyone trying to prove himself capable in the new medium. Directors, stars, and writers who were enjoying tremendous success in silent films suddenly found their heads on the chopping block. Even cameramen suffered, the most famous case being that of James Wong Howe, who chose this inopportune time to take a vacation to the Orient. He had been very successful in silents, but upon his return he couldn't get a job. Studios insisted that he didn't know talkie technique, and therefore wouldn't hire him. It took several years for Howe to regain this lost ground.

Hal Mohr's interview in this book best captures the situation the cameraman faced in the early talkie era. But while it is true that sound technicians were most despotic during this time, one should not fall for the legend that every early talkie was filmed like a stage play, with a

An elaborate set-up for an apparently simple scene in GOLDEN BOY (1939) *with William Holden, Adolphe Menjou, and Barbara Stanwyck. Director Rouben Mamoulian is standing to the left of the camera, and Freund is signaling to his crew from in front of the spotlight.*

stationary camera and stilted, awkward techniques. Some filmmakers *did* understand sound and realized immediately that it was merely an addition to the medium they had already mastered.

One need only go to the field of comedy, again, for an easy example. Laurel and Hardy, the consummate clowns of the late 1920s, had a few awkward efforts at the outset of sound, but by June of 1929 they showed, in MEN O'WAR, how easily they could adapt to talking pictures, without sacrificing cinematic know-how or eliminating visual humor.

SUNNY SIDE UP (1929), directed by David Butler and photographed by Ernest Palmer and John Schmitz, opens with a five-minute crane shot that examines every square inch of a tenement block, roaming up and down the street, into windows and along the sidewalk. WOMAN TRAP (1929), directed by William Wellman and photographed by Henry Gerrard, features an impressive tracking shot down a hospital corridor, during which the microphone picks up snatches of conversations as it passes people in the doorways. THE BIG TRAIL (1930), directed by Raoul

Walsh and photographed by Arthur Edeson, is one of the best outdoor epics ever filmed, and, but for one obvious glass shot representing a sunset, the photography is sparkling.

One device used in early talkies that makes for great annoyance today was the use of silent footage whenever possible. Sometimes the simplest scenes would be shot silent, in order to save time, money, and trouble in setting up sound equipment. One almost wonders if a microphone was present more than a few days when Roland West directed his famous film ALIBI (1929), photographed by Ray June. Presumably, 1929 audiences didn't notice that most of the sound was post-dubbed, and that much of the action took place in long-shot in order to enable this process to go "unnoticed." But today it is disconcerting to watch important scenes, such as those in the speakeasy, and see the obvious lack of care in matching the sound to the previously filmed action.

On the other hand, some early talkies used silent footage so deftly one hardly notices it. An example is the musical SWEETIE (1929), directed by Frank Tuttle and

Shooting the first "all-talking" feature film, LIGHTS OF NEW YORK (1928).

Rehearsing a shot for MGM's BROADWAY MELODY *(1929); note the hanging microphones. Star Charles King is between the musicians, gazing at director Harry Beaumont. James Gleason, co-author of the dialogue, is leaning on the piano, which is being played by composer Nacio Herb Brown. The actor with his thumbs under his vest is Jed Prouty.*

photographed by Alfred Gilks. This breezy little musical takes place on a college campus, and most of the exterior establishing shots are silent (one sure way to tell, of course, is that the action is much faster in silent footage, it having been shot slower than sound-film speed). But these shots are shown so briefly, and overdubbed so well, that they blend into the talkie footage perfectly.

Many filmmakers did not learn, however. Some films *were* shot like stage plays (with acting to match), and some directors continued to use silent footage well into the 1930s. One of the key scenes in William Dieterle's excellent THE LAST FLIGHT (1931), in which Johnny Mack Brown is killed during a bullfight, is rendered ludicrous by the obvious insertion of silent footage—moving so fast that the scene seems more comical than tragic.

It is nothing short of tragic that Hollywood lost the very brilliance it had sought to achieve for so long in one fell swoop. A handful of creative artists continued to shine during the transitional period of the talkies, but not until the early 1930s did the cameraman regain his former stature, and begin to take up where he had left off in 1929.

One filmmaking artist who first came to prominence at the beginning of the decade was Slavko Vorkapich, whose first film of note was THE LIFE AND DEATH OF

A HOLLYWOOD EXTRA (1928), described by the Museum of Modern Art as one of the first American expressionist films. Written and directed by Robert Florey, with close-ups by Gregg Toland, it was designed, photographed, and edited by Vorkapich. The whole film was made for $99 in Florey's kitchen, Toland's garage, and other such exotic locales. It remains an avant-garde classic today, and it is safe to conjecture that its reception was the springboard for Vorkapich's unusual career.

Born in Yugoslavia in 1898, he was educated in Budapest and Belgrade. As a young man he traveled to Paris, and then New York, where he worked as a commercial artist. He moved again, to the West Coast, and in 1922 secured a job designing the sets for Rex Ingram's THE PRISONER OF ZENDA. From that time on he remained in Hollywood, making portraits, short subjects, and doing special work for Paramount. In 1930 he signed a contract with RKO, where he stayed for four years, making the credit line "Montage effects by Slavko Vorkapich" a familiar slogan to astute film-goers.

One of Vorkapich's earliest film assignments was a very ordinary soap opera called NO OTHER WOMAN (1933), starring Irene Dunne and Charles Bickford. What placed it out of the ordinary was Vorkapich's work: a surreal composite of newspaper headlines when Bickford is sent

A Vitaphone sound stage of the early 1930s, complete with soundproof "ice boxes" for the cameras.

to prison, an impressionistic sequence depicting his two years in prison within a minute's time, etc. Elements of the avant-garde, filmed with a great sense of pictorial beauty, hallmarked Vorkapich's montage work.

In 1934 he produced one of his most brilliant pieces of film, the prologue to Ben Hecht and Charles MacArthur's CRIME WITHOUT PASSION. Hecht wrote, years later, "There was also a brooding fellow named Vorkapich [on the film] whom we had hired through a misunderstanding. We had thought he was a movie cutter. It developed he was a montage expert. Not wanting to waste Vorky's talents and paychecks, Charlie and I wrote a montage prologue for our movie. Vorky put together four handsome minutes of Furies flying through the canyons of New York." It is an eye-popping opening for the film.

By the late-1930s, Vorkapich was on call quite often at MGM. His opening sequence for THE SHOPWORN ANGEL (1938) summarizes the varied aspects of World War One—almost a mini-documentary—within a few short minutes. His impressionistic depiction of love, introduced

by Nelson Eddy and Jeanette MacDonald's spree at an ethereally lovely springtime fair in MAYTIME (1937), is one of the most beautiful sequences ever filmed, framed by a large bouquet of white flowers against a stark black background, with an invisible hand tying them up with a ribbon.

Vorkapich continued to free-lance, as well as to make his own experimental films, for many years. During World War Two he directed a number of short subjects. He also pioneered another field, that of film instruction, at the University of Southern California, and later at the Museum of Modern Art. One of his students was Conrad Hall, who talks about Vorkapich's influence in his interview in this book.

Several other men chose another specialty during the 1930s: process-screen work, or as it is sometimes called, rear projection. In the early days of filmmaking, virtually all special effects were done in the camera with special mattes, multiple exposure, and other tricks of the trade. By the 1920s, the "matte shot," in which a character is

Lionel Barrymore and John Arnold with Arnold's patented soundproof camera, which Barrymore used when he directed MADAME X *and* THE UNHOLY NIGHT *at MGM in 1929.*

superimposed against another background by special work in the laboratory, came into use. The device was used sparingly, however; most filmmakers preferred to keep their films as realistic as possible (a notable exception was Cecil B. DeMille, who used matte shots as early as 1922 in MANSLAUGHTER, and later became one of the prime culprits when it came to bad optical effects). In the early 1930s, however, another device was introduced: the process screen. This enables a character to stand in front of a screen on a sound stage and appear to be anywhere in the world—with the background projected on the screen behind him. This observer does not pretend to understand the technical workings of this device, but one thing is certain: there is good process work, and there is bad. When it is good, it serves a definite function, saving a filmmaker the trouble and expense of going out on location with an entire company. When it is bad, it betrays the essence of the motion picture and is a discredit to the filmmakers who expect their audience to believe the story they are telling.

The telltale signs of process work are easy to spot: the background is not as brightly lit as the characters in the foreground. The background may be grainy or fuzzy. The proportions of the characters in the foreground may not match that of the objects in the background. Fox's Will Rogers vehicle MR. SKITCH (1933) was supposed to have Rogers and family traveling west, yet it was clear they never stepped out of the studio to make the film. This is true of many pictures, but one becomes painfully aware of the phoniness when Rogers and Charles Starrett, the leading man, are supposed to be walking through Grand Canyon National Park. They are walking on a treadmill, well-lit, sharply focused in the foreground, as the sights of Grand Canyon, in gray contrast, pass behind them, out of proportion and just a little too fast. Rogers' STATE FAIR (1933) also had a lot of process work, but cameraman Hal Mohr explains in his interview how they tried to work around it. For a *good* example of process work, see THE CLOCK (1945), another example of a film shot entirely in a studio, even though it takes place in New York City.

The master of process-screen photography is Farciot Edouart. A career choice came rather naturally to the young man born in California; his father was a portrait photographer, and the youngster was exposed to the magic of photography early in life. In 1915, he became an assistant cameraman at Realart Studios in Hollywood. When the United States joined World War One, he enlisted in the Signal Corps, but through red tape was not assigned for photographic work. Instead, he ended up taking the Corps' cinematography course at Columbia University. He was so good that after graduation he was asked to stay on as an instructor. After a stint as teacher, he went on to Europe for active duty, both during and after the war. By 1921, he was settled again in Hollywood. He joined Paramount Pictures, where he spent most of his career. At first he made "glass shots," paintings of set extensions on optical glass which, when positioned in front of a camera, would make the set seem like more than it was. From there he progressed to the complicated "blue-backing" process. This was essentially the matte-work system of the 1920s, an incredibly exacting method of placing actors in a studio against an artificial background and making it look real. But it was Edouart's training ground, and when in 1930 the process screen was introduced, he adopted it immediately, and became one of its chief practitioners in Hollywood (his closest peer was Vernon L. Walker, another fine technician whose home base was RKO). Edouart's official title was Head of Paramount's Transparency Department. The more general title of Special Photographic Effects went to Gordon L. Jennings, whose equally outstanding work encompassed miniatures and other such production details.

The fact that the quality of their work varied sharply from picture to picture can probably be attributed to the technical caliber of their collaborators—that is to say, the cameraman and director on the specific film.

It is a fact, for instance, that Cecil B. DeMille, for all his skill as a director and his greatness as a showman, did not have an eye for such details as the quality of process work. Indeed, one would think that a director of DeMille's stature would simply shoot on location when certain scenes were necessary; but instead, one repeatedly finds the most flagrant use of interior sets and process shots for the most elementary sequences in DeMille's films. THE PLAINSMAN (1936) is full of unconvincing process work that puts a damper on the action sequences of that film (to make matters worse, the footage was reused by Paramount three years later for their film GERONIMO. It was just as bad as ever—one simply cannot get excited about a group of cowboys fighting against a tribe of Indians who are riding on a fuzzy screen behind them).

Then, for contrast, examine the work of Alfred Hitchcock from this same period. In FOREIGN CORRESPONDENT (1940), a key sequence takes place at sea, with a dozen survivors of a plane crash sitting on the detached wing of the submerged aircraft in a stormy sea. The scene was shot in a studio tank, with the waterline blending into the process screen just behind the airplane. Yet only the most meticulous examination of the sequence would reveal this procedure—most assuredly, few people in a typical audience would be able to detect how it was done. The film was photographed by Rudy Maté, designed by William Cameron Menzies, with special effects by Lee Zavitz. A year later, in Hitchcock's MR. AND MRS. SMITH, Carole Lombard and Gene Raymond are stranded at the top of a parachute jump. In reviewing the film, the *American Cinematographer* magazine praised Vernon L. Walker's achievement: "His work here is excellent, for although you know it must be a process shot, you are never forceably reminded of the fact."

That phrase captures the essence of special effects: really good effects should make you forget that they *are* effects. Take, for example, the case of an actor playing a dual role. If the optical work is skillful, you may forget that you're watching one man photographed twice. If the work is below par, you won't be able to think of anything but.

Double exposure scenes are usually the work of the cameraman himself, or, in some instances, a collaboration between the cameraman and the special effects expert. One of the earliest examples of great double exposure work was in Mary Pickford's LITTLE LORD FAUNTLEROY (1921), photographed by Charles Rosher. *Wid's Daily* (the forerunner of *Film Daily*) said in its review of the film, "The double exposures are the finest that have ever been made in the history of the business. When Mary Pickford kisses herself as 'Dearest,' and hugs herself, and when both characters walk off together, one ahead of the other—well, it's almost uncanny."

Rosher explained to Kevin Brownlow in *The Parade's Gone By* how he built a special camera stand to ensure perfection. "Steel girders formed the framework; the base was lined with sandbags, and a huge, hollow block of steel supported the pan and tilt head. The contraption could be moved around on casters, but when I'd lined the shot up, packs secured it to the floor. Jacks held the pan head rigid, too, once it had been positioned. In front of the camera was the matte frame, and I moved the matte as Mary moved. The whole setup was so solid that you could jump around the floor without shifting it a thousandth of an inch!"

Many years later, James Wong Howe dazzled audiences with his work in the exquisite PRISONER OF ZENDA

Technicians prepare to film a process shot of Dick Powell and Lizabeth Scott at sea in PITFALL (1948). *The sea will be projected from behind onto the screen in back of them.*

William Cameron Menzies checks a camera angle against one of his preliminary compositional sketches for THE DEVIL AND MISS JONES (1941).

(1937). A film replete with visual splendor, one of its many highlights was a scene where Ronald Colman, as a happy-go-lucky vacationer, shakes hands with his look-alike, the future king of a Ruritanian country. Howe told Jack Jacobs how he did it: "Split screen was used, of course, but not the usual straight line split. I placed a three-by-four-foot optical glass three feet in front of the camera. Ronald Colman shook hands with a double. The double's head and shoulders were matted out with masking tape on the glass. The scene was photographed, the camera shutter was closed, and the film was wound backward to the beginning of the scene. We then masked out everything but Colman's head and shoulders and re-photographed the scene. This required great accuracy on the part of everyone involved, especially on Ronald Colman's part as he spoke and reacted to himself. We did all this fourteen times. The third try was the best."

Not as famous, but equally beautiful, was Harry Stradling's work on THE CORSICAN BROTHERS in 1941, with Douglas Fairbanks, Jr., playing twin brothers. Once again, the double exposure scenes were amazingly real. For an idea of how the same idea can be ruined, one need only turn to another Dumas swashbuckler, THE MAN IN THE IRON MASK, filmed in 1939. Producer Edward Small (who also did CORSICAN) was pinching pennies throughout the production, but with the skill of director James Whale, the finished product showed few signs of its economic background. One exception was a scene where Louis Hayward confronts his look-alike: the feat was accomplished by having Hayward step in front of a process screen of himself and conduct a conversation. It was an idea that probably looked good on paper, and done with fine process work, it could have been effective. Unfortunately, it was not.

Some cameramen had to be engineering geniuses to calculate certain devices, and in an age before there were scores of experts to handle any problem that might arise, the cameraman had to be a one-man edition of *Popular Mechanics*. Almost every veteran cinematographer can tell you at least one unique gimmick he had to dream up to meet a certain situation. It was a case of not having any precedent to follow; these men had to devise a solution to every problem, and in doing so, they blazed new trails in cinematography.

Consider this newspaper account of a difficult shot that was needed for D. W. Griffith's THE SORROWS OF SATAN

(1926): "Fred Waller, trick camera expert ... was to photograph the figure of Satan, falling as a tiny figure out of Paradise, down through space, increasing to enormous proportions as he falls, and splashing into Hades. The camera was placed on a truck that moved forward on a long track to create the effect of the figure's increase in size. The figure itself dropped in a slanting line across a large white drop. Waller had to make exact mathematical calculations coordinating the movement of the camera with that of the falling figure and allowing for dimensions of height, width, and thickness. Also—and here is where the fourth dimension comes in—he had to allow for the retarded speed of the falling body as it increased in size. This made necessary what appears to be a fourth dimensional calculation. He used to be a professor of differential and integral calculus and molecular physics, and anybody familiar with these subjects can figure it out for himself and see just how simple it all is." Unfortunately, this prodigious effort was for naught; the shot described did not appear in the final print of the film.

Or take the famous MGM picture THE LADY IN THE LAKE (1946), Robert Montgomery's first directorial effort, photographed by Paul C. Vogel, in which he decided to shoot the whole movie with the camera as hero. Superficially, it sounds simple, but it required much experimentation and many difficult setups. For instance, when Montgomery wanted the "hero" to light a cigarette, it required three men: one to act as left hand, one to act as right hand, and one man lying under the camera puffing smoke upward in front of the lens. Breakaway sets were used so the "hero" could walk around at will. When leading lady Audrey Totter was to kiss the hero, she had to kiss upward, so it would look natural on screen.

While many men were specializing in these unusual areas of photography, others in the 1920s and 1930s were concentrating on another seemingly less complicated, but actually equally exacting field: color photography. From the 1920s through the 1950s, color in movies was something special; it was not taken for granted, as it is today. It was an expensive process, and studios used it only for special films.

The chief exponent of color in Hollywood was the Technicolor company. Founded by Daniel F. Comstock and Herbert T. Kalmus, who had been experimenting with a color-film process since 1915, the firm was incorporated in 1922 after achieving its first success in a Metro picture called TOLL OF THE SEA. Technicolor at this time was a two-color process (red and green) made possible by the exposure of two negatives, which were combined on the finished print. The novelty of color, especially this pleasing early color (which, although it excluded blues, did have a pleasant effect, and particularly appealing flesh tones) enabled Kalmus, who became president of Technicolor, to convince various studios to let him film portions of their most important films in color. Most of the companies took advantage of this system and used Technicolor inserts in such major productions as BEN HUR, THE TEN COMMANDMENTS, THE MERRY WIDOW, and THE PHANTOM OF THE OPERA. Features filmed entirely in Technicolor included Douglas Fairbanks' THE BLACK PIRATE, but these full-color features were still rare.

When a studio wanted a color sequence, they contracted with Technicolor, which assigned one of its own cinematographers to join the production staff, with a special Technicolor camera. Often the Technicolor cameraman would shoot the sequence himself, but just as often he would serve as "consultant" to the cameraman on the feature, checking to see that there was enough light, that the colors would not clash, that there would be separation (i.e., making sure the color of a man's suit would not blend into the color of the background), etc. Arthur Miller's interview in this book provides a first-hand account of working under these conditions.

One of the principal Technicolor cameramen was Ray Rennahan. He filmed the landmark picture TOLL OF THE SEA, the first three-color Technicolor film, a short subject called LA CUCARACHA, and the first three-color Technicolor feature, BECKY SHARP, in 1935. Three-color Technicolor opened new horizons for Kalmus and Company, as well as for the motion picture industry, which had been tiring of the two-color process. Three-color produced a lush, vivid (and, some modern critics contend, unreal) result, covering the entire color spectrum in a dazzling array. The popularity of the new process could be seen in Technicolor's record books: their laboratory processed five million feet of film in 1932 (just before three-color was introduced)—and in 1946 it developed over one *billion* feet.

Ray Rennahan became one of the busiest men in Hollywood. In 1941 he said, "There's a definite advantage to working as we Technicolor cinematographers do. We *do* get around! I think we get a greater variety of work and experience than almost any other group of cinematographers. It's not only that we're constantly working in different studios, on different pictures, and with different production cinematographers as partners. We also run the fullest possible range of production conditions and subject matter. One day, for instance, I may be working on a really big major production, like GONE WITH THE WIND or my present assignment, BLOOD AND SAND; a few days after that assignment closes, I may be sent to some other studio to direct the photography of a little three- or four-day short subject, or even a commercial film, in either of which instances time and resources are likely to be as limited as they were abundant on the major studio 'special' ... and the results on the screen have still got to be good."

The experience paid off for Rennahan, however. After having collaborated with most of the top cameramen in Hollywood, he left Technicolor and became a solo cinematographer, almost concurrently with the development of Monopack Technicolor, which employed one negative instead of three, eliminating the need for a special Technicolor cameraman. With his unusual background, Rennahan naturally specialized in color films, and his first endeavor, FOR WHOM THE BELL TOLLS (1943, on which he was assisted by Karl Struss), was an auspicious debut, followed by such films as LADY IN THE DARK, DUEL IN THE SUN, CALIFORNIA, THE PALEFACE, A CONNECTICUT YANKEE IN KING ARTHUR'S COURT, and THE WHITE TOWER. Rennahan remained active through the late 1950s, and has served as president of the American Society of Cinematographers.

After Hollywood accustomed itself to the talking picture, in the early 1930s, imagination and creativity returned to filmmaking, and a new crop of outstanding cameramen established themselves. Chief among these was Gregg Toland, who had started in the silent era, and by the late 1920s was assistant cameraman to George Barnes, working at the Samuel Goldwyn studio. Eventually he became a chief cinematographer, collaborating with Barnes on several films, and working on his own for both Goldwyn and other studios. But in 1934, Toland started to

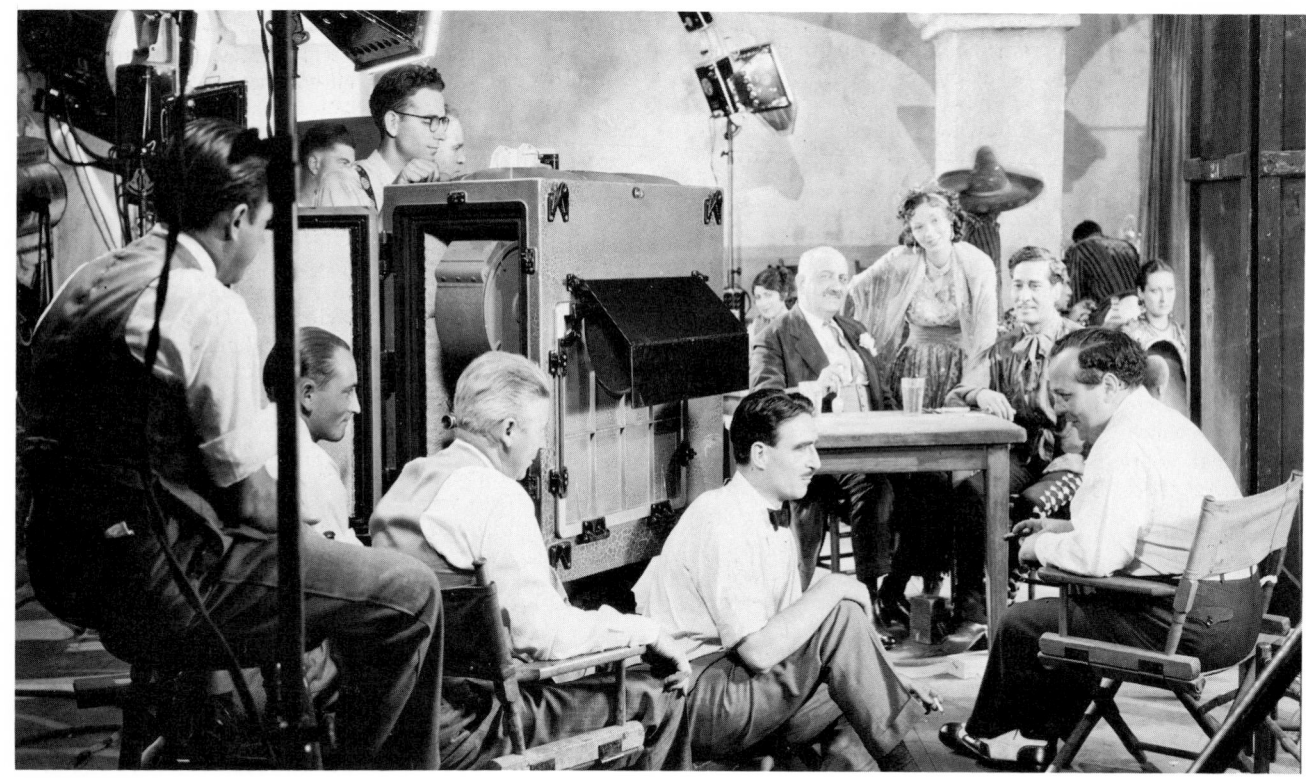

The first three-color Technicolor camera is seen filming the first live-action three-color film, the short subject LA CUCARACHA (1934). Cameraman Ray Rennahan talks with director Lloyd Corrigan; in the background are cast members Paul Porcasi, Steffi Duna, and Don Alvarado.

The Technicolor camera goes outdoors for RAMONA (1936), with specialty cameraman William V. Skall checking a light reading; his camera operator Arthur Arling is behind him, while the man in the straw hat is assistant director Robert Webb.

display the qualities that were to separate him from the ranks of competent cameramen and make him stand out as one of the greats. This development was made possible largely by Sam Goldwyn. Goldwyn was a rarity among producers in Hollywood; he owned his own studio and personally supervised every film made there. Naturally, he was interested in making money, but more than most of his colleagues, he was also interested in quality, and would go to any lengths to achieve the finest results possible. In addition, he admired and fostered talent; he knew how good Toland was, and eventually signed him to the most lucrative contract awarded any cameraman in Hollywood.

1934 was the turning point, for it was that year that Goldwyn brought a Russian actress named Anna Sten to America, determined that she should rival such continental stars as Garbo and Dietrich. The producer let it be known that nothing would be spared in the making of Miss Sten's films. Thus, NANA, WE LIVE AGAIN, and THE WEDDING NIGHT were incredibly sumptuous productions, affording Toland the opportunity to create pictorial beauty as he never had before. Historian George Mitchell called Toland's work in WE LIVE AGAIN "some of the most breathtaking photography ever recorded by a motion picture camera."

On loan-out to 20th Century Fox, Toland shot such beautiful films as LES MISÉRABLES (1935) and THE ROAD TO GLORY (1936), but most of his great work was done for Goldwyn, in collaboration with director William Wyler. The films are among the all-time classics of Hollywood: THESE THREE (1936), DEAD END (1937), WUTHERING HEIGHTS (1939), THE WESTERNER (1940), THE LITTLE FOXES (1941), and THE BEST YEARS OF OUR LIVES (1946).

The creative spark of this team was best captured by Richard Griffith in his monograph on Samuel Goldwyn. Discussing WUTHERING HEIGHTS, he wrote of a photographic problem the film posed for Wyler and Toland: "The setting for the film was not the moors of Yorkshire, but a wilderness of the imagination. To have reproduced on the screen any large expanse of landscape would have been to chain the story and its characters to the actual. Instead, Toland and Wyler devised a close-in camerawork which, in every shot, seemed to show only a small part of the whole scene, in which roads, crags, housetops, and human figures were revealed in outlines against dense grays or blacks. Thus was created a chiaroscuro country of the mind in which the passionate Brontë figures can come credibly alive. It was a daring experiment, owing something to the example of the once-admired German studio films of the twenties, and like them it might have seemed today to exude a faint odor of plaster and machinery. That the spell holds is due to the fact that cameraman and director were aware of the peril in which they stood; instead of proudly parading their artifice, they make all

Setting up an overhead shot for the grand finale of FOOTLIGHT PARADE (1933) *is cameraman George Barnes, as Busby Berkeley, director of the dance sequences, gives instructions.*

Genius at work: Orson Welles and Gregg Toland set up one of the warehouse scenes in
CITIZEN KANE (1941).

vague, moony, nebulous; each shot is whisked away and replaced by its reverse angle as quickly as the action allows."

Every film Toland shot during this period is worthy of detailed discussion—indeed, it seems sacrilegious to omit mention of any—yet one film stands out, reasserting its brilliance and significance year after year: CITIZEN KANE (1941). Orson Welles has said that Toland came to him when the film was being prepared and asked to work on it. The astounded Welles asked him why. "It's your first film," Toland replied, "and you won't know what you can't do." Indeed, the film attracted much attention for doing what had been considered tabu: showing ceilings on sets (many setups were lit upward), for example. Welles received acclaim for his work as director, co-scenarist, and principal actor, but Toland was not lost in the shuffle. Astute observers realized the importance of the step he had taken in using depth of field, or as Toland

called it, forced focus. This involved shooting scenes from a considerable distance—certainly farther back than one normally would go—achieving the effect of keeping both foreground and background of the scene in focus, and letting the eye take in much more than it would be able to in a conventionally filmed sequence. Forced focus was not a gimmick; it was a cunning device that worked particularly well in this film. CITIZEN KANE stands as one of Toland's great achievements.

He worked with John Ford on two of that director's finest films, THE GRAPES OF WRATH and THE LONG VOYAGE HOME, and during World War Two distinguished himself in the field of combat photography, as well as with a documentary film, DECEMBER 7TH, that won an Academy Award when released theatrically. He continued to work for Goldwyn after the war, but for the most part his films were glossy star-vehicles and soap operas, fine as entertainment but not particularly challenging for the

Erich von Stroheim directs GREED *(1925) while William Daniels (left) and Ben Reynolds man the cameras.*

cameraman. (One notable exception was Walt Disney's SONG OF THE SOUTH.) Toland hoped to go on to greater things when heart disease struck him down at the age of forty-four; he died on September 28, 1948. Now, some twenty years after his death, he is still revered and studied by film buffs and students alike, who realize the greatness of his work.

While most cameramen working under the studio system were versatile, of necessity, nevertheless certain ones had specialties for which they were known. Several names became synonymous with the term "glamour photography." One of the first was William Daniels. Born in Cleveland, Ohio, in 1895, he studied at the University of Southern California, and, presumably, it was while attending school that he was first attracted to the motion picture business nearby. In 1917 he obtained a position as assistant cameraman at the Triangle Studio; like many

others at this time, Daniels was young, enthusiastic, and quick to learn. By 1918 he was a chief cameraman at Universal Pictures, and it was here that he met a unique actor-director named Erich von Stroheim, forming an association that spanned several years and included the director's greatest films, FOOLISH WIVES (1921) and GREED (1923). The latter film, shot in large part in Death Valley, was Stroheim's masterpiece, a meticulous production that at once earned him the title "genius" and branded him a merciless, eccentric madman. The rigors to which his company was subjected during filming are legend, and the final product, lovingly assembled by Stroheim, lasted forty reels—nearly eight hours. Reluctantly, Stroheim cut his film in half in order to reach a compromise point with his studio, Metro, but the company took the film out of Stroheim's hands and cut it in half again before releasing it. Even in its current state, GREED remains a brilliant film. No small credit is due cameraman Daniels, who managed to capture both the harsh reality Stroheim favored in certain scenes, as well as the highly dramatic moods of others, with unnatural lighting and morbid atmosphere.

Filming GREED brought Daniels to MGM, where he remained under contract for the next twenty-two years. It was here that he earned his reputation as a glamour specialist, particularly for his work with Greta Garbo, whose favorite cameraman he was. Norman Zierold explained, "Daniels studied Garbo's face and body with great care. He saw immediately that she was least attractive in repose, best in close-ups or long-shots, indifferent in the intermediate range. She was better seated or lying down than standing—Daniels later shot some of her best scenes, in FLESH AND THE DEVIL and QUEEN CHRISTINA, with Garbo reclining."

MGM in the 1930s was, of course, *the* glamour studio of Hollywood, and Daniels upheld the tradition with such lush, luminescent films as DINNER AT EIGHT, GRAND HOTEL, NAUGHTY MARIETTA, and MARIE ANTOINETTE, along with most of Garbo's pictures. At this time, Walter Blanchard wrote of Daniels in the *American Cinematographer,* "[He] has always striven to avoid what he considers the two greatest—though diametrically opposite—photographic pitfalls: on the one hand, routine, 'formula' photography; on the other, exhibiting too spectacularly individualistic a style. . . . In seeking to avoid these pitfalls, Bill Daniels has developed a style completely his own. Two successive Daniels pictures may not look in the least alike, yet both will be instantly recognizable to the camera-minded viewer by the sure precision that marks every phase of their camera treatment—a certain singing smoothness which for all its variety of technique and artistic mood is as distinctive as anything on the screen."

Daniels stayed with MGM through 1946, leaving to join Universal, where initially he had his first opportunity in many years to break away from glamour and remind people of his talent as a cameraman. BRUTE FORCE, a tingling prison picture, WINCHESTER 73, a grim Western, and HARVEY, a whimsical fantasy, were among his all-time finest efforts. And his work on Jules Dassin's classic semi-documentary, NAKED CITY, won him an Academy Award.

Daniels free-lanced for the rest of his career, working on such diverse assignments as PLYMOUTH ADVENTURE and CAN-CAN. Probably his finest work in the 1960s was on

Daniels films Greta Garbo and Dorothy Sebastian in A WOMAN OF AFFAIRS (1929) *while director Clarence Brown looks on, at the left.*

Peter Ustinov's LADY L (1966), a visually beautiful film in which Sophia Loren never looked more ravishing. Daniels even tried his hand at producing in the 1960s, on two Frank Sinatra pictures, ROBIN AND THE SEVEN HOODS, and ASSAULT ON A QUEEN, but he remained faithful to his first love, cinematography. He died in June, 1970, shortly before his last film, MOVE, was released.

William Daniels had a long, distinguished career as a cinematographer, but, he told Norman Zierold in his book *Garbo*, "The saddest thing in my career is that I was never able to photograph her [Garbo] in color. I begged the studio. I felt I had to get those incredible blue eyes in color, but they said no. The process at the time was cumbersome and expensive, and the pictures were already making money. I still feel sad about it."

Another glamour specialist whose career spanned many years was Harry Stradling. British-born, in 1910, he was the nephew of Walter Stradling, for many years Mary Pickford's cameraman. The younger Stradling spent most of his life in this country, establishing himself as a chief cameraman in the 1920s, but assigned to unimportant films (he even photographed short subjects for Pathe in

1929). It was not until the mid-1930s, away from the United States, that he distinguished himself in the motion picture world. The film that marked the turning point of his career was LA KERMESSE HÉROÏQUE (CARNIVAL IN FLANDERS) (1935), a delightful French film which won instant acclaim around the world. One of its admitted aims was to capture the quality of Flemish paintings on the screen; director Jacques Feyder and Stradling worked so well together, not only in achieving this goal, but in producing a great film, that when Feyder received an offer from British producer Alexander Korda to make a film in England, he took Stradling along with him. The result was another excellent, although often neglected film, KNIGHT WITHOUT ARMOUR (1937), starring Marlene Dietrich and Robert Donat. Besides presenting low-key, impressionistic backgrounds representing Moscow, the film handed Stradling the task of filming one of the screen's great stars, Marlene Dietrich, not long after her famous series of visual orgies with Josef von Sternberg. Stradling met the challenge, and conquered it with finesse. KNIGHT WITHOUT ARMOUR is a beautifully photographed film.

It led to other prestigious British assignments—indeed,

Daniels checks a light reading on location for VALLEY OF THE DOLLS (1967) *in New England.*

Harry Stradling and director William Wyler (in director's chair) film a scene with Barbra Streisand (holding dark fur) for FUNNY GIRL *(1968).*

some of the most important films being made in England at the time—PYGMALION, THE CITADEL, and JAMAICA INN. After this string of successes, Hollywood beckoned, and Stradling returned to America, resuming his career in Hollywood as one of the top men in his field. Of his work on Alfred Hitchcock's MR. AND MRS. SMITH, the *American Cinematographer* wrote, "His treatment of Carole Lombard is a definite asset to that young lady. She is not and never has been a subject suited to conventional camerawork and lighting. Stradling gives her a simple, forceful key-lighting rather reminiscent of the style with which Josef von Sternberg, ASC, made Marlene Dietrich famous. For Miss Lombard this treatment does two things: it first accentuates her good features (while concealing her less favorable ones) and, secondly, gives her a more decided visual personality, which is greatly to her advantage. To put it bluntly, she looks better in this picture than she has in many another."

(Miss Lombard, who had a small scar on one cheek, was very aware of photography, and Stradling complimented her at the time, telling an interviewer, "She knows as much about the tricks of the trade as I do! In close-up work, I wanted to cover her scar simply by focusing the lights on her face so that it would seem to blend with her cheek. She was the one to tell me that diffusing glass in my lens would do the same job better. And she was right!")

Stradling did exceptionally fine work in such films as SUSPICION (again for Hitchcock), THE PICTURE OF DORIAN GRAY, which won him his first Academy Award, and A STREETCAR NAMED DESIRE. While never stuck in a single category, through the 1950s and 1960s, his name was always most closely linked with glamour and color. Among his assignments were the leading Technicolor films of the era, and he reaffirmed his skill in creating pictorial beauty in 1964 when he shot Cukor's MY FAIR LADY, winning a second Academy Award.

When Barbra Streisand was signed to do the movie version of her Broadway hit FUNNY GIRL, Harry Stradling was faced with the challenge of giving the star a distinctive screen image. He had to diminish her unphotogenic qualities as much as possible, yet retain the image that made Streisand unique to begin with. Through careful lighting and positioning, and some of the most expert diffusion work ever seen, Stradling won out on all points, making her most appealing, without sacrificing anything of Barbra's personality.

When Miss Streisand won the Academy Award for FUNNY GIRL, she thanked the many people who had helped her, including "dear Harry Stradling." The actress was intelligent enough to know just how valuable his contribution was, for she insisted on having him on her subsequent films, HELLO DOLLY! and ON A CLEAR DAY YOU CAN SEE FOREVER, the latter film, directed by Vincente Minnelli, giving Stradling a particularly good vehicle for his talent. Unfortunately, it was to be his last film. He died in early 1970 while filming THE OWL AND THE PUSSYCAT; like so many of his colleagues, he was active right up until his death, because, as with many others, cinematography was a way of life for Harry Stradling.

The extent of a cinematographer's contribution to the making of a film varies from one picture to another. Most of the time it is a collaboration between the director and the cinematographer; but even this is inconsistent, depending on the director's attitude, capability, and personality, as well as the cameraman's. One cameraman found himself in somewhat a unique situation during the 1930s; he was Lee Garmes, already a highly respected and talented man who was always something more than just a cameraman. Born in 1897, he started in the movie business in 1916, and worked as a second unit director, then assistant director with George Fitzmaurice, one of the leading directors of the time. He gravitated to camera work, and had extended working relationships with such directors as Rex Ingram and Mal St. Clair on great silent films including THE FOUR HORSEMEN OF THE APOCALYPSE, THE GARDEN OF ALLAH, and THE GRAND DUCHESS AND THE WAITER.

In the 1930s he photographed many of the Josef von Sternberg classics—MOROCCO, DISHONORED, AN AMERICAN TRAGEDY, SHANGHAI EXPRESS (winning an Academy Award for the last)—as well as other memorable films like Rouben Mamoulian's CITY STREETS and Rowland V. Lee's ZOO IN BUDAPEST, films made more memorable because of Garmes' skill.

Garmes always yearned to direct, and had several near-misses. In 1933 he was announced as the director of Lilian Harvey's American-made vehicle MY WEAKNESS, but was replaced before filming began. He acted as associate producer on several British films (including the abortive Alexander Korda version of CYRANO which was to star Charles Laughton), and again was announced to direct a film, starring Elisabeth Bergner, that never came to fruition. Garmes did not get his chance to direct until 1938, on a Jack Buchanan musical, THE SKY'S THE LIMIT.

He went on to film GONE WITH THE WIND (in collaboration with several other cameramen), THE JUNGLE BOOK, SINCE YOU WENT AWAY, NIGHTMARE ALLEY, ROPE, DETECTIVE STORY, and many other fine films. But he never had any assignment to compare with the offbeat trio of films he made with Ben Hecht and Charles MacArthur in 1934–1935 at Paramount's studio in Astoria, Long Island. Hecht and MacArthur, Hollywood's leading scenarists and bon vivants, signed a contract with Paramount to produce a series of independent productions which the studio would release. The two were to write, produce, direct, and supervise each film; one of their first tasks was to hire Lee Garmes as cinematographer.

Once in Astoria, however, it became evident that Hecht and MacArthur were too busy having a good time to tend to the serious and time-consuming job of setting up the production of a motion picture. Hecht wrote, years later, "My memory of our Astoria moviemaking doesn't include any glow of success or burn of failure. It is a memory of a two-year party that kept going seven days a week." He and MacArthur wanted to film the movies simply and economically; they felt directing to be unimportant, if there was a good script to start with. They considered shooting tests, making retakes, using different camera setups, all a waste of time.

But they trusted and respected Garmes, and before too long bestowed upon him the title of "co-director." It is safe to assume that without him, the movies never would have been completed. The finished products were CRIME WITHOUT PASSION, a bizarre story of a heel, played by Claude Rains; ONCE IN A BLUE MOON, an attempt to transfer stage-star Jimmy Savo's magic to the screen, and THE SCOUNDREL, a magnificent vehicle for Noel Coward, supported by a cast that included Alexander Woollcott and other Hecht–MacArthur cronies (a fourth film, SOAK THE RICH, was not filmed by Garmes, but by Leon Shamroy). They are all fascinating, decidedly offbeat films; probably the best is CRIME WITHOUT PASSION, which, although it does have an excellent script, with particularly good dialogue for Rains, owes the most to Garmes. It is filled with unusual camera angles, bizarre lighting, and even has a surrealistic courtroom montage at the beginning.

Hecht and MacArthur were right in placing great importance on a good script, but if they supplied the content for their films, it was Lee Garmes who provided the form. Hecht knew it, too, even if he didn't want to admit it on the printed page; when he was given the opportunity to direct again, later in his career, he always hired Garmes. The results were always intriguing: ANGELS OVER BROADWAY in 1940 (on which Garmes again received co-director credit), SPECTER OF THE ROSE in 1946, and ACTORS AND SIN in 1952.

Lee Garmes (seated) and crew do a complicated scene with Olivia de Havilland for LADY IN A CAGE (1964).

Director Archie Mayo (white shirt) and cameraman Sol Polito (directly below camera lens) ready a shot for THE PETRIFIED FOREST (1936) *with Humphrey Bogart, Bette Davis, and Leslie Howard. Onlookers include cast members Dick Foran, Slim Thompson, Joe Sawyer, and (seated far right) Charley Grapewin.*

Most of the studios had regular production teams in the 1930s and 1940s, both in front of and behind the camera; these people worked together to give each studio its own distinctive style, which could easily be recognized by any discerning movie-goer. You knew it was a Warner Brothers movie by the type of subject matter, the thunder of Max Steiner's music, the hard-boiled dialogue, snappy pace, inevitable presence of Frank McHugh or Alan Hale ... and the photography of Sol Polito. Born in 1892, Polito drifted into the movie industry in the teens, and became a cameraman. By the 1920s, he was a very competent craftsman, working on Westerns and action pictures by the score. In the late 1920s he joined First National Pictures, shooting Ken Maynard Westerns and various program pictures. With the Warner Brothers–First National merger, and the emergence of Warners as one of the leading studios in the talkie era, Polito's assignments became more important. With Darryl F. Zanuck in charge of production, Warners concentrated in the early 1930s on tough, lightning-paced pictures "torn from today's headlines," as some of the ads used to say. Polito's sharp, straightforward photography complemented the style of these films perfectly; among his pictures were FIVE STAR FINAL, UNION DEPOT, THE DARK HORSE, BLESSED EVENT, THREE ON A MATCH, and I AM A FUGITIVE FROM A CHAIN GANG. He photographed some of the Busby Berkeley spectaculars, as well as assorted vehicles for James Cagney, Edward G. Robinson, and Bette Davis, teamed with Warners' corps of first-rate directors (Michael Curtiz, Ray Enright, Lloyd Bacon, etc.).

But Polito was not a man of limited talent; like actors and directors, he had simply been typecast with a certain kind of picture. As Warner Brothers' style changed in the late 1930s, so did Polito's—abandoning the harsh, realistic lighting of his early pictures, for softer, more attractive effects. The height of his metamorphosis can be seen in what is probably Polito's finest film, THE SEA HAWK (1940), one of the all-time great swashbucklers, directed by Curtiz and starring Errol Flynn. There are individual scenes in this film—one, in which Flynn's pirate crew mounts a neighboring ship—that are simply breathtaking. Yet at no time is there a beautiful shot for its own sake; every frame is utilized to move the story forward. Tony Thomas, Rudy Behlmer, and Clifford McCarty, in their book *The Films of Errol Flynn*, wrote, ". . . Sol Polito's high-contrast black and white photography is a highwater mark in opulent, dramatic lighting and composition in the classic style. His and Curtiz' love of the moving camera—in, out, down, up, sweeping, or cruising laterally—was extraordinarily effective."

Director William Keighley and Polito rehearse a scene with Billy Mauch for THE
PRINCE AND THE PAUPER (1937).

In the late 1940s, Polito left Warner Brothers—it hardly seemed possible—and did a few more films before
retiring. His retirement came at around the same time
that Warners, along with most other studios, started to
slide downhill from the peak it had reached in the 30s and
40s. Perhaps it was appropriate for this master
cameraman to leave the studio at this time, rather than
suffer the indignity of training his expert eye on much of
the filmmaking that followed.

This identification of a certain cameraman with a certain studio was not always pleasing to the Hollywood
corps of cinematographers. Once a studio established a
style, it was imposed on everyone working there. In 1942,
an editorial on the subject appeared in the *American
Cinematographer:*

If anyone suggested seriously that Joe Louis defend
his championship with one hand tied behind him, or
that Joe DiMaggio bat with a cricket player's under-
hand stance, the country would ring with indignation
at stupid officialdom's attempt to shackle an outstanding performer. But in some of our studios,
something very similar seems to happen. They sign up
the best directors of photography available to them—
men who have made top reputations for individual

skill and artistry. And, judged by the results on the
screen, they seem to shackle these highly paid artists
by insisting that all photography on the lot conform
to rigid, if perhaps unwritten, regulations dictated by
the personal preferences of someone in authority. . . .
The result is [that], photographically speaking, one
picture from one of these studios looks very much
like other pictures from that studio. Any of them
might conceivably have been photographed by the
same man.

This is the same problem many artists faced during the
reign of the studio system in Hollywood. Actors, writers,
directors, as well as cameramen, were often made to
conform. But a handful of artists, in every category,
fought for artistic freedom; some won it because their
work was successful at the box office, others because they
knew how to deal with the all-powerful studio bosses.
However obtained, this freedom enabled talented men to
create, and it is their work which stands the test of time,
and which we are discussing here.

At the 1964 Academy Awards, James Stewart was
presenting the Oscar for Best Cinematography. In the
color category, he read the first two nominations: CLEO-

PATRA, Leon Shamroy, and THE CARDINAL, Leon Shamroy. Stewart hesitated a moment, then quipped, "There's three years of a man's life right there!" A glance over his filmography shows that Leon Shamroy has devoted *fifty* years of his life to the motion picture business, most of that time as a cinematographer. And if Sol Polito's name is indelibly linked with Warner Brothers, then Leon Shamroy's ought to be synonymous with 20th Century Fox. He has been with the studio almost continuously for over thirty years.

Like many other cameramen, Shamroy first learned the business by working in a film laboratory—coincidentally enough, the Fox lab—in 1920. He progressed from there to become a cameraman by the mid-1920s, filming many of Charles Hutchinson's popular action pictures for Pathe; films with titles like THE TRUNK MYSTERY, PIRATES OF THE SKY, and LAND OF THE LAWLESS. In 1928 he collaborated with Paul Fejos on an avant-garde film, THE LAST MOMENT, photographing it and earning co-producer credit as well. The film was Fejos' ticket to Hollywood (see Hal Mohr's comments in his interview in this book), but it led Shamroy in quite a different direction. He spent a year working with pioneer documentary filmmaker Robert Flaherty on an unrealized project, and another period filming scenes of the Far East as part of the Huntington Ethnological Expedition.

Back in Hollywood in the early 1930s, he joined the B. P. Schulberg unit at Paramount and filmed many first-rate pictures. One of his first, JENNIE GERHARDT (1933), a filmization of Theodore Dreiser's novel, starring Sylvia Sidney, was one of his loveliest works, with period setting and costumes produced on an impressively lavish scale. Other pictures followed at a steady clip, including a side-trip to the Hecht-MacArthur unit, where he replaced Lee Garmes as cameraman on the team's last independent picture, SOAK THE RICH. On loan-out, he filmed Fritz Lang's lovely YOU ONLY LIVE ONCE (1937), an atmospheric tale which many have called the forerunner of the 1960s' BONNIE AND CLYDE.

After a brief stay at the Selznick studio, Shamroy was signed by 20th Century Fox, where he immediately won many of the studio's most prestigious assignments. He fared particularly well with period films (THE ADVENTURES OF SHERLOCK HOLMES, LITTLE OLD NEW YORK, etc.) but tackled such diverse pictures as TIN PAN ALLEY and BUFFALO BILL. He distinguished himself particularly in the photography of Fox's Technicolor product, and won three Academy Awards, for THE BLACK SWAN (1942), WILSON (1944), and LEAVE HER TO HEAVEN (1945), all filmed in color.

In the 1950s, Shamroy worked on most of Fox's big pictures. He filmed THE ROBE (1953), the first feature film in CinemaScope; the incredibly widescreen aspect ratio (2.66:1) on this initial endeavor provided Shamroy with a challenge the equal of which he had not faced in many years. Despite unperfected lenses and general experimentation with the tremendous screen image, THE ROBE's photography caused more comment than the film's content. Whether by chance, or simply because he had been so successful with the new process, Shamroy became one of the industry pioneers in the mad scramble for new film formats in the 1950s and 1960s. He continued to film Fox's major CinemaScope pictures like THREE COINS IN THE FOUNTAIN and THE EGYPTIAN. Then in 1956 with THE KING AND I he was one of the first to utilize Fox's CinemaScope 55 process. This involved a 55mm strip of film, several times larger than conventional 35mm. The larger frame made for increased clarity in both color and definition. After shooting THE KING AND I in this process, it was decided that equipping theaters with special projectors for CinemaScope 55 would be too troublesome, and the picture was reduced to standard 35mm film. Nevertheless, the results were an improvement over those obtained with standard CinemaScope.

James Limbacher, in his book *Four Aspects of the Film,* commented, "THE KING AND I [was] marked by extremely good color rendition and very sharp focus and depth. In 1961, Fox re-released THE KING AND I in large negative form for showing at the Rivoli Theater in New York—the only time that CinemaScope 55 was shown in its original form."

That wasn't the end of widescreen experimentation, however. Two years later, Shamroy photographed SOUTH PACIFIC in still another process, Todd-AO. This was a 65mm film size which, again, yielded superior results. The reason it succeeded where CinemaScope 55 failed was that the Todd-AO projector was more versatile, being able to adapt to practically any film gauge. Once again, the photographic technique of the film put the rest of the production to shame (several of Shamroy's later pictures were also shot in Todd-AO: PORGY AND BESS, CLEOPATRA, and THE AGONY AND THE ECSTASY).

On the set of SOUTH PACIFIC, Shamroy told an interviewer, "I've made tough pictures, in the early days when we didn't have much money, but this—it's one of the biggest, but it's the toughest I ever worked on in my life! Not even to mention weather, the locations were tough—you couldn't reach them—the equipment was tremendous ... yet, you know, there's nothing like adversity for success. You work five times as hard and it shows—not in a physical sense, but in a sort of spiritual sense. You don't get any of that run-of-the-mill nonsense."

Shamroy's use of color in SOUTH PACIFIC was unique. The film was an exercise in filters—perhaps overdone a bit, but indisputably striking to the eye. Shamroy explained to Anne T. Suivne, "Everybody thinks of the South Seas as sparkling. It isn't. You get the sun here, and a rainbow here, and then it's gloomy over there. As we were walking through [the native village], I suddenly thought, 'I'd like to get something like Gauguin did with that magenta—' and that's why I used a magenta filter actually. Then, near the waterfall, I thought of Rousseau—you know, the French primitive painter—his detail, the green, the yellow seeping in. And also Covarrubias, those green ferns he had— And, over all, maybe some of the golden sunlight of Van Gogh. I shot 'Happy Talk' through a medium yellow filter—it was a dull, cloudy day, but it came out sunlight!"

Only by such experimentation, and the urge to try something new, can a cinematographer stay young and active in the film world. Shamroy has never fallen into any of the potential pitfalls, even after following such spectacular films as CLEOPATRA (for which he did win the Academy Award) with such inconsequential films as DO NOT DISTURB with Doris Day.

Most recently, Shamroy has faced a new challenge: television. He is currently shooting his first TV series, quite a step for a man who has been in demand for feature films, and thus far has been a TV holdout—but appropriately enough, it is a 20th Century Fox production, ARNIE. *TV Guide* reported that after one take during filming, the show's star, Herschel Bernardi, thanked Shamroy "for making a middle-aged Jew look like a young Gentile," and Shamroy replied, "Yeah, that's what Danny Kaye told me."

The demands of TV filming are rigorous, and coming up with quality results is extremely difficult. But if anyone can do it, it is Leon Shamroy.

How does one summarize the outstanding work of cameramen in Hollywood? It is an impossibility, for the complete story of cameramen's work is the complete story of motion pictures. Yet certain men and their achievements stand out.

Joseph L. Walker once told an interviewer, "Years ago, I decided that the real foundation of photography was the lens that made the picture. And as photography was my bread-and-butter, I decided I'd better know something about lenses. And I've been learning about them ever since." Walker's collection of lenses was the envy of every cameraman in Hollywood, and what is more important, Walker knew how to use them. His base of operations for over twenty years was Columbia Pictures, and his name is associated with virtually every great film the studio produced during that time: IT HAPPENED ONE NIGHT, ONE NIGHT OF LOVE (in which he faced the challenge of making unglamorous opera star Grace Moore an appealing heroine—and won), MR. DEEDS GOES TO TOWN, LOST HORIZON, ONLY ANGELS HAVE WINGS, THE JOLSON STORY, AND BORN YESTERDAY, to name a few. His skill is evident even in an early endeavor like the recently discovered Frank Capra film THE MIRACLE WOMAN (1931), which boasts nothing less than impeccable photography, from scenes like the one with Barbara Stanwyck and David Manners in a room lit only by a fireplace behind them, to heavily diffused day-for-night shots at the shore. Capra says today, "We worked together very closely on visual effects. He would try *anything*. We developed the idea of using a four-inch lens on closeups of women, where everything behind them would fall completely out of focus." Walker's last picture was AFFAIR IN TRINIDAD, in 1952. Since that time he has devoted himself to the technical gadgetry he has always loved. He is the inventor of the Electra-Zoom lens utilized in television camera work, and is often credited as a pioneer in the field of zoom lenses for cinematography as well.

Ray June graduated from Cornell University in his home town of Ithaca, New York, and journeyed to Hollywood. While still a young man, he became chief cameraman in the 1920s, shooting dozens of program pictures. The coming of sound brought a change in his luck; he photographed the famous early talkie ALIBI, and soon found himself in demand for top-drawer films. In 1931 he filmed what may be his all-time best picture, ARROWSMITH, beautifully directed by John Ford. Two years later, his low-key photography for I COVER THE WATERFRONT attracted notice, succeeding in striking the happy medium between the harsh realities of the story and the

Leon Shamroy works out a scene with Linda Harrison and Charlton Heston for PLANET OF THE APES *(1968).*

Frank Capra smiles for the still photographer on the set of DIRIGIBLE *(1931); long-time associate Joseph Walker is behind the camera to the right of him.*

romanticism of the leading characters. Among his other films were such Goldwyn pictures as ROMAN SCANDALS, KID MILLIONS, and BARBARY COAST, and MGM films like TREASURE ISLAND, CHINA SEAS, and WIFE VERSUS SECRETARY. Continuing to work for MGM through the 1950s, June proved himself a master once again with the brilliant color photography of Stanley Donen's FUNNY FACE in 1958, with Audrey Hepburn, Fred Astaire, and Paris as it has seldom been photographed by others.

J. Peverell Marley first came to prominence as Cecil B. DeMille's chief cameraman in the 1920s, succeeding Alvin Wyckoff. He photographed THE TEN COMMANDMENTS, KING OF KINGS, THE ROAD TO YESTERDAY, THE VOLGA BOATMAN (in collaboration with Arthur Miller—and which collaboration brought about one of the most beautiful of all silent films), and DYNAMITE, among others, building himself a truly impressive reputation. By the mid-1930s he was photographing the prestige pictures for the newly formed 20th Century company, which was soon to merge with Fox and become 20th Century Fox. HOUSE OF ROTHSCHILD, BULLDOG DRUMMOND STRIKES BACK, and FOLIES BERGÈRE were among the elegant pictures he filmed for 20th Century. The distinction between competence and excellence was never so clear as in FOLIES BERGÈRE; the basic film was shot by Barney McGill, but the two spectacular musical numbers were done by Marley. They

stood out from the rest of the film like neon signs—vivid and crystal-clear, with ingenious compositions, while the balance of the picture could only be called adequate.

Under the 20th Century Fox regime he continued to receive top assignments: KING OF BURLESQUE, IN OLD CHICAGO, and SUEZ, to name a few. In 1939 he photographed THE THREE MUSKETEERS (which he had also shot in its 1935 version) and, with the aid of expert art direction, and a top director (Allan Dwan), turned a modest production into an opulent swashbuckler which remains a fine film today. Like many cameramen, Marley married some of the actresses he photographed, notably Linda Darnell, but in the early 1940s he found himself shooting less important pictures for Fox—not even his wife's starring vehicles. So after Army duty during World War Two, he left Fox for Warners, where he shot NIGHT AND DAY and LIFE WITH FATHER, among others; one of his notable achievements at the studio was in 1953 with the 3D production of HOUSE OF WAX. Also in the 1950s, his career came full cycle when he returned to his former boss, Cecil B. DeMille, as one of several photographers on the director's last two films, THE GREATEST SHOW ON EARTH and THE TEN COMMANDMENTS. And in 1957 he capped his career with one of his finest achievements: Billy Wilder's SPIRIT OF ST. LOUIS, photographed with Robert Burks. The film was an admitted challenge to both Wilder and his

Another production shot from DIRIGIBLE. *As Capra said in his autobiography, "Blankets on cameras to keep them quiet, not warm."*

Nick Grinde perches alongside Joseph Walker's well-muffled camera to direct Regis Toomey and Barbara Stanwyck in a scene from SHOPWORN *(1932).*

Ray June (standing) and Tay Garnett shoot a scene with Clark Gable and Wallace Beery for CHINA SEAS *(1935).*

DeMille and crew (among them cameraman Alvin Wyckoff) film a scene for MALE AND FEMALE *(1919).*

Peverell Marley behind the camera, Robert Z. Leonard directing in front; the film is A
LADY OF CHANCE *(1928), with Johnny Mack Brown and Norma Shearer.*

cinematographers, an exercise in creativity under confining
conditions (namely Lindbergh's cockpit). Under contract
to Warner Brothers, Marley continued to photograph their
glossy star-vehicles and programmers into the early 1960s.
He died in 1964.

Many film technicians can be credited with longevity; it
is only a handful who have remained at the top all that
time. One of these men is Charles B. Lang, Jr., for forty
years one of the best cinematographers in Hollywood.
Born in 1902, he studied law at the University of Southern
California, but eventually succumbed to family influence
and joined the laboratory staff at Realart, which was
headed by his father. This was his entree to motion
pictures, and before long he was working his way up
through the ranks of assistant cameramen to become
second cameraman at Realart. When the studio folded, he
found odd work as first cameraman on independent
"quickies," but gladly gave it up to join Paramount as
second cameraman in 1926. He seized his first opportunity
to work as first cameraman at the studio the following
year, on a Betty Bronson comedy called RITZY. It was
considered something of a disaster, photographically and
otherwise, and Lang was instantly demoted. Analyzing
what went wrong, Lang later said that his trouble was not
having an individual style, but merely imitating Victor
Milner, Harry Fishbeck, and other cinematographers with
whom he had worked. Finally, in 1929, he returned to the
position of first cameraman with a deeper understanding

of his craft, and remained one of Paramount's best
cameramen for over twenty years.

Lang won his first Academy Award for photographing
Frank Borzage's A FAREWELL TO ARMS (1932), and it
remains one of his outstanding achievements today, a
genuinely beautiful film, filled with what Lang called
"effect lighting" and meticulously conceived mood scenes.
He followed this with standout work in such films as
DEATH TAKES A HOLIDAY, LIVES OF A BENGAL LANCER,
PETER IBBETSON, DESIRE, MIDNIGHT, ZAZA, and A FOR-
EIGN AFFAIR. His work on SEPTEMBER AFFAIR (1950), a
lovely picture directed by William Dieterle, is among his
best. Since 1952 Lang has free-lanced, and brought his
skill to such films as THE BIG HEAT, GUNFIGHT AT THE O.K.
CORRAL, and SOME LIKE IT HOT, the last proving once
again that skilled black and white photography can rival
color work any day. Most recently he has photographed
some of the most polished films to come out of Hollywood, visual treats such as CHARADE and HOW TO STEAL A
MILLION, as well as the effective chiller WAIT UNTIL DARK.
His latest credits include CACTUS FLOWER and the romantic film A WALK IN THE SPRING RAIN. And so, in the 1970s,
Charles Lang continues to dazzle just as brightly as he did
when he started over forty years ago.

What of Lucien Andriot, Joseph August, George Barnes,
Floyd Crosby, Clyde DeVinna, Elmer Dyer, George
Folsey, Tony Gaudio, Bert Glennon, Ernest Haller, Sam
Leavitt, Ted McCord, Oliver Marsh, Ernest Miller, Victor

Marley lets Margo and Burgess Meredith look at a scene from WINTERSET (1936) *from his point of view.*

Milner, Nicholas Musuraca, Ernest Palmer, Joseph Ruttenberg, John Seitz, Leo Tover, Karl Struss, Gilbert Warrenton, Stanley Cortez, Robert DeGrasse, Milton Krasner, William C. Mellor, Russell Metty, Joseph Valentine, Paul C. Vogel, Daniel Fapp, Burnett Guffey, Joseph LaShelle, Ernest Laszlo, Frank F. Planer, Philip Tannura, Robert Surtees, and so many others who have turned in fine work over the years? They all deserve discussion, but this book cannot hope to do justice to them. When the definitive encyclopedia of cinematography is written, their names will certainly rank among the top in their field.

Cinematography is a specialized field; at best, it affords unlimited creativity and artistic satisfaction. But practically speaking, the cameraman must often subordinate his feelings to those of the director. This is no discredit to the cameraman, for, after all, the director is the boss. Numerous cameramen, however, have felt the need to expand their horizons, and so have turned to direction. In such a case, the photography of a film is usually left to another man, but even so, the cameraman-turned-director is certain to have a greater concern and understanding for the visual aspect of his film than most directors without any experience behind the camera. There are many examples of cameramen who have successfully graduated into di-

recting careers; we shall discuss a few of the most prominent within this group.

George Stevens has had a distinguished career as a director; his films include ALICE ADAMS, SWING TIME, GUNGA DIN, I REMEMBER MAMA, A PLACE IN THE SUN, SHANE, and THE DIARY OF ANNE FRANK. But his first contact with motion pictures was as a cameraman. He recently recalled for us, "I had been interested in photography as a kid, as a hobby. I was in the theater world, looking for a job in the film business. There were no unions, so it was possible to become an assistant cameraman, if you happened to find just when they were starting a picture. There was no organization; if a cameraman didn't have an assistant, he didn't know just where to find one. And I learned a little bit about it; I was on a picture for four or five days. I had an opportunity to be on a set, and the assistant cameraman kept showing me things. One day I climbed a fence, and knew they needed an assistant cameraman, so I told them I was an assistant cameraman. A couple of days later, I was, but the first day or two it was pretty disas-

Opposite: *Charles Lang, Jr. (right of camera) and director Billy Wilder (left of camera) get a rear view of Tony Curtis and Marilyn Monroe in this production still from* SOME LIKE IT HOT (1959).

SL(532)PUB-14

Cinematographer George Folsey is at the camera while crew members move the base of his high-flying crane for this production number from GOING HOLLYWOOD (1933) with Marion Davies and Bing Crosby.

Jean Renoir, cameraman Lucien Andriot, and camera operator Fred Kaifer on location for THE SOUTHERNER (1944).

Bert Glennon (in white hat) anchors a camera to the top of a coach for an exciting action scene in John Ford's STAGECOACH (1939). That's Andy Devine at the reins.

Director Otto Brower (slightly hidden behind lens) and cameraman Nick Musuraca film William Gargan and Frances Dee in HEADLINE SHOOTER (1933).

trous. I knew something about photography, and I caught on quick.

"When I stayed on with [Hal] Roach, I started doing some things that they weren't doing, because they were very old-fashioned about the photography in their comedies. I worked first with Fred Jackman, who was making pictures with Rex, the King of the Wild Horses. I was a cameraman on that, and he was director; his brother was cameraman. He was first cameraman, and I—well, I wasn't second cameraman, because we did separate work—*associate* cameraman. I knew about panchromatic film, and they didn't. I had bought the plates from England, a photo store there; we got some extraordinarily good effects, and he liked it. I finished those pictures, and there was nothing left to do but photograph comedies if I

Director Mitchell Leisen (chin in hand) prepares a shot with Leo Tover's camera crew for I WANTED WINGS (1941) *with Ray Milland and Wayne Morris.*

wanted to stay with Hal Roach. I didn't like comedies, I hated two-reel comedies, but I got on the Laurel and Hardy pictures, and that was great.

"Roach used to direct a picture every now and then, and he was directing this one. About noon he said, '*You* direct it.' He would make one picture a year, or something, and he would always get the wrong story, and he'd get into trouble with it. So I said, 'Not for me.' I wouldn't do it; I wouldn't know what the hell to do with it. I thought what he was doing was silly enough, without me trying it. He insisted, and I said, 'No, I can't do it, Hal.' So he said, 'Well, what do you want to do?' I said, 'If you want me to direct a picture, let me get my own story, so I'll know what I'm doing.' So I did, and it was THE BOY FRIENDS series."

THE BOY FRIENDS films, all but forgotten today, were delightful two-reel comedies, very much oriented to slapstick and sight-gags. They had Hal Roach's mark on them, yet they were distinctive, filled with unusual camera angles and photographic ideas that are elementary today, but

were quite imaginative then—especially at the Roach studio.

Stevens has carried this visual awareness with him throughout his career; indeed, one of his trademarks is a visual device, the long, slow fade, probably best used in A PLACE IN THE SUN (1951) to juxtapose the conflict of the two life-styles facing Montgomery Clift. Stevens' success as a director has made many forget his work as a cinematographer, but the fact remains that his camerawork was outstanding, evidenced by the sparkle of the Laurel and Hardy, Charley Chase, and other comedies he filmed during the late 1920s, which can still be admired today.

Rudolph (Rudy) Maté was born in Cracow, Poland, in 1898, to an upper-class family that could afford to give their son a fine education. He studied at the University of Budapest, but a postwar depression in 1919 sent him job-hunting. He found work in a film laboratory, and followed the route of so many other careers: from lab technician to assistant cameraman. The taste of cinematography whetted Mate's appetite, and he journeyed to Vienna, where he talked his way into a job as chief cameraman for Alexander Korda (little dreaming that director Korda was also a novice at the time). Finally he settled in Paris, where he became one of that country's foremost cinematographers, particularly excelling in his work with Carl Theodor Dreyer: THE PASSION OF JOAN OF ARC (1927) and VAMPYR (1932). His outstanding reputation in Europe put him in demand, and in 1934 he accepted a contract offer from Fox Films in Hollywood. His first year in America, however, was largely unrewarding, with such ordinary films as CHARLIE CHAN'S COURAGE assigned to him (the main exception being the ten-minute Hades sequence in DANTE'S INFERNO).

That short sequence in DANTE'S INFERNO was a dazzling one, however, and it opened some eyes. Maté left Fox to free-lance, and photographed the prestige picture DODSWORTH for Samuel Goldwyn. From that time on, his films were of the highest caliber, and Maté earned a reputation in Hollywood equal to the one he enjoyed abroad. In 1940 he did one of his finest jobs, working with Alfred Hitchcock on FOREIGN CORRESPONDENT. Shortly thereafter, he was chosen by Samuel Goldwyn to replace Gregg Toland for the duration of Toland's wartime duty. Maté displayed

his talent in Goldwyn's THE PRIDE OF THE YANKEES (1942), the exceptional biography of Lou Gehrig directed by Sam Wood, starring Gary Cooper. Maté explained a cunning trick that was but one of many factors contributing to the excellence of the film: he conceived the idea of lighting Cooper from below (generally tabu) during the early part of the picture; this tended to erase the wrinkles in Cooper's face and make him look more youthful. Later, as the character aged, Maté diminished and finally eliminated the unusual lighting.

While working at Columbia during the 1940s, filming most of Rita Hayworth's films (COVER GIRL, GILDA, DOWN TO EARTH), Maté received his first opportunity to direct. Signed as cameraman on IT HAD TO BE YOU (1947), a Ginger Rogers–Cornel Wilde comedy, he was soon assuming more and more directorial responsibility, along with nominal director Don Hartman (more a writer than a director). Soon he needed another cameraman to take over *his* responsibilities (Vincent Farrar), and on the final product, Maté received credit both as co-director and co-cinematographer. This experience, however, served two purposes: it created an interest in directing for Maté, and it showed Columbia chieftain Harry Cohn that Maté was

Director Joseph Pevney (under boom) and cameraman Russell Metty set up a shot with James Cagney and Dorothy Malone for MAN OF A THOUSAND FACES (1957).

Cinematographer Burnett Guffey and director Fritz Lang go over a scene with Glenn Ford and Gloria Grahame for HUMAN DESIRE (1954).

capable of directing a film. Indeed, it was Columbia that gave him his first solo opportunity, on a thriller, THE DARK PAST. It turned out well enough to make Maté decide to remain a director, and it opened more doors for him. There followed what is probably his best film, D.O.A., a fast-paced melodrama whose realistic format has been copied many times, seldom with the success of the original. Another of his better films was the George Pal science-fiction opus WHEN WORLDS COLLIDE (1951). But throughout the 1950s, Maté's misfortune was the paucity of decent material in Hollywood; he turned out some first-rate, compact films (SECOND CHANCE—filmed in 3D, THE FAR HORIZONS, FOR THE FIRST TIME), but nothing outstanding; and the balance of his films could only be called workmanlike. He produced several of his pictures, including THE LION OF SPARTA; his final film, in the 1960s, WAS SEVEN SEAS TO CALAIS, a rather humdrum ending to a distinguished career on two continents. Maté died in 1964.

Ted Tetzlaff was born in 1903 in Los Angeles; his proximity to the movie industry is probably the explanation for his interest in films. While still a young man, he joined the camera staff at Fox, where he got his training and experience. By the late 1920s he was a chief cameraman at the fledgling Columbia Pictures, filming a steady stream of program pictures every year. Not until 1935, when he moved to Paramount, did Tetzlaff get the chance to photograph "A" pictures (RUMBA, HANDS ACROSS THE TABLE, etc.). So good was his work at this time that he secured a directing contract from the studio in 1941; the problem was to find suitable films for him to direct. WORLD PREMIERE (1941), starring John Barrymore, was not the greatest film for a directorial debut, and Tetzlaff decided to wait rather than accept another such picture. He returned to cinematography, and did a beautiful job on Mitchell Leisen's THE LADY IS WILLING (1942), one of the lushest pictures ever to come out of Columbia, with Marlene Dietrich; THE MORE THE MERRIER; and Alfred Hitchcock's NOTORIOUS, a beautifully photographed thriller.

Working at RKO as a cameraman, Tetzlaff investigated the possibility of directorial work and found that he could make the move, but only if he would work in the B-picture unit. He decided to do so, and turned out some creditable Pat O'Brien vehicles before embarking on an inexpensive thriller called THE WINDOW (1949). The Cornell Woolrich story of a boy who witnesses a murder, it

Cameraman Joseph Valentine and director Henry Koster film a balcony scene with Leopold Stokowski and Deanna Durbin for 100 MEN AND A GIRL (1937).

Director Robert Wise and cinematographer Ernest Laszlo are hoisted aloft to shoot a scene from STAR! *(1968).*

starred Bobby Driscoll as the youngster, and Paul Stewart as the murderer. It was turned out very quickly, and just as quickly earned itself a reputation as the "sleeper" of the year; a terse, tingling, thoroughly engrossing melodrama that was among the best of its genre. Over the next few years, Tetzlaff showed that just because a picture is made on a low budget doesn't mean it can't be good (A DANGEROUS PROFESSION, UNDER THE GUN, etc.). But as the 1950s waned, and the B picture faded out, so did Tetzlaff's career. His last films were hardly distinguished, not even up to his own standard from the early 50s. But a distinguished career as a cinematographer, and a fairly good one as a director, marked by one film that is widely considered to be a classic, is not a bad record for anyone.

Mrs. Natalie Kalmus, wife of Technicolor founder Herbert T. Kalmus (and the omnipresent "Technicolor consultant" on so many films), was once quoted as saying that the finest Technicolor film she had ever seen was THE RED SHOES. This writer votes for another British film, BLACK NARCISSUS. Both films were photographed by Jack Cardiff, one of the best cameramen of all time, who captured color as few others have been able to. Born in Yarmouth, England, in 1914, Cardiff had his first taste of show business as a child actor. Growing up, he developed a liking for more technical work, and pursued an interest in cinematography. He was assistant cameraman when Technicolor's Ray Rennahan went to England in 1936 to film that country's first color feature, WINGS OF THE MORNING, with Annabella and Henry Fonda. It was invaluable ex-

Cameraman Rudolph Maté (left), director Harry Lachman (in cap), and crew are trying out an unusual shot for DANTE'S INFERNO *(1935).*

Maté perches atop a huge camera platform for another angle on DANTE'S INFERNO; *with him are assistant art director Lewis Creber, assistant cameraman Werner Cruze, and Claire Trevor.*

perience for Cardiff, and evidently he learned a great deal, for not long afterward, he was director of photography on most of England's important Technicolor films: FOUR FEATHERS (1939), CAESAR AND CLEOPATRA (1946), and the brilliant series of films produced by The Archers (Michael Powell and Emeric Pressburger), A MATTER OF LIFE AND DEATH (STAIRWAY TO HEAVEN) (1946), BLACK NARCISSUS (1947), and THE RED SHOES (1948), to name several. NARCISSUS is perhaps the loveliest color film ever made, a beautiful display of pastel colors that dazzle with their richness, yet at no time appear garish, as much 1940s' color in Hollywood tended to do. THE RED SHOES, which won Cardiff an Academy Award, included a fantasy ballet sequence that enabled him to let his imagination run wild in overall conception, not just the color. The result was a brilliant sequence, the highlight of an already brilliant film.

On these outstanding films was Cardiff's reputation built, and with such follow-ups as PANDORA AND THE FLYING DUTCHMAN, THE AFRICAN QUEEN, THE MAGIC BOX, and WAR AND PEACE was it enhanced. In 1958 he was sufficiently established to venture into the field of directing, with a modest and not too successful thriller called INTENT TO KILL. Other routine films followed, including the first picture in Michael Todd, Jr.'s late, unlamented process, Smellavision, SCENT OF MYSTERY. But in 1960, Cardiff directed a meticulous, sensitive adaptation of D. H. Lawrence's SONS AND LOVERS that won world-wide acclaim and established him as a director of formidable talent. The realization of a coal-mining town, the interpretation of the difficult story (it was one of the first attempts to film Lawrence), and the handling of the actors were all superb. After this triumph, Cardiff defied convention by making an unusual move—returning to cinematography. He explained, "I haven't anything I want to direct in the immediate future, so I can go back to handling the camera with no loss of face."

Besides having "no loss of face," Cardiff racked up another winner with his next film, FANNY, considered one of the highlights of his career, and another testament to his skilled use of color. He did return to directing, however, and carved out a sturdy career for himself, with competent work on a variety of films, some of which have been duds (THE LION, MY GEISHA), and others which have reasserted his directorial talent (THE LONG SHIPS, DARK OF THE SUN). Since SONS AND LOVERS, his best picture has been the excellent biography of Sean O'Casey, YOUNG CASSIDY, which was started by John Ford, who only worked a short time on the film.

Cardiff's cinematographer on SONS AND LOVERS was a man with a solid background in British film, Freddie Francis. Born in 1917, Francis was a still photographer when just seventeen years old, and steadily progressed to become a chief cameraman at British International Pictures during the 1940s. In 1947 he turned in a first-rate job on the outstanding production THE MACOMBER AFFAIR, and through the 1950s continued to excel in such films as BEAT THE DEVIL, TIME WITHOUT PITY, and ROOM AT THE TOP. His work on SONS AND LOVERS, with Jack Cardiff directing, won him an Academy Award, and his next film, THE INNOCENTS, turned out to be what many consider his finest effort, a thoroughly absorbing film with the *impression* of ghosts subtly conveyed through his fine black and white photography.

These two personal triumphs enabled Francis to secure a director's berth in England, and since 1962 he has turned out a large number of horror films. He has a cult following among film buffs, but his current status is something of a disappointment when one considers the level of his work as a cinematographer. Some of his films, particularly DR. TERROR'S HOUSE OF HORRORS and TORTURE GARDEN, have been quite good, while others, like MUMSY, NANNY, SONNY AND GIRLY, have been atrocious. Francis is obviously a talented man, and one can't help but feel that with a wider range of subject matter, and better filmmaking colleagues, he could emerge as a first-rate director.

Cinematographers continue to turn to directing as an outlet for their talents, with varying degrees of success. William Fraker, who has distinguished himself with such pictures as BULLITT, ROSEMARY'S BABY, and PAINT YOUR WAGON, has made his debut as a director with MONTE WALSH, starring Lee Marvin and Jeanne Moreau. If this melancholy Western is indicative of his skill, he should have a long and successful career ahead of him. Other cameramen, like the late Karl Freund and James Wong Howe, have dabbled in direction, but returned to cinematography.

The most impressive transition has been that of Haskell Wexler. Born in Chicago in 1926, to a noted and wealthy family, Wexler's interest in film was apparent from the start. As a teen-ager, he started shooting his own home movies, and after graduation from the University of California, he became a professional cinematographer. He returned to his native Chicago, where he made educational and industrial films for eleven years; two of his documentaries were nominated for Academy Awards. In 1959 Wexler photographed the unusual semidocumentary THE SAVAGE EYE, produced and directed by Ben Maddow, Sidney Meyers. and Joseph Strick. This "brutally honest" view of Los Angeles received widely mixed reviews, but the undeniably provocative nature of the film gave forward steps to the careers of both Strick and Wexler.

By 1961 Wexler was photographing such interesting black and white features as ANGEL BABY and THE HOODLUM PRIEST. Established in Hollywood, he continued to turn in first-rate work on AMERICA, AMERICA, A FACE IN THE RAIN, and THE BEST MAN. In 1965 he took on the added responsibility of producing, first with a documentary, THE BUS, and then with the Tony Richardson filmization of THE LOVED ONE. All of these were fine examples of modern black and white photography at its best, but Wexler's next film brought him official recognition of that fact: WHO'S AFRAID OF VIRGINIA WOOLF won him the Academy Award for the best black and white cinematography in 1966. It was indeed a photographic marvel, and a tribute to Wexler's, as well as Mike Nichols', creativity, that the film, basically a theatrical experience, also realized its full potential cinematically. It being Nichols' first film assignment, the need for an experienced cinematographer was obvious, and the director has acknowledged the fine support he received.

Wexler then turned to color for the first time, in IN THE HEAT OF THE NIGHT. But in deference to the subject matter at hand, he tried to achieve what has been called a "black and white color," a desaturated and realistic look that is as appropriate to a film like HEAT OF THE NIGHT as it would be inappropriate to something along the order of TRUE GRIT. With the same director, Norman Jewison, Wexler then shot another color film, THE THOMAS CROWN AFFAIR, and did the exact opposite. He made the colors rich and vivid, in keeping with the depiction of Steve McQueen's lavish life-style. The results were extremely

Haskell Wexler explains a scene to Peter Bonerz for MEDIUM COOL *(1969).*

effective. Additionally, THE THOMAS CROWN AFFAIR was highlighted by four attractive multi-image sequences, which were Jewison's idea, but were carried out in large part by his expert cameraman.

These successes behind him, Wexler then embarked on his most ambitious project to date, MEDIUM COOL. Wexler co-produced, directed, wrote, and photographed this arresting film—one of the few times a director of photography has taken screen credit as camera operator as well. The idea was beginning to take shape when the Democratic National Convention was scheduled for Chicago. Wexler made the convention, and the subsequent street violence, an integral part of the story; like the rest of the film, the scenes involving the convention and riots were authentic (Wexler himself was tear-gassed at one point).

Seldom has a fictional film created such a feeling of reality; appropriately, few films have gone to such lengths to make everything about them real. No sets were used, virtually no lighting, and all sound recording was authentic—there was no post-dubbing whatsoever. It is a tribute to the actors that their performances hardly seem to be performances. Robert Forster, who played the cameraman "hero" of the film, became so absorbed in his role that he asked Wexler if he could experiment with the camera; some of Forster's footage eventually wound up in the film.

Since many non-actors appeared in the film, Wexler used special methods to get the best results from them. None of the players saw a complete script; they were only told their lines so the reaction at hearing the others' dialogue would be natural and unaffected. "Professional actors can improve their performance in a scene through various retakes," Wexler explained, "but non-actors tend to become self-conscious and unnatural if required to rehearse or repeat a scene. We used a multiple camera setup on numerous scenes to secure the proper surprise, shock, or other reaction we wanted from our amateurs on the first take, since they did not anticipate what other people in the scene would say or do."

Thus was MEDIUM COOL created—a process of feeling through various scenes with intelligent actors and dedicated amateurs, using the most mobile camera equipment available for the greatest freedom in shooting, and letting everyone participate in the creative process, for the best possible results.

(An amusing sidelight concerns one of the most striking sequences in the picture, where Forster chases his current bed-mate through the winding geography of his multi-room apartment, followed close behind by Wexler's wide-angle camera. When it came time to shoot the scene, Wexler suggested that it would be more realistic if the

Wexler is on the camera cart, shooting a scene for MEDIUM COOL *with Robert Forster and Peter Bonerz.*

actors played it in the nude. The actress quickly obliged, but Forster objected, protesting that it wasn't in the script, and had not been agreed upon in advance. After much cajoling on Wexler's part, Forster said, "All right, I'll tell you what. I'll play it nude if you'll shoot it nude." Ever the dedicated filmmaker, Wexler cleared the apartment of all crew members, stripped, mounted his Eclair on his shoulder, and shot the scene as Forster requested.)

With MEDIUM COOL, Wexler proved himself a master, and a compleat filmmaker, not just a skilled cinematographer. Where he will go from here is known only to Wexler himself; he can certainly pursue any aspect of motion picture he chooses, for it is clear that any project he tackles will be in capable hands.

What of today's cinematographers? Many ASC veterans are still at the top of the heap, and for good reason—there is nothing so valuable to a film as a cinematographer who knows his business. James Wong Howe is as much in demand today as he ever was, not only because of his outstanding track record, but because he is always experimenting, ready to try something new. When he recently filmed THE MOLLY MAGUIRES (his fourth picture for director Martin Ritt), he broke precedent by eschewing the traditional "brute" lights for the more modern,

not universally accepted "bank" light fixtures. He used no light at all on many scenes, including one interior shot which was illuminated solely by candlelight.

Perhaps Howe's masterpiece (at least a strong contender) is John Frankenheimer's SECONDS (1966), one of the most outstanding films of the 1960s, and one of the most brilliantly photographed films of all time. The bizarre storyline, about an organization that gives middle-aged men new bodies and identities, gave Howe an opportunity to try unusual effects with his camera. He utilized the "fish-eye" lens with excellent results, before TV commercials killed the idea with overuse; provided the opening sequences with a startling dreamlike aura by creating a subtle soft focus around the edges of the frame; and made optimum, realistic use of New York locations such as Grand Central Station without the aid of artificial lighting.

Probably no cinematographer has received as much attention in recent years as F. A. "Freddie" Young, whose collaboration with director David Lean is as famous today as Billy Bitzer's was with Griffith fifty years ago. And like so many other filmmakers who have received sudden recognition of late, Young is hardly an overnight success. He will soon be seventy years old, and his credits include many of the most famous British films of all time: NELL GWYNN, VICTORIA THE GREAT, GOODBYE MR. CHIPS, and

49th PARALLEL, as well as such other memorable movies as TREASURE ISLAND, IVANHOE, and LUST FOR LIFE.

Young's remarkable three Academy Awards, however, have all been for his films with David Lean: LAWRENCE OF ARABIA, DR. ZHIVAGO, and RYAN'S DAUGHTER, all three of which, made on an epic scale in large-screen processes, have given Young the opportunities to "show off" his skill, as it were. There remains the danger so often mentioned by cinematographers of having this grand show of photography become *too* obvious, taking precedence over the action in the film, but that question aside for the moment, one cannot belittle the beauty of Young's work on the screen.

While Howe, Charles Lang, Robert Surtees, and other great cameramen continue to shine, a new breed of cinematographers has established itself in Hollywood, and many of these young men are doing remarkable work. One of the brightest is Laszlo Kovacs, who fled from his native Hungary in 1956 when the country was torn by revolution. Eventually settling in Hollywood, he became part of the crowd at American-International Pictures, the industry's chief supplier of exploitation films. Little did anyone dream that out of AIP would emerge such suc-

cessful filmmakers as Roger Corman, Dennis Hopper, and Peter Bogdanovich. Some of their work at AIP, however, can charitably be described as "embryonic," and little more. *Variety* reviewed one of the many tawdry motorcycle films produced at AIP and photographed by Kovacs, and commented that "the most depressing thing about this latest adventure of the Rover Boys is that such first-rate color camerawork was thrown away on such trivia. . . . The cinematography even manages to give overphotographed California highways a new and interesting look."

It was not just one critic's opinion. Many people started noticing the quality of Kovacs' work, especially in the much-praised but little-seen Peter Bogdanovich film TARGETS (1968). This was Kovacs' first opportunity to break away from AIP, and once again he dazzled everyone with his excellent camerawork. When Dennis Hopper asked him to shoot EASY RIDER, Kovacs demurred, not eager to be associated with still another motorcycle opus. He consented after Hopper made it clear that the film, while still low-budget, would be of a much higher caliber than any of the AIP efforts. EASY RIDER went on to become one of the biggest hits of 1969, and while there were differences of opinion as to its worth as a film, there was no disagree-

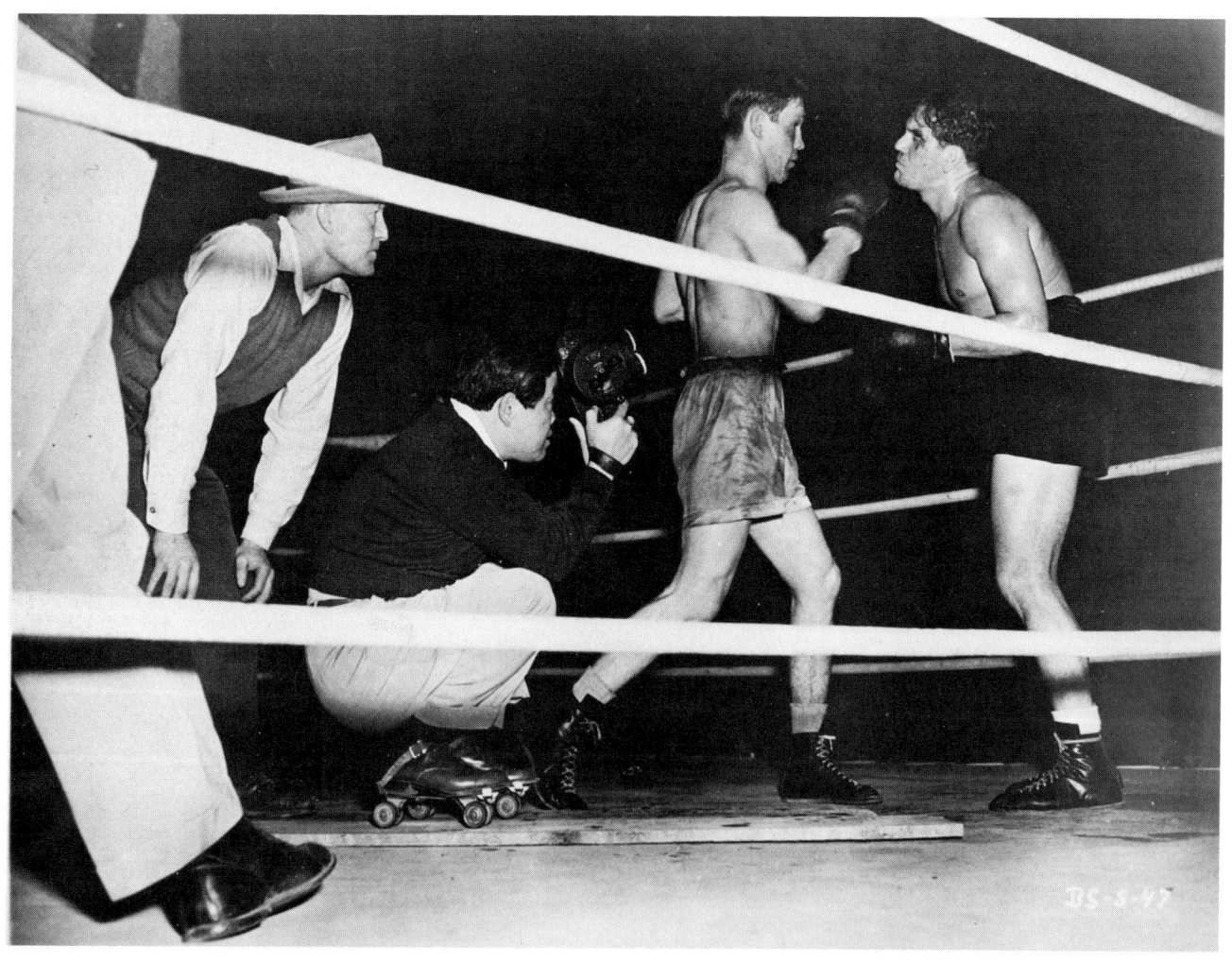

James Wong Howe dons roller skates and uses a hand-held camera to intensify the excitement of a prizefight in BODY AND SOUL *(1947) with John Garfield.*

ment about Kovacs' contribution. *Variety* called it "brilliant."

Perhaps his best work to date, however, was in GETTING STRAIGHT, directed by Richard Rush, more conventional cinematically than many of his other films, yet eminently effective, with fine color results. Bob Rafelson, another EASY RIDER alumnus, hired Kovacs for his FIVE EASY PIECES (1970), another low-budget, high-quality film that permitted Kovacs to attempt a hybrid of his "naturalistic" camerawork from earlier films with a more polished type of photography that the film warranted. The result is a very *real* effect, but not harsh, as it might have been in the hands of a less capable cameraman. Asked about the working relationship of FIVE EASY PIECES, director Rafelson told us, "Lesley feels his function is to entirely oblige the director, and I feel it's *my* job to oblige him. He's fantastic."

The prolific Kovacs also photographed Dennis Hopper's THE LAST MOVIE and Paul Mazursky and Larry Tucker's ALEX IN WONDERLAND, with apparently no end in sight to the string of successes he plans to tuck under his belt.

Another "new" cinematographer in American films is not young at all, nor is he new to filmmaking. His name is Gabriel Figueroa, and in his mid-sixties, he is just achieving recognition in Hollywood, having been a leading Mexican cinematographer for years. He photographed seven of Luis Buñuel's classic films, beginning with LOS OLVIDADOS (1950) and continuing through SIMON OF THE DESERT (1965). Figueroa's previous contributions to American films have been those shot on location in Mexico. One would think that his beautiful work on John Ford's THE FUGITIVE (1947) would have resulted in a hearty welcome from Hollywood, but for the most part Figueroa remained in Mexico, turning out consistently superior work for whatever director happened to film on location there.

John Ford recalled for Peter Bogdanovich, "It [THE FUGITIVE] had a lot of damn good photography—with those black and white shadows. We had a good

This photo and the seven that follow show the innovative Howe at work with director John Frankenheimer and star Rock Hudson on SECONDS *(1966). Notice that despite the variety of locations, indoor and outdoor, Howe tried to use natural light wherever possible, and employed lightweight cameras in order to bring the audience "into" each scene. As you can see in the last picture of this sequence, he was not above holding a camera light himself to help make a shot work smoothly.*

cameraman, Gabriel Figueroa, and we'd *wait* for the light—instead of the way it is nowadays where regardless of the light, you shoot."

Through the 1950s, Figueroa's work in domestic Mexican pictures and in international classics directed by Buñuel, continued on the same plateau. Not until 1964 did he contribute his talent to another American film, John Huston's THE NIGHT OF THE IGUANA, for which he was nominated for an Academy Award.

Most recently, Figueroa filmed what must be one of the loveliest outdoor color films ever shot, Don Siegel's TWO MULES FOR SISTER SARA (1970). Filmed in widescreen, using many pleasing filters for various effects, SISTER SARA captured a vividness of color never thought to exist in the barren country where most of the shooting was done. He followed this with what may be his first non-Mexican-located film, KELLY'S HEROES, an elaborate World War Two comedy directed by Brian Hutton. Reviewing HEROES the same month as SISTER SARA, *Playboy*'s film critic, having praised the latter's photography, referred to KEL-LY'S HEROES as "another feather in the cap of cinematographer Gabriel Figueroa . . . expertly filmed." It was a tribute not only to Figueroa, but to the growing awareness of cinematography as a vital force in the art of filmmaking.

In cinematography, as in few other fields, age is irrelevant. Men in their sixties and seventies are experimenting as boldly as newcomers, and novices in their twenties and thirties are perfecting techniques that belie their youth.

Most importantly, there is always room for creativity and invention in the field. Nothing is constant in cinematography; there are no techniques that can't be improved upon, no equipment that can't be further developed, no rules that can't be broken. Just as we have looked back on the great achievements of the past, we can also look forward to even greater accomplishments in the future, in this tremendously exciting, vibrant field, made up of men behind the camera who have dedicated themselves to this most fascinating of all the arts.

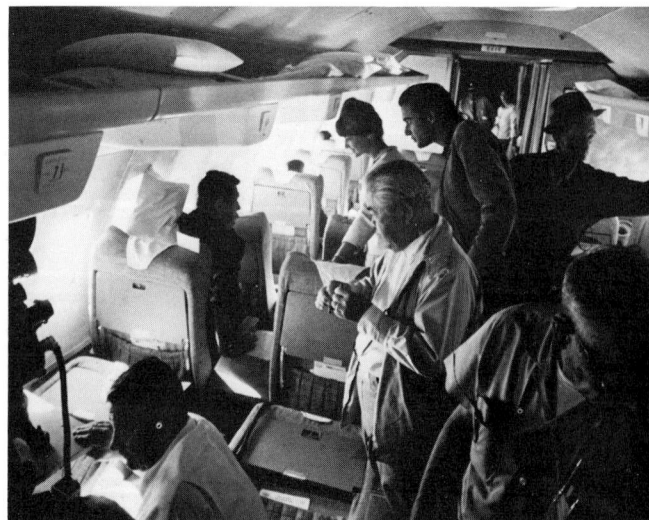

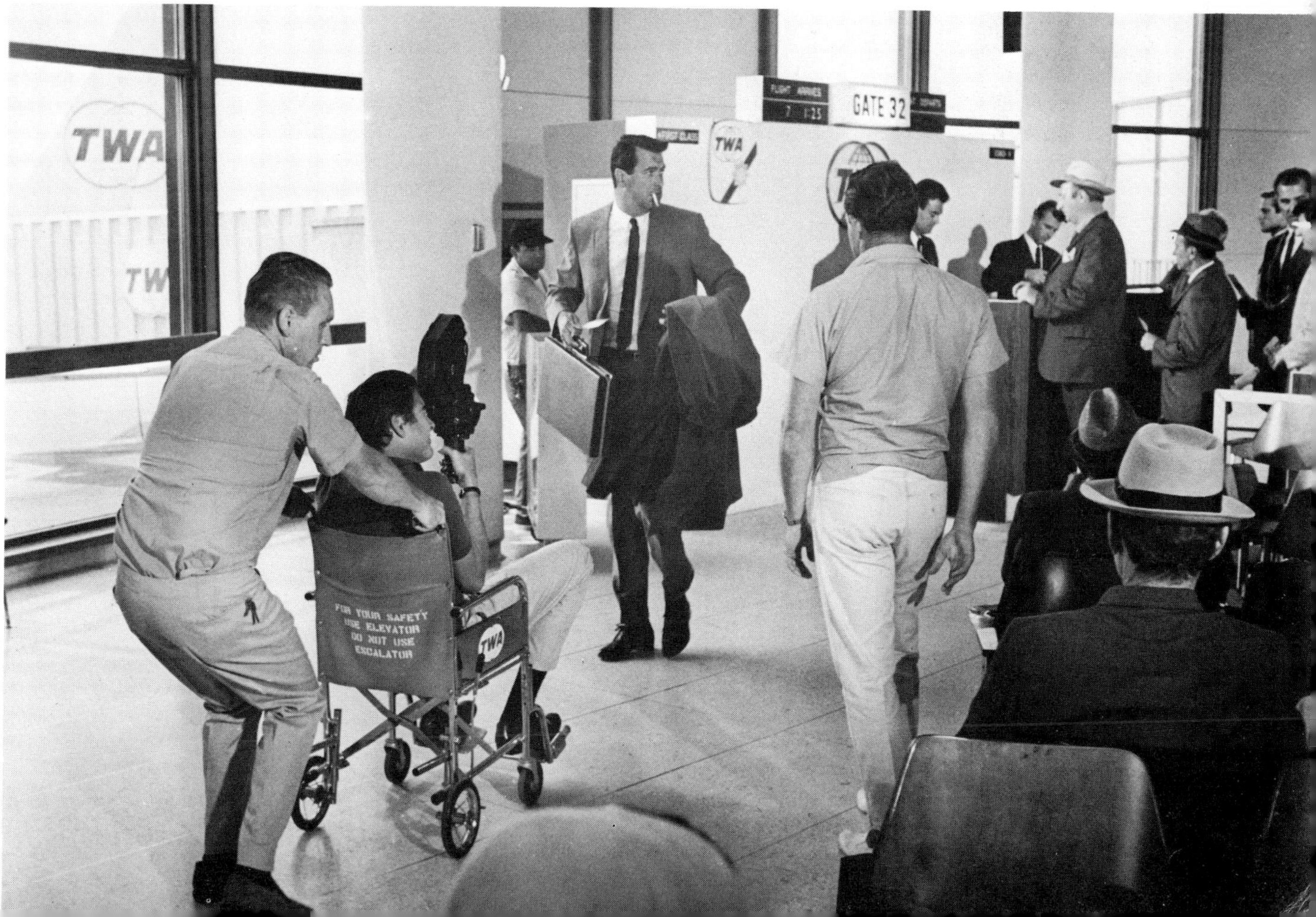
TWA
GATE 32
FOR YOUR SAFETY
USE ELEVATOR
DO NOT USE
ESCALATOR

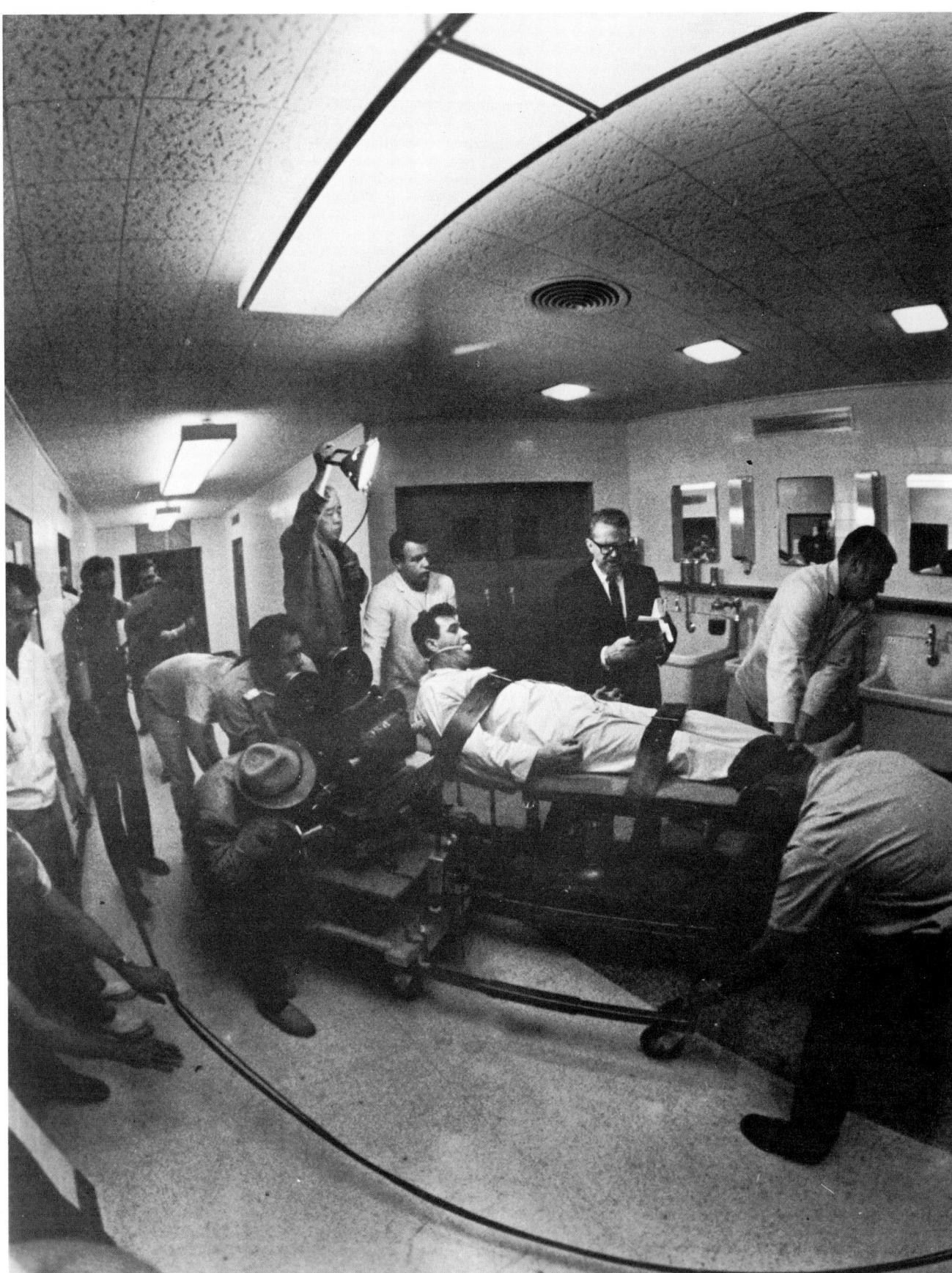

How to film a panoramic shot, ca. 1920.

In the days before unions, anyone who was handy might be pressed into service on the camera crew. Here, some extras lend a hand on a tracking shot for TRAVELIN' ON *(1922). William S. Hart is walking alongside the wagon.*

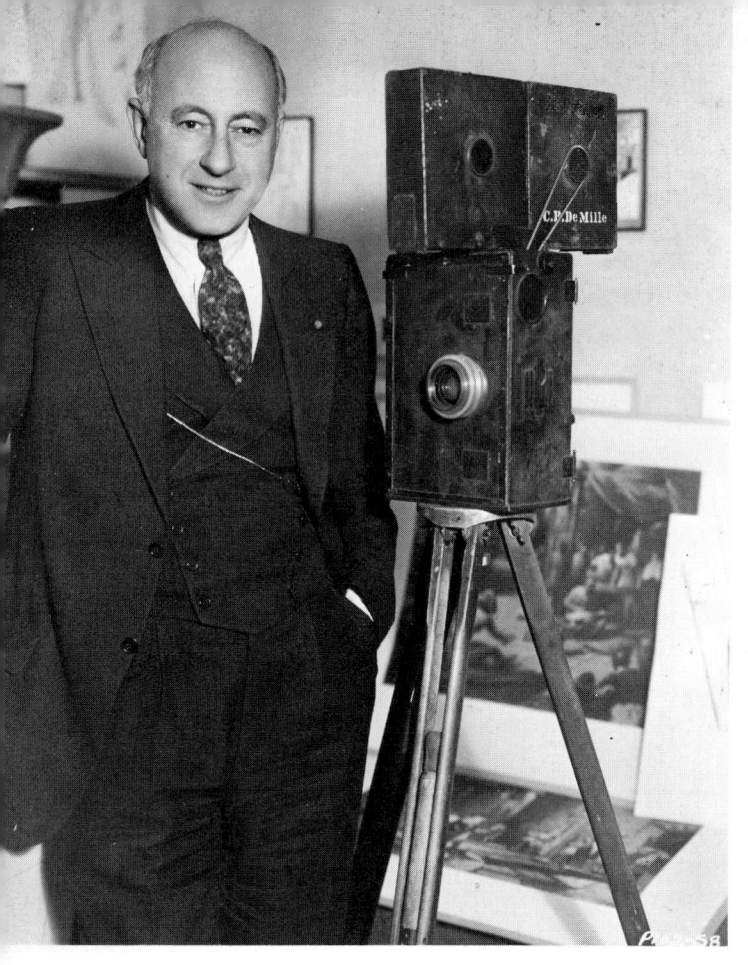

Left: *Cecil B. DeMille poses in 1934 with the Pathé camera that filmed his first movie, the pioneer Hollywood feature* THE SQUAW MAN (1914). Below: *A hand-cranked camera (operated by Fred Guiol) captures the comedy of Harold Lloyd, Bebe Daniels, and Snub Pollard in* JUST NEIGHBORS (1919). Opposite Above: *Director Charles Reisner and cameraman Edwin DuPar use intense lighting to get an authentic night scene for* THE BETTER 'OLE (1926) *with Syd Chaplin. Opposite Below: Fred Niblo directs Joan Crawford in* DREAM OF LOVE (1928), *with Oliver T. Marsh at the camera.*

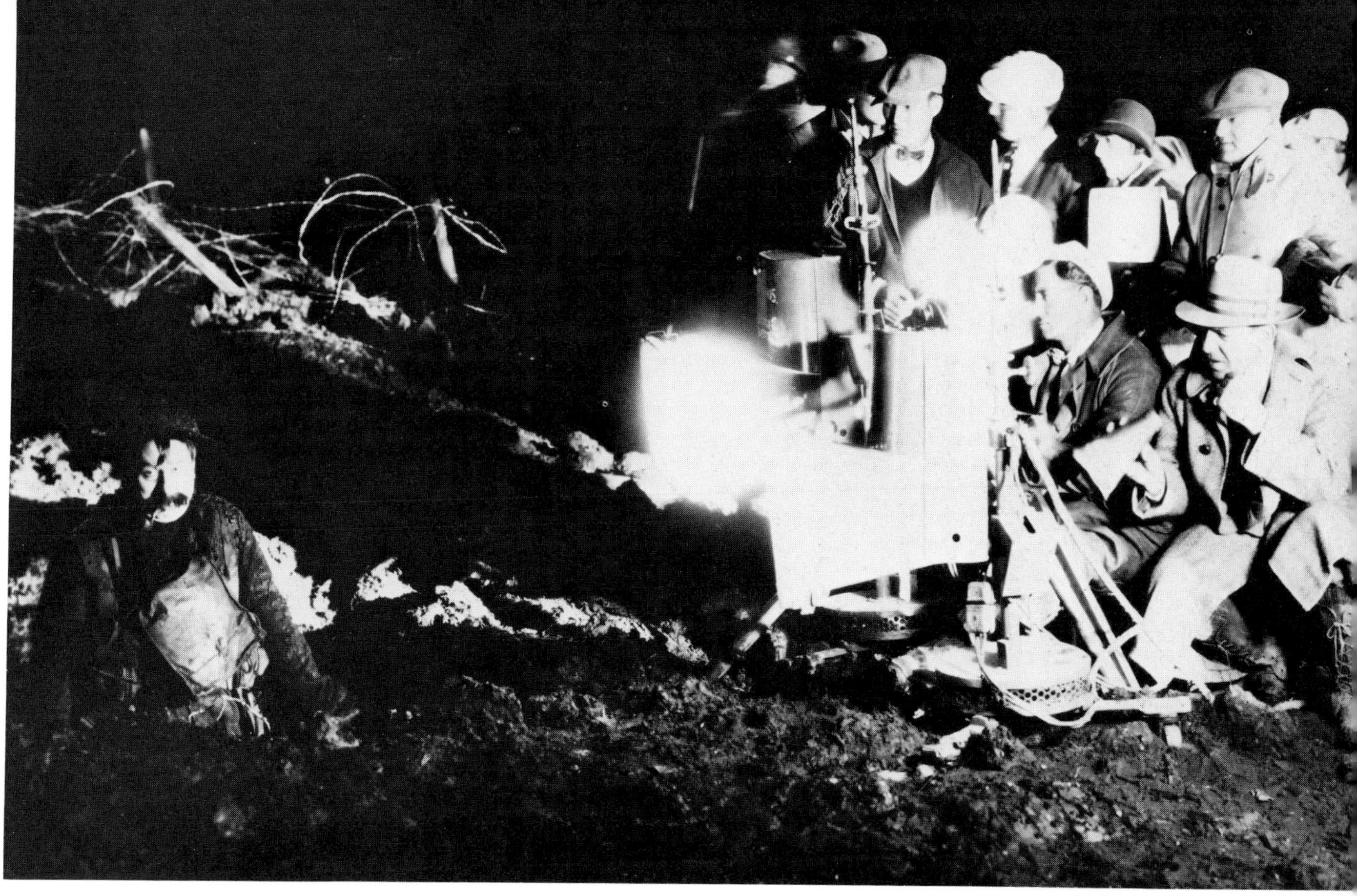

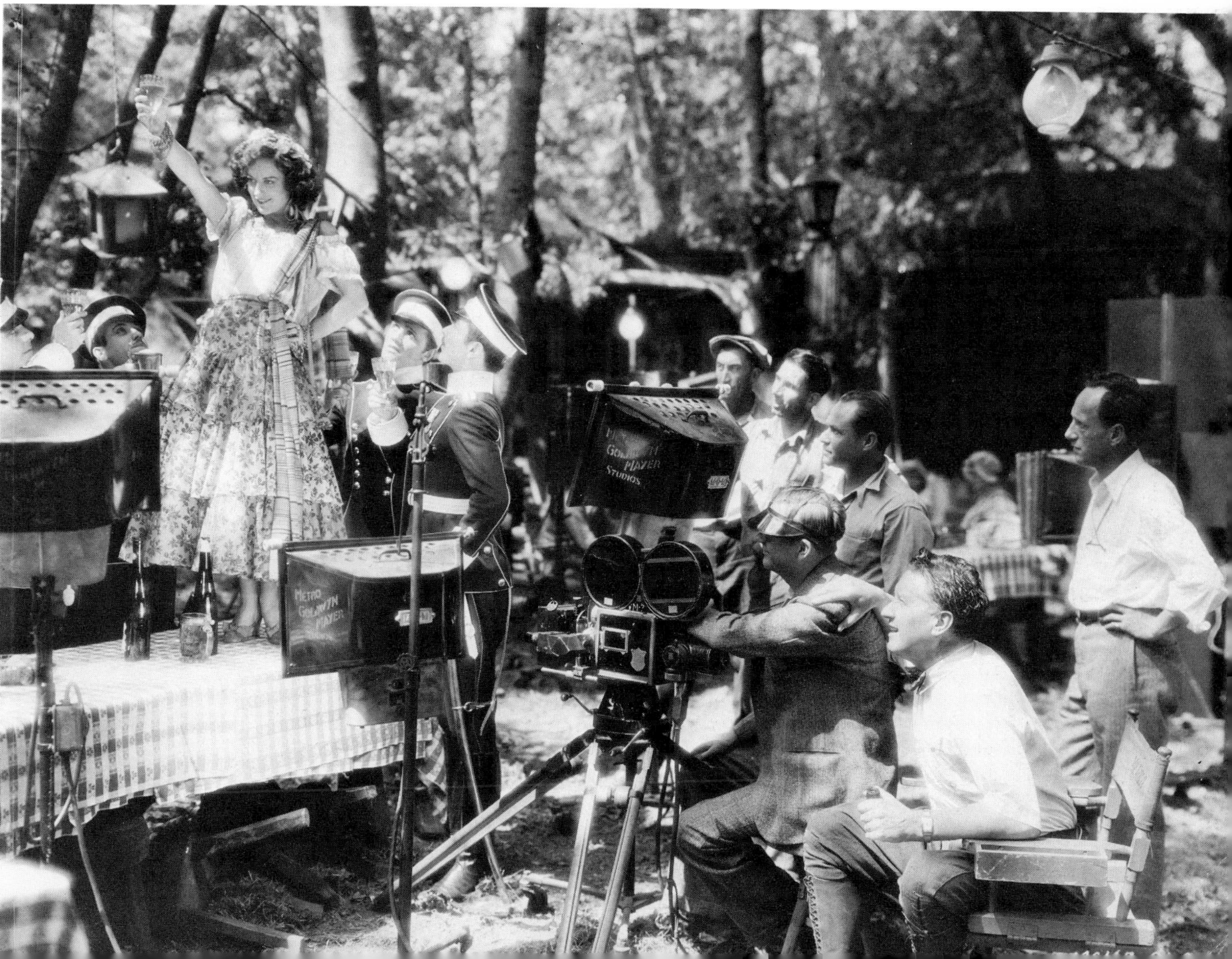
METRO GOLDWYN MAYER

A "second unit" hard at work on UNDER TWO FLAGS *(1936).* Victor McLaglen is leading
the detachment.

Second-unit director Otto Brower gets more action for UNDER TWO FLAGS.

Director H. C. Potter and his camera crew take to the floor to shoot an intimate scene with Brian Aherne and Merle Oberon for BELOVED ENEMY *(1936).*

The camera rolls along specially built tracks so it can scan the line of young ladies and come to rest on a close-up of Simone Simon in GIRLS' DORMITORY *(1936).*

90
PARAMOUNT STUDIOS
STUDIO EQUIPMENT CO
90
90

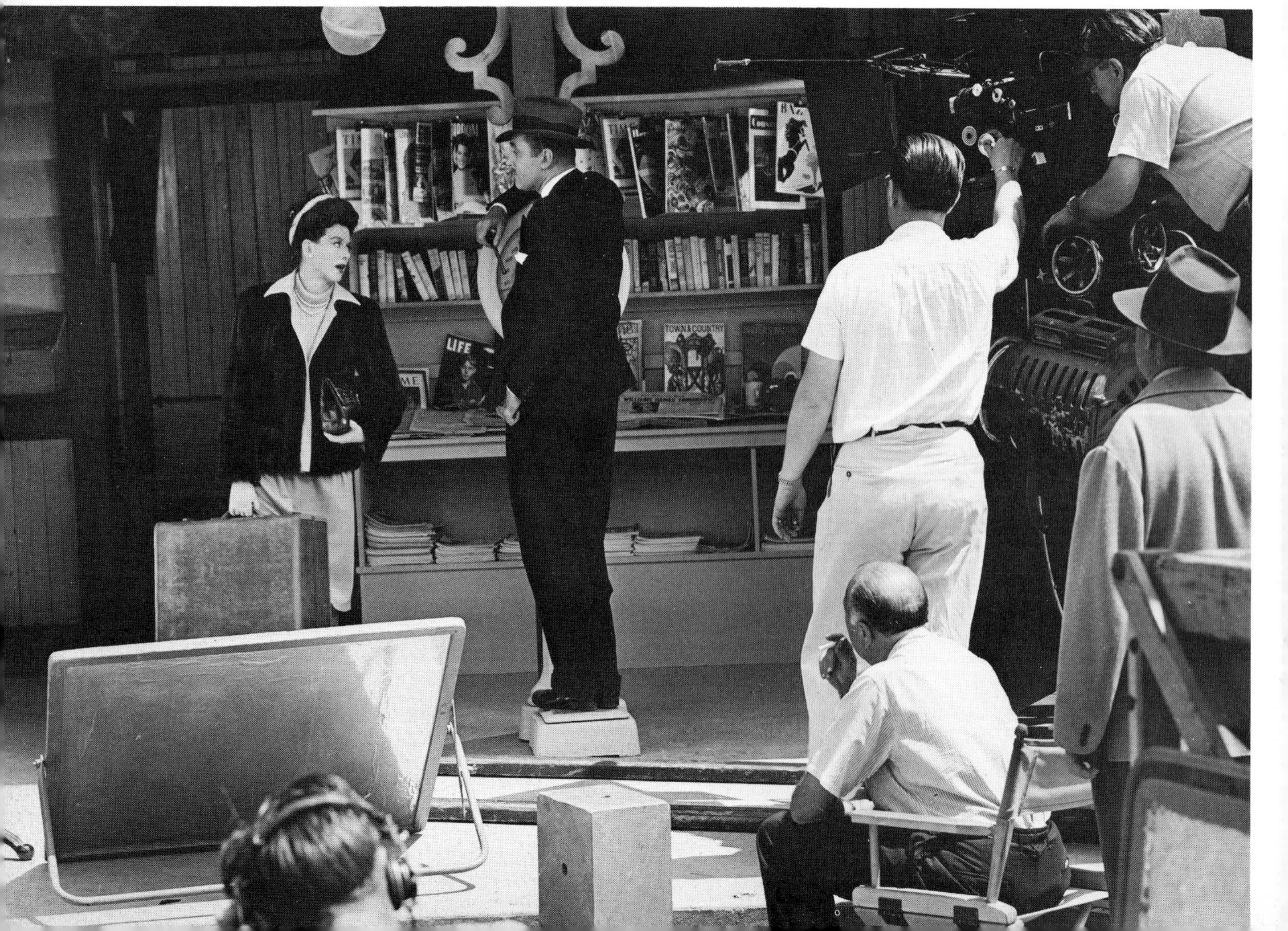
LIFE
TOWN & COUNTRY

Opposite Above: *Camera operator Guy Roe shoots a scene for cameraman Bert Glennon (not seen) and director Edward H. Griffith, as assistant director Edward Beroudy peeks around the doorway. The film is* ONE NIGHT IN LISBON (1941) *with Fred MacMurray, Patricia Morison, Madeleine Carroll, and John Loder.* Opposite Below: *Joseph Walker's camera crew films a simple sidewalk conversation between Rosalind Russell and Brian Aherne for director Irving Cummings'* WHAT A WOMAN! (1943). Left: *Stan Laurel and Dante the Magician run through a scene for director Alfred Werker (crossed legs, center) and cameraman Glen MacWilliams on* A-HAUNTING WE WILL GO (1942). Below: *Billy Wilder provided moviegoers with a realistic look at a movie sound stage, courtesy of fellow Paramount director Cecil B. DeMille, in* SUNSET BOULEVARD (1950).

PRESS
WARNER PATHE NEWS
WARNER-PATHE NEWS
WARNER-PATHE NEWS
WARNER-PATHE NEWS

Opposite Above: *New postwar lightweight cameras are displayed by a crew from Warner-Pathé Newsreel in the early 1950s.* Opposite Below: *William Boyd (right) visits Cecil B. DeMille, Charlton Heston, and cameraman Loyal Griggs on location for* THE TEN COMMANDMENTS (1956). Left: *John Wayne, cameraman Russell Harlan, and Howard Hawks discuss an action scene for* HATARI! (1962). Below: *Director Howard Hawks checks a camera set-up for his ambitious CinemaScope production* LAND OF THE PHARAOHS (1955).

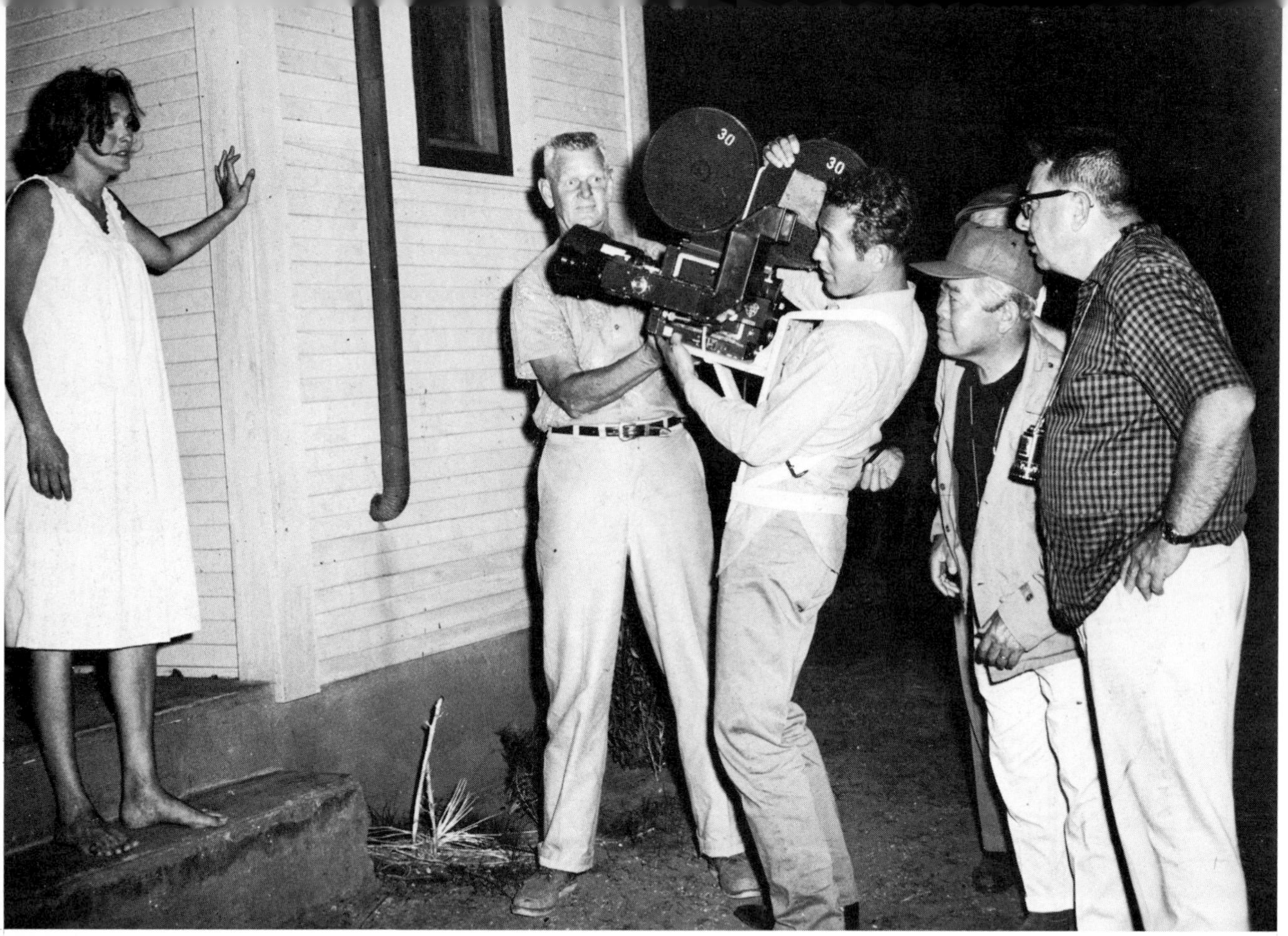

Above: *Director Martin Ritt and cameraman James Wong Howe let Paul Newman try to film a hand-held shot of Patricia Neal for* HUD *(1963) . . . and (Below) several years later, actor-turned-director Paul Newman sets up a shot with wife Joanne Woodward for his film* RACHEL, RACHEL *(1968).*

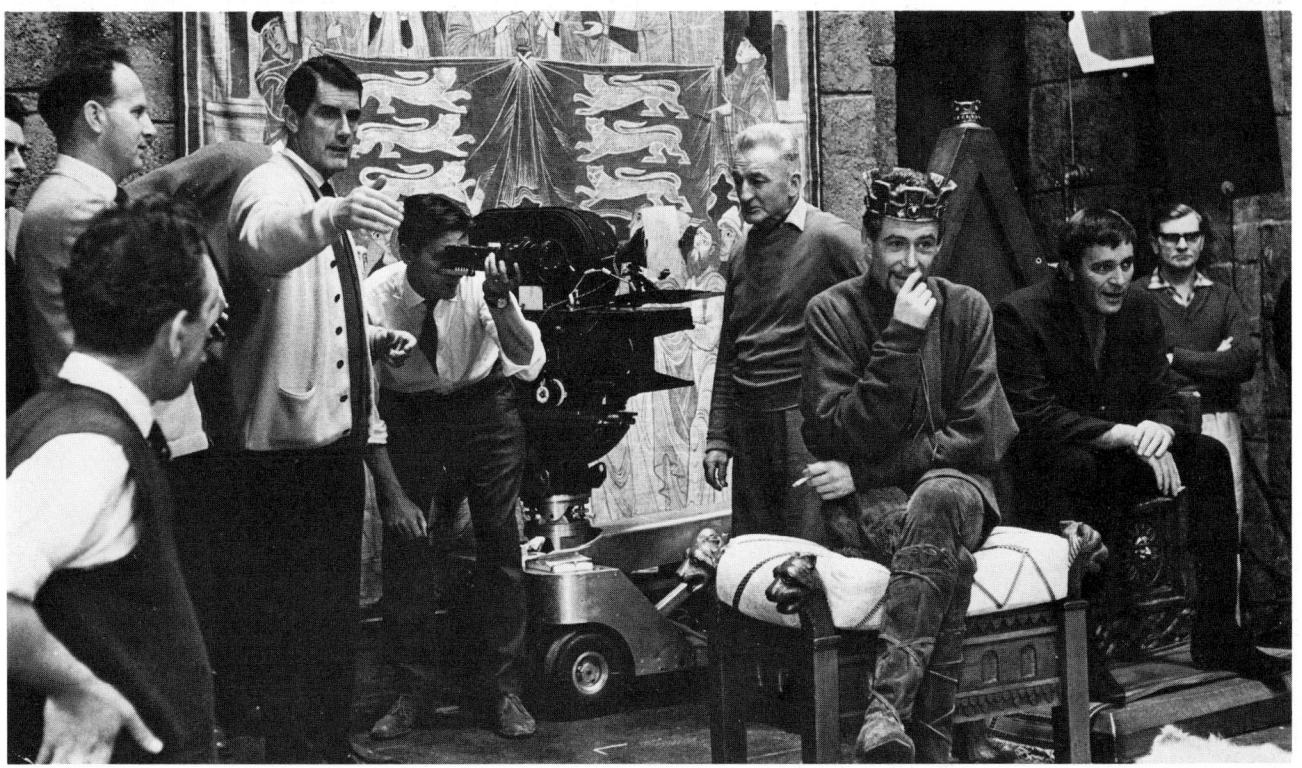

Above: *Director Peter Glenville instructs cameraman Geoffrey Unsworth how to shoot a scene for* BECKET *(1964) while Peter O'Toole and Richard Burton wait for the scene to begin.* Below: *Director Henry Hathaway checks a scene with his Technirama 70 camera for* CIRCUS WORLD *(1964).*

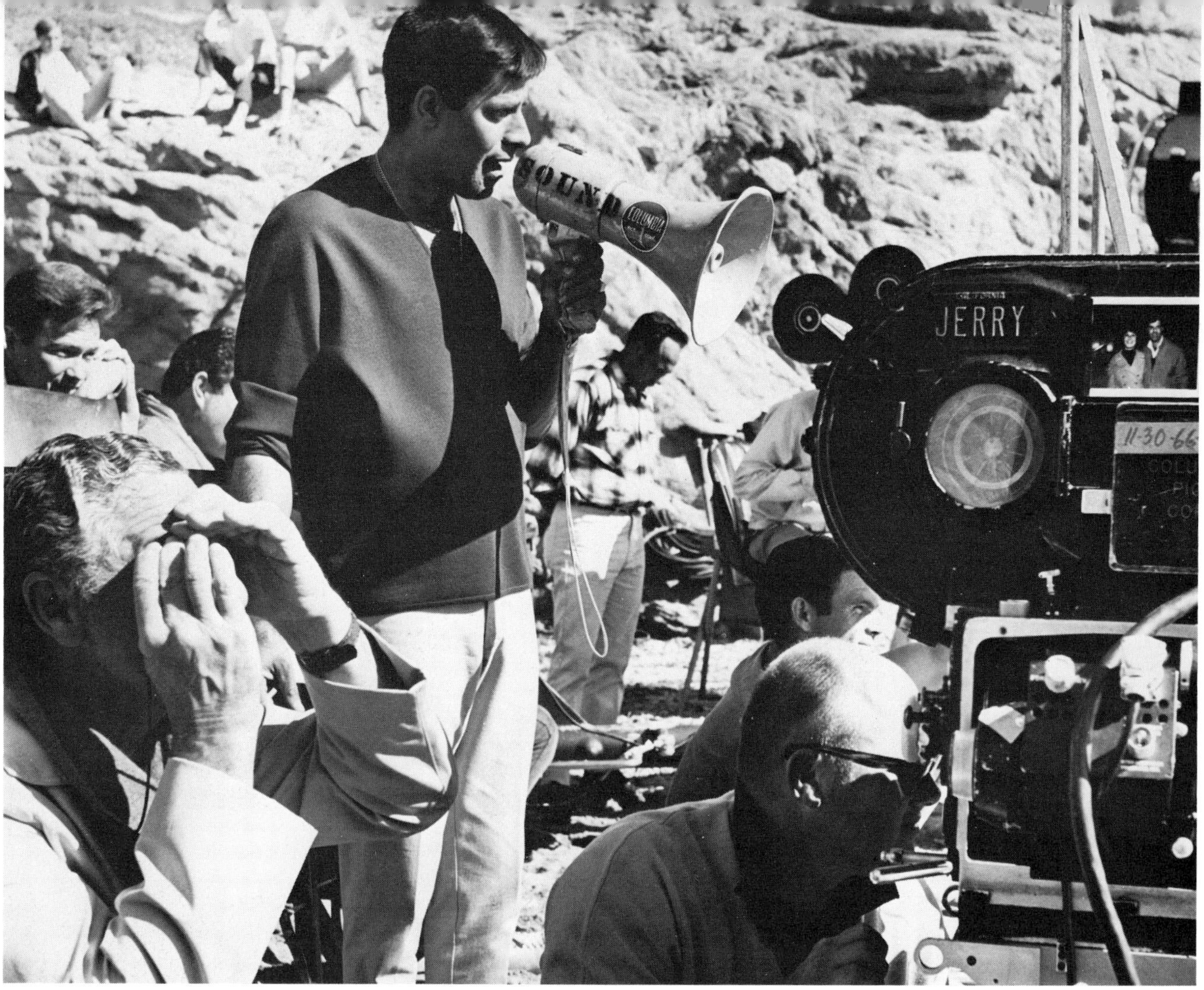

Above: *Jerry Lewis directs his film* THE BIG MOUTH (1967) *while his long-time cameraman W. Wallace Kelley checks the light.* Left: *Harry Stradling's camera crew moves in for a close-up of Barbra Streisand in* FUNNY GIRL (1968). Opposite Above: *A tracking shot of Jack Elam, Gary Lockwood, and Henry Fonda for* FIRECREEK (1968) *is rehearsed by director Vincent McEveety (in white trousers) and William Clothier (behind camera).* Opposite Below: *Cinema vérité at work: a hand-held camera used to film Leacock-Pennebaker's* MONTEREY POP (1969).

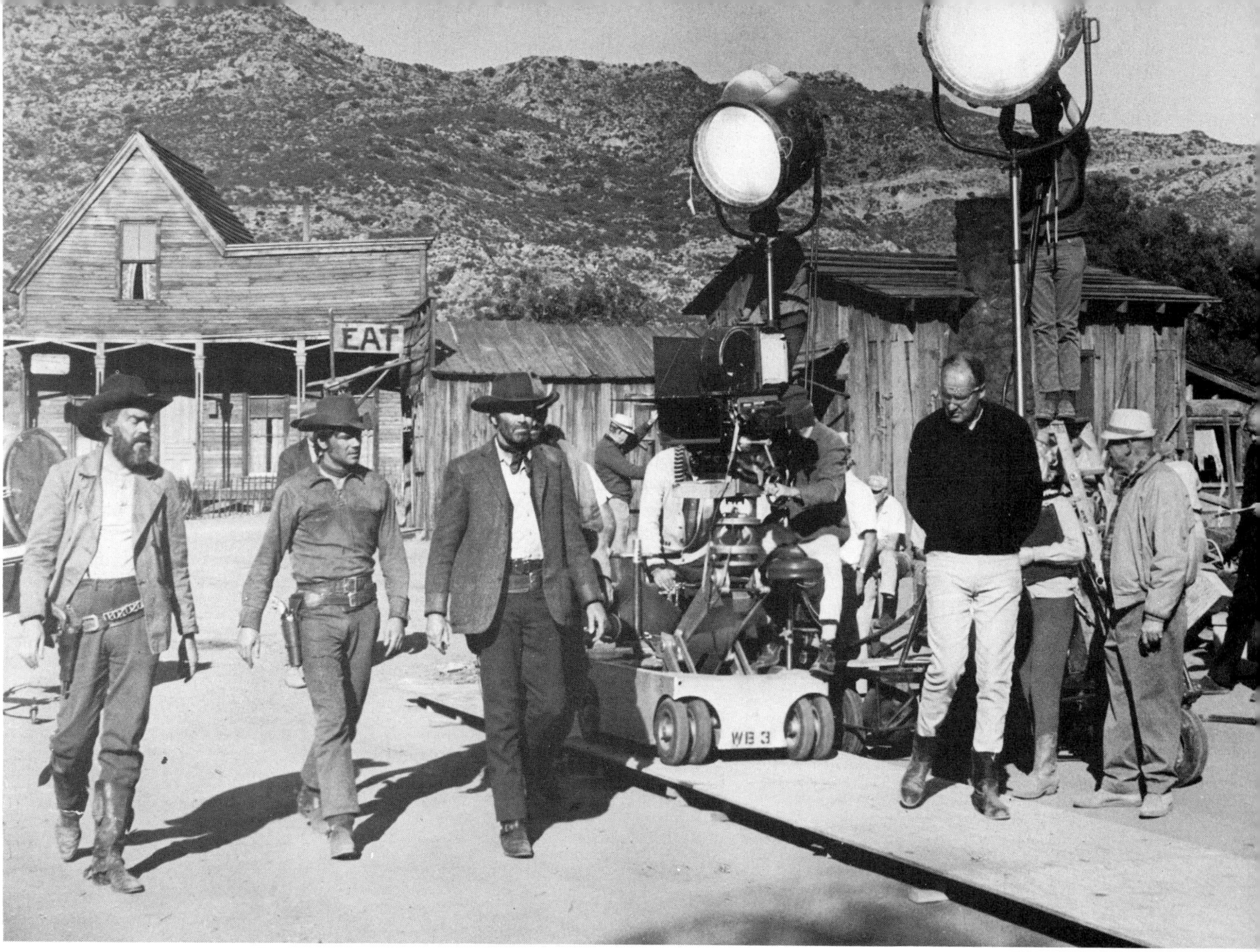

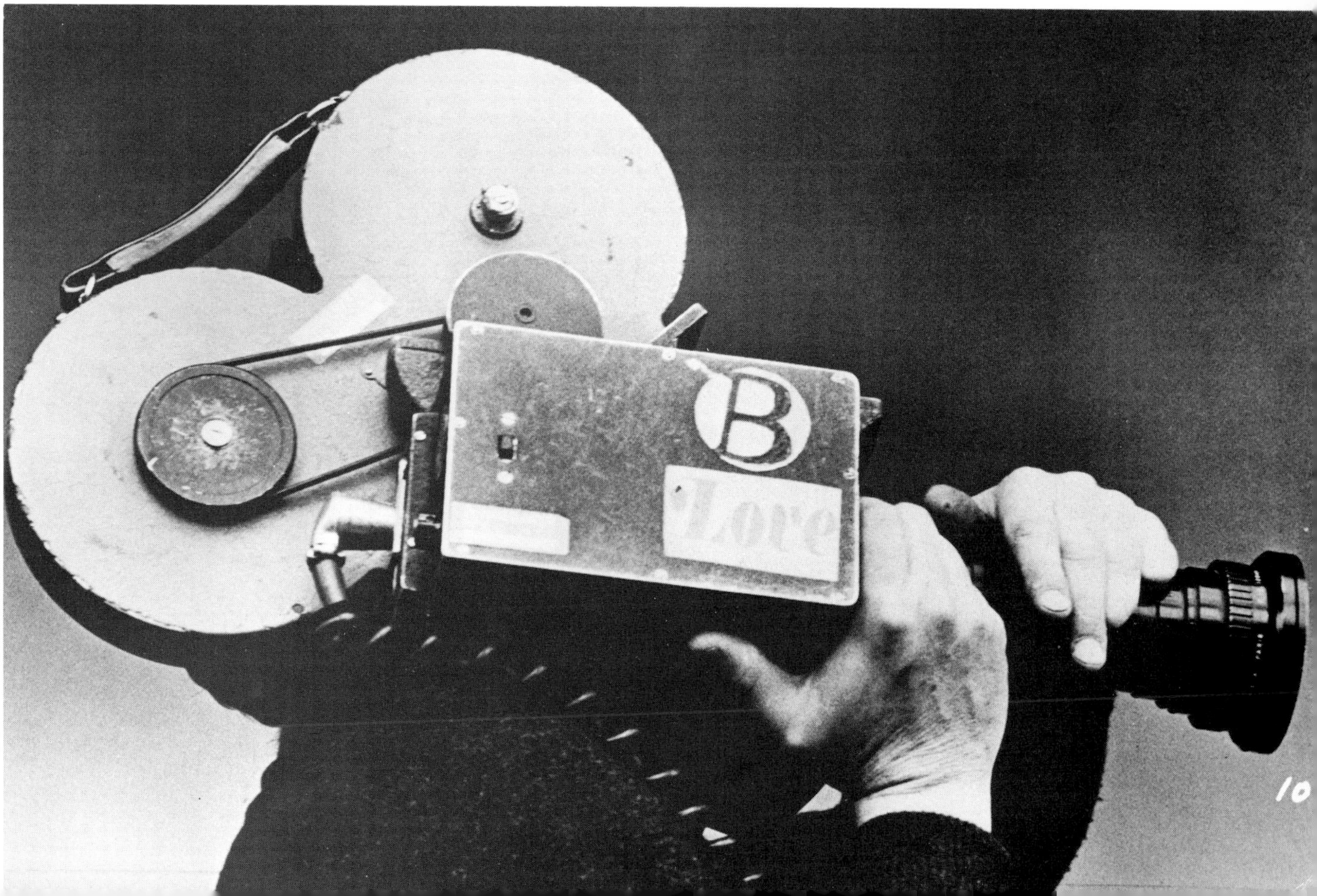

10

FIVE INTERVIEWS: Introductory

These five cameramen represent a cross-section of the scores of outstanding craftsmen who have made films in Hollywood for the past sixty years. Three are pioneers who started with the industry; one began with the talkie era; and one is among the younger breed of cinematographer.

Cameramen are naturally technicians, but these five are also artists. In our conversations, we tried to cover the important technical aspects of their work; how they learned their craft, how new developments affected them, their work with color and widescreen, etc. It is hoped that their thoughts will provide an insight into each man's individual talent and create a better understanding of their artistic endeavors.

If some of the conversations sound more anecdotal than technical, one should remember an important point: filmmaking is a human experience, involving a large number of individuals who must somehow work together on one product. If films were made by machines, one could talk about how a movie was programmed, without worrying about personalities and working relationships. Such is not the case, however, and interaction among cameramen, directors, actors, writers, producers, and others has always been responsible for what eventually showed up on the screen. The reader will find apparent contradictions in the five interviews, but these are not discrepancies at all. They are honest, *personal* reactions of how each man viewed his working experiences. And just as no two people are alike, no two reactions to an individual or situation will be exactly the same.

It is hoped that these five interviews, spanning the length of the motion picture business in Hollywood, from the turn of the century to 1970, will provide a rounded picture of the filmmaking process, both yesterday's and today's.

Interview with *ARTHUR MILLER*

Arthur C. Miller's status among his peers can be best described by relating an incident that occurred during our interview in Miller's office at the American Society of Cinematographers, of which he was vice-president. At one point George Folsey, a fine cameraman himself, joined us and said, "I couldn't go by without stopping in to say hello to the Master."

To most cinematographers in Hollywood, Miller *was* the Master, not only because of his exceptional photography, but because of his intense dedication to his craft. As Miller himself put it, "This has been my whole life." Although prevented from shooting films since 1951, for health reasons, he worked tirelessly at the ASC, as administrator as well as supervisor of such projects as the important handbook published periodically by the organization.

Photography was the dominant factor in Miller's life from boyhood, and during his peak years in Hollywood, no one was more devoted to his work than he. In the 1940s, he won three Academy Awards, for his work on HOW GREEN WAS MY VALLEY, THE SONG OF BERNADETTE, and ANNA AND THE KING OF SIAM. When Sam Spiegel and John Huston formed Horizon Pictures in 1950, they signed Miller to a contract as a cinematographer. His first picture was to have been THE AFRICAN QUEEN, but a medical examination caused his doctor to forbid his working from that time forward. It deprived the industry of one of its great cameramen, but it did not stop Miller from becoming the leading figure at the ASC, always working for the improvement of motion picture photography, as well as preserving its heritage through the ASC archives and publications. In 1968, he collaborated with his original mentor, Fred J. Balshofer, on a book, *One Reel a Week,* which is one of the most informative and instructive volumes ever written on the early days of filmmaking.

A ready conversationalist, Miller did not hesitate to give us his candid opinions about his career and colleagues. The interview reveals the intensity of his interest in cinematography, and if it tends to ramble at times, it is worth noting that Miller's ramblings have more value than what a lot of other people may say more concisely. Unfortunately, this is the last interview Arthur Miller ever granted. He died on July 18, 1970, a few weeks after speaking with us.

LM: One thing that astounds me is how someone like yourself just suddenly "became" a cameraman. You started off, like so many others, at the very beginning of the business, and became in such a short time a person of rare ability. This certainly didn't just *happen*, did it?

MILLER: Well, at the time I started, in 1908, I would say there were no more than a dozen men, at most, who knew how to make a motion picture—how to take a camera, photograph with it, go in and develop the negative, make a print, and run it on a machine. Learning to be a cameraman then wasn't anything like it is today. We had two films: Eastman film, that nobody could get but the Patents Company, and we used Lumière film, which was manufactured in France. It came to us unperforated, we had to perforate our own film. My first job was in a laboratory; I'd perforate as much film as we needed the next day. We didn't shoot a half million feet of film in those days; if we shot eight hundred feet in a day, this was a lot of film. A picture ran anywhere from $5 to $1,000. I had been interested in photography as a little bit of a kid, with my brother; we had a Brownie No. 1, which made 2¼ by 2¼ pictures. That was the first camera to use film, or celluloid. They sold MQ$_2$ tubes, and in my mother's soup plate, my brother and I would mix eight ounces of developer; there were six pictures on a roll. You'd dip it in the soup plate until it was developed, with a ruby-red light, then into the hypo, and then you'd put it into the wash and fix it. There were fancy beer trucks in those days that used to deliver the beer kegs to the saloon; every corner in Brooklyn had a saloon. The fellows that drove these trucks were very proud of their teams of horses—the brass shining, and the harness and everything. When the guys would untie the horses and go into the saloon for a short beer, my brother and I would take pictures of the horses drinking in the trough, and then when the guys would come out, we'd ask them to stand by the front wheels and get a shot of them. And when they'd come around the next week, we'd sell them prints, three for fifteen cents. That way we'd buy more material, and make more pictures. I had some wonderful stuff made with the Brownie No. 1. When I was thirteen, I went to work for a horse dealer, delivering horses. Coming home from delivering some horses one day I saw this crowd gathered outside a German beer garden, and I sat there astride this horse bareback. A guy came over and asked if I wanted to work in moving pictures. I said, "Doing what?" He said, "You can ride a horse bareback, can't you?" I said, "Yeah, I can ride anything with four legs." He said, "Could you be here tomorrow morning at eight o'clock?" I said yes, and I went to work for this fellow. The first day we went out to a golf course in Brooklyn, and I rode this horse all over, got chased, and all. It always intrigued me, how did they develop this long piece of film? When we got home that first day, the boss told me I could help the man with the camera—well, I couldn't even lift one of the cans —I weighed less than a hundred pounds. But I told him about the pictures I had made, and he didn't quite believe me because he thought I was working for the Patents Company—I was asking him all about the camera. That was Fred Balshofer, and he didn't tell me until we were doing our book together that he'd thought I was a spy for the Patents Company. But I was fortunate; the business was young, and it was a gradual thing. You learned that three-quarter light was the best coming over your shoulder, not directly, as Eastman said, and putting reflectors on the dark side. If you're shooting against a dark background, you open up a little more; if you're shooting against a light background, stop down a little. I've got tapes of thirty cameramen, and in those tapes the same question arises: How did you judge your exposure? And you get thirty different answers. Some say, "I looked through on the ground glass and stopped the lens down until the detail started to disappear in the shadows." Well, if you think that through, if he was on the desert, the pupil of his eye would be down to nothing. If it was a nice day like this, the pupil would be larger. So it was never constant—never. So how could he judge when the detail was beginning to disappear? Others say, "Oh, I don't know, I just look up and make a guess at it," and that's what I think most people did. We had latitude in the film; we only had one film.

LM: Did you feel restricted at this time as a cameraman?

MILLER: Well, the Biograph had a standing rule that all their exteriors would be shot in back-light. They liked the sun coming through Mary Pickford's hair, and Lillian Gish's hair. So cameramen were copycats; one copied the other, I copied someone, someone else copied me. A fellow sent me a review of a picture I did, HOW GREEN WAS MY VALLEY. It said, "If Gregg Toland invented depth of field"—of course he didn't—"it was Arthur Miller who perfected it in HOW GREEN WAS MY VALLEY"—which is also false. But this is the way this critic saw it. What Gregg Toland did in CITIZEN KANE was to use wide-angle lenses on the longer shots, and as he got closer, he never used wide-angle lenses, because the distortion would become too great if someone leaned forward. He worked f.9 inside, and that takes an awful lot of light. But there wasn't anything new, because this had been done in another picture I saw, and I used it myself in a picture called MAN HUNT. I'm not sure that was before CITIZEN KANE or not, although I didn't go for the distortion with the lenses, where a guy takes three steps and advances 150 feet. That's what you see in television pictures today; you look at a guy up at the well and he walks down to the entrance of the house, just count how many steps he travels that distance. To me this was never real. My opinion of a well-photographed film is one where you look at it, and come out, and forget that you've looked at a moving picture. You forget that you've seen any photography. Then you've succeeded. If they all come out talking about "Oh, that beautiful scenic thing here," I think you've killed the picture. A good picture, as we all know, starts with a story. The next thing is to tell that story pictorially. And the next thing is to put dialogue in it that doesn't annoy people—just enough, and the way people talk. That's my opinion of a moving picture. I saw one the other night, THE OUT-OF-TOWNERS. This is my idea of entertainment. Fast-moving, pictorial, not overloaded with dialogue. You could see that picture without dialogue and you'd know what it was all about. This was the secret of John Ford's pictures. You could run any of his pictures silent, and you'd still know what they were all about. Most pictures you can't. So the whole secret is, to get down to one word,

realism. Realism at its prettiest: a girl looking her best—not overdone, just looking her best, without makeup, looking that way. Then you've got photography. I made a picture in 1920, PETER IBBETSON; it had depth of field, it had all the things. . . . For instance, we had a hanging scene, where the guy goes to the gallows, and you just figure these things out. I thought, "A guy going to the gallows in the sunshine is no fun; this affects nobody. So get the atmosphere to fit the scene." Hell, I'd never done any great pictorial things, at that time I'd just been starting to get some lessons in art; so I made it an early morning fog scene, and it came out *gorgeous*—you know, early morning, daybreak, this guy going to the gallows. I wouldn't claim I invented anything—it was necessity. I used Nujall Oil, out of a spray gun. Today they use what they call a B-gun, which gives smoke, but I didn't know this, so I just had a couple of guys with spray guns full of Nujall. Everybody was sick for days afterward from breathing this Nujall all day. I needed something, and I said, "I wonder what a lot of thin oil in the air would do," and at least for three years after that everybody used Nujall. Now I'm not saying I did it first, some other guy might have done it elsewhere, because the guy that tells you, "I did something first" in the movies, just cross it off. Nobody knows who did *what* first, and most people can hardly remember why they did it. When they talk about "Who made the first moving shot?" up in 1911 in the Biograph company, you came out on the stage, with a camera and tripod, set the tripod down on the floor, and a stage-crew was on the tripod—you screwed it into the floor. You screwed your camera down onto the floor solid—it didn't move. The actors were in the back of the set, and they would move up to the camera. Now who was the first one to take the screws out of there and say, "Let's move the camera"?

LM: A cameraman had to be a technician in those days, didn't he? He could also be an artist, but . . .

MILLER: First he had to be a technician.

LM: But you did become an artist.

MILLER: You can't help it, if you're interested in your work. In 1915 I went to Detroit on a job, and I had evenings to myself, so I went to an art school. I didn't go to learn to paint or draw, I just went to learn composition. Then I was fortunate enough to work with Henry Stanlaws, as I tell about in my book; I learned more from this man—you could never pay for what I learned from this man being by my side, day after day. He rubbed off on me, and that's the way I got it. I think all cameramen develop a sense of composition. Whenever you go in an automobile with a cameraman, they always see everything in that frame line; they say, "That'd make a swell shot," or if they're driving across the country they say, "Gee, this would be a location you could use for the Sahara Desert." They're always thinking that way. You know all this business with making a frame out of your hands . . . well, a cameraman looks and he judges. I could tell you what a two-inch lens would take in, what a three-inch would take in, without any of this business. I've worked with the best and the worst of the directors, and the best of them never looked through a camera. Jack Ford, who I think is not only the best director that I ever worked with, but the best director in the picture business—film ran in his bloodstream—not only didn't he look through the camera, he never looked at the rushes. Never looked at them a day in

Arthur Miller shooting THE ETERNAL CITY (1923) *with director George Fitzmaurice and stars Barbara La Marr and Bert Lytell.*

his life. I'd go in with the editor and look at the film. He'd say to the editor when he'd show up, "How was the photography?" The editor would say, "It looked good." He'd say to me, "How was the action?" I'd say, "It looked fine."

One day I asked him, "Why don't you ever go in to see the rushes?" He said, "If I don't remember what I shot yesterday, then I don't belong in this business."

LM: Did technological advances make shooting films more enjoyable or less enjoyable for you?

MILLER: More. Competition was always the thing. You see, cameramen are a funny breed of zebras. They all gather here [at the ASC] and have drinks together, and have dinner together, and run films. It isn't the way it used to be, but competition was really vicious—but on a friendly basis. It's a hard way to put it. I never asked a cameraman in my life how he did something that he didn't tell me himself. We used to do all our trick lap dissolves and things in the camera. The last time I ever did this was

a picture I did with Ricardo Cortez for C. B. DeMille. In the picture this guy got shot, they brought him in the operating room, and as they put him to sleep, he goes through the whole story in his mind. I had an assistant by the name of Clarence Shleifer, who'd won a contest, he'd come from somewhere in the Middle West, and the winner of this contest was to come out to the Pathe Studio and get a job as assistant cameraman. Clarence arrived, and on that picture, I went down to the backlot and rigged up a little darkroom, and had a lathe bed set up, from the machine shop, and on one end of it I had a Bell and Howell camera, and at the other end I had a Pathe camera, sort of an optical printer, and we did all sorts of things. We made slides of hardener and hypo and then held a candle under it; the thing would run, and we'd fade out on it, put another one in, take back the film and fade in on it, make a smear. Crazy things. And he got hooked on this. When I went over to Fox to work, he went along with me. I was there about a year, and he met a fellow by the name of Cosgrove, who was making glass-shot paintings. He got offered a job by this fellow, came to me and said, "Would you feel bad if I left you to work for this fellow Cosgrove?" I said, "No, Clarence, it'll be fine if he'll give you more money and a year's contract. Show me that first and then I'll tell you how I feel." So he came back and he said, "He'll give me a year's contract and so-much money a year." I said, "Sign it," and he turned out to be quite a guy; he did all the trick stuff on GONE WITH THE WIND. He became an expert at that. Another kid that I had was Fox's still cameraman, and he was inclined the same way. He came to me one day and said, "I've got a chance to get a job down in the special effects department." I said, "Billy, I know that's what you want, go ahead." His name is Billy Abbott, and he's the head of the place. George Folsey used to be my assistant, Harry Stradling was my assistant—I've had many of them.

LM: One of the most striking films of yours is THE VOLGA BOATMAN for DeMille.

MILLER: That picture was made when panchromatic was first coming in. In the book, I tell you I signed a contract to do THE KING OF KINGS with this old bald-headed guy, it's the absolute truth. I talked it over with him; I didn't know anything about panchromatic film, other than the fact that I'd shot a roll in Rome, on THE ETERNAL CITY. I thought, "Well, I guess there's something to this," especially for shooting night stuff in the daytime. But came THE VOLGA BOATMAN and I had this all figured out. But I didn't know what the effect would be if I photographed in orthochromatic makeup with panchromatic film; the makeup was for the blue end of the spectrum—the lips were deep purple, and if you saw them under the banks of Cooper-Hewitt lights we had inside, they looked like death warmed over. We were going on location, and I didn't have time to figure out what would happen if I photographed them in panchromatic with the orthochromatic makeup. So I talked to the old boy and I said, "Look, when we get up there"—we went up the Sacramento River, that was the Volga—"we'll shoot the long-shots, then we can finagle the people over, put them in front of some trees or something, and shoot the close-ups, and I'll put in orthochromatic film. Cut the two together and you'll never know the difference." So I did this, and I guess I got on his nerves. I'd been shooting down the river, with a lot of guys pulling the boat, singing the boatmen thing that I got tired of hearing. I was down low with the camera, shooting these guys, with sun in back of me, with the blue sky up above—that's why I was down below, I wanted a lot of blue sky. Now I wanted the reverse of them, going away, so all I had to do was turn the camera around and look up the river, and I was looking into the sun, so I'd get the streak on the water. I didn't know what the hell I'd get with panchromatic film; I'd never tried it, and I didn't want to take a chance. It would only have taken me a minute and a half to change the magazine, so I said to this assistant of mine, "Give me a roll of ortho," and I did, the old man looked down and said, "I don't understand this; first you want this film, then you want another film. Just what do you want?" I looked up at him and I said, "All I want right now, for Christ's sake, is for you to let me alone so I can get the film on the camera, get the camera set, and get the boat going up the river before the sun drops down into the picture!" Well, nobody ever talked to Mr. DeMille like that, I'm sure. I was brought up differently. I was never brought up to salaam people, and I

never expected anybody to salaam to me; we're all just human beings. Then he pulled another trick. On the rushes, I had the light tests printed from 0 to 22 and you could look at them and pick out any light where it would print. But THE MERRY WIDOW had just been made, and it was shot in a low-key light. We were running the rushes in a small theater in a small town; I went in the night before to see THE MERRY WIDOW, and the screen was black. So I asked the operator, "What the hell are you doing? Can't you get some more light on the screen?" He said, "No! The guy who shot the picture didn't use enough light." So I knew what was going to happen, and I arranged with my grip a piece of cardboard about four feet square, on two sticks, and I had two guys there. As soon as the rushes came on, and you couldn't see them, I had these guys hold this thing up close to the projector! Well you know, he didn't believe me? He saw them on the cardboard, and he didn't believe that they were OK? I showed him the tests, but he had so many goddamn yes-men around him, bowing and scraping, saying, "Yes, Mr. DeMille," he made us go over to Sacramento which was eighty miles from where we were, and got a theater, got the operator out of bed, went to this theater and ran these rushes, at three in the morning. And of course there was nothing the matter with them. You'd sit in a projection room and you wouldn't hear a sound until you'd hear Old Baldy say, "Gee, that looks kind of nice," you'd hear "Oooh," "Oooh," all over the place. It would just turn your stomach. But finally I got away from there, and went to work for a man named Bill Seiter . . .

LM: . . . a fine director . . .

MILLER: Oh yeah, and a wonderful man. And from there, I went to Fox.

LM: When you were at Fox, did you have a choice of what pictures you were to do?

MILLER: Oh no.

LM: Do you remember one called ME AND MY GAL?

MILLER: Yeah, that was the first one I ever did, with Spencer Tracy.

LM: There's one shot—I wonder if you remember it— where some gangsters are trying to get into a bank from a room above, and they cut through the ceiling. When the piece of the ceiling is cut through, we see this from below, and when it falls onto the level below, the camera shakes.

MILLER: I did that; I had the camera on a rubber-tire dolly, and just hit it. Now, this wasn't original, because I had seen the earthquake picture over at the Chinese theater, and I saw what effect it gave. That's what they did all through it; you'd hear the rumble first, everything would start to shimmy, and then it would hit. They rolled their dolly. I did it in THE RAINS CAME exactly as they did it in OLD SAN FRANCISCO, running the dolly against a bumper, and you'd get quite a shiver. All I did was go to Johnny Arnold, who was the head of the camera department, asked him how they did it, went back to the studio and did it.

LM: There was one called THE MAN WHO DARED that was quite good.

An actual enlargement of one of Miller's light tests for BRIGHAM YOUNG, FRONTIERSMAN (1940), *with Tyrone Power and Linda Darnell.*

MILLER: Oh, yes; you know that picture was made for pennies. Didn't we have a tunnel in that, down in the mines? We made that for peanuts, a real quickie. I think we made it in sixteen days. Preston Foster had another picture to do, and they put this director, MacFadden, on it. He said to me, "Can we make a picture in sixteen days?" I said, "I don't know if you can, but I can. But you'll only get one crack at each scene, you know; you can't fiddle around and make thirty takes." He said, "I'm willing, my job hinges on this." We started to shoot, and he'd look around, I'd say OK, and that was that. It was a pretty good picture.

LM: Did you ever do trick work with minimal sets, to make them look like more than they really were?

MILLER: We did an interior which was practically the interior of the Taj Mahal, and it was all cardboard cut-outs. That was THE NAULAHKA, with Tony Moreno. I brought Billy Menzies—William Cameron Menzies—into the business on that picture. I met him in a restaurant I used to go to; he was going to art school half a day and working in an antique shop the other half a day.

LM: How about HANDY ANDY?

MILLER: That was Will Rogers—dear old Bill. A nice guy. I was with Will Rogers on a set the day he left to go to San Francisco; he'd just finished a picture called DOUBTING THOMAS, and the director I'd known very well, Dave Butler. I went over to see Butler, and Rogers had just finished. He said, "Well, I'm going to go up to meet Wiley, up in San Francisco. I don't know whether I should go or not; I don't like to fly around in a lot of snow." He went anyway. You know, he lived out here, where the tourists go now, out in Santa Monica Canyon. About four o'clock he'd begin to sing "Santa Monica Canyon Is Calling Me," and he'd get Butler's goat. But we always finished a week ahead of schedule. He'd come to me and say, "Get the names of the crew." I'd get the names of all

Miller (left), assistants, and Walter Pidgeon prepare to shoot a scene for MAN HUNT (1941).

the electricians, the grips, give them to him, and he'd give them all a check for a week's salary, because we finished a week sooner. He thought he was doing them out of a week's salary.

LM: What was the first time you worked in color?

MILLER: The first color I ever shot was in Technicolor. I shot the first piece of Technicolor with artificial light, in 1924, on a picture called CYTHEREA. I was working for Sam Goldwyn. He called me, and said, "A man came over from Technicolor, and he'd like to do an episode of the picture, and if I don't like the color, I don't have to buy any of it. If I like it, I can buy as many prints as I want. I figured if it's worthwhile, maybe I'd buy prints for the big cities." I said, "What have you got to lose?" He said, "Well, do you know anything about color?" I said, "No. Why don't you send a guy over." So a fellow showed up with the equipment, a fellow by the name of Ball; the camera was a Bell and Howell, but it pulled two frames. We had no light meters, so I started putting light in. He told me not to use all arcs, so I said OK. I made hand-tests in my little box, with ortho film, and it turned out so black, so overexposed. Finally the leading man Lew Stone called me over and said, "I can't stand this, it's getting too hot in here." So I said to the fellow Ball, "We're going to lose these actors." He said, "Well, can you put a little more light under this couch." It was right near the edge of

the set, and I said, "I can do it, and I will, but it usually isn't very bright under a couch." He said, "I have to go on the theory that where there's no light, there's no color." So he wasn't so dumb. We shot the thing, and Goldwyn bought for all the big cities this one sequence in color. They did a lot of that from then on.

LM: Were you pleased with the results?

MILLER: Yes, I was. It was as good as any color I'd ever seen; this did have a sharp image on both the magenta and the blue-green.

LM: How did you adjust yourself to preparing for color, then?

MILLER: Well, you'd do all right; you would jiggle your light bar up and down, until you got the flesh tones. When you got the flesh tone right, you let the rest go; if it turned out to be a bluish-looking horse, he had to be a bluish-looking horse. The flesh tone was the key.

LM: How did working in that early color compare with doing a later film like THE BLUEBIRD?

MILLER: I did that, and another one in color, THE LITTLE PRINCESS. I didn't have much faith in exactly how this was going to work out. You see, to do a picture with a child like Shirley Temple—you know what a thousand-foot candle is? A thousand-foot candle, when you turn it on, jolts

Fritz Lang (extreme left) and Miller sit on the camera platform as it tracks along with Pidgeon's pursuers in MAN HUNT.

you right out of your seat. So Zanuck called me into the office and said, "We'd like to do a picture with Shirley in color. Is that possible?" I said, "In Technicolor, if you go by what the Technicolor people have you do, no, we can't do it. Because you have to have one-thousand-foot candles." He said, "What's a one-thousand-foot candle?" I said, "I'll set a one-thousand-foot candle up down on the stage, and if you drift through today, stop in, I'll put it on, and I'll have it marked where you can stand and look at it, and see how strong it is." So I had an arc set up, and he came in, I set him on the spot, and said to the gaffer, "Hit it!" When he hit it, Jesus, Zanuck said, "Do actors work in front of lights like that?" I said, "They do. You must agree that a kid can't stand that kind of light. However, if you want to do a picture in Technicolor, and you get permission from Dr. Kalmus that we don't have any restrictions about how much we have to use, as long as we give him a negative that's satisfactory for them to come up with color they're satisfied with, we can do it." So he called Kalmus, the head of Technicolor, and a fellow by the name of George Dye came over with a camera. I went down on the back lot with Shirley, her mother, and a makeup man, and I shot a long-shot of her standing in the middle of the street, walking over to go in the house—Jimmy Dunn comes over and talks to her, and she goes in the door. Now we copied the doorway, built it on a stage, and I used five- to six-hundred-foot candles, put

the lights up high, so they were out of her vision, and filler down below, played with her, and made the shot. The thing went to Technicolor and came back; I spliced the two together. Zanuck looked at them and said, "I don't see anything wrong with that—what's supposed to be wrong with it?" I said, "I don't see anything wrong with it either. I think it's pretty good, under the circumstances. But the main thing is, we can make the picture, if Dr. Kalmus says that's all right." Kalmus looked at it, and we got the word that we could go ahead and shoot. And that's the way I made both pictures with this child, with at least 400 to 450 foot less than the supposedly required amount. If I'm a guy who works in charcoal and can work in pastel, and I'm going to do a portrait of you, if I take my canvas and charcoal and do a sketch, I'd have tones, shadows. Now supposing I did it with pastel crayons—I'd give you the same tones, wouldn't I? There is no difference. The same thing in film. What makes it easy in color is if you put green against blue, you've got separation. In black and white, you have to create these separations with your lighting; that's what separates the men from the boys. I did a picture, THE SONG OF BERNADETTE with Henry King, and Jennifer Jones sees the Lady in the film. I figured that this was one of those holy-holy pictures, we might as well ease into this thing; before she sees the Lady, try to suggest that there's something different about this girl. I never said anything to King, but in her home, with her father and mother, and wherever she sits at the table, in back of her, there's just a slight glow of light on the wall. Not obvious, not a spotlight. Wherever she stopped against the wall, nobody noticed it—it was that slight. We had some little friendly words; we shot three days, and King said to me, "Jesus, if I knew we were going to shoot this thing from the floor, I'd have brought my overalls." So about three weeks went by, and the cutter came and said she had three reels made up. King said to me, "Do you want to see them?" I said, "Sure." So we went into the projection room, just King and I, and the editor. We looked at it, and the lights went on, and the first thing he said was, "It looks kind of good, it looks beautiful." I said, "Did you notice the shot from the floor?" He said, "My God, I didn't notice it at all. But you know, there's something happening in this picture. I noticed every place she stops, there's a little glow of light behind her!" So then, after she saw the Lady, I really went overboard.

LM: You worked with a lot of directors. In some cases, did you find that you had more responsibility for getting the picture on film than in others?

MILLER: Oh yeah, according to the director. I found out that the less the director would bother you, the more you could help him. This sounds funny, but a guy will come in today and say, "Put on a two-inch lens," or "Put on a three-inch lens." If I were to ask him, "Why do you want a three-inch lens instead of a 40mm?" I guarantee you he couldn't tell me. I spent sixty years at this business, and I know how you use lenses. You don't only have them so you can get close to somebody you can't reach otherwise—you use them for different purposes. For instance, I made a picture, THE PURPLE HEART, and these fellows were shot down in Japan, six or seven of them, and tried in a Japanese court. In back of the three judges was the Japanese flag. I had it made loose, so I could raise it a little, lower it a little, or turn it a little. Because when I'd get one judge, I could balance him off with the composition of the red ball on the flag; if I had two judges and the ball came over his eye, I could always move it over a little and get composition. Now sometimes when I'd want to emphasize this thing, above the importance of the judge, I'd put on a long-focus lens, get back farther, and make the flag predominant. If I want to emphasize the judge, I'd get closer, use a wide-angle lens—I'd still have the flag, but it would be smaller in the background. And you'd use this with your actors—you make one more important than another by the focal length of the lens you use—there are all sorts of things you can use this for. True, there are places where you're cramped against the wall, and the only reason you use a wide-angle lens is so you'll get the set in without knocking the walls of the studio down. But when a director says, "Put on a four-inch lens," if he could tell me why, I wouldn't mind, because if he told me why, I might learn something—I'm always willing to learn. He could say, "I want it because I don't want too much depth of focus; shoot it with a four-inch and try to cut the shutter, and leave the lens wide open—you'll get less depth of focus." Then the guy would be talking sense. Now I'd figure out, "Why did he want less depth of focus?" and nine times out of ten it'd come to me what he had in mind in his continuity, and I wouldn't only give him what he wanted, I'd give it to him better. I'd exert every thought I could get in my little noggin to help him achieve this thing that he was after. But when they come

and tell you to put on this or that—they usually do this when there's a group of people around. Ford, I don't think Jack Ford ever told me what lens to put on—he knew nothing, he never looked in the camera. He'd say, "What do you get?" I'd say, "From there over to the end." And no marks on the floor for the actors—they might look down for their marks. This man directs less than any man in the business. As a matter of fact, he doesn't direct—he doesn't want any actor to give an imitation of him playing the part. He wants the actor to create the part—that's why he hired him, because he saw him in this part. You'd sit at a big coffee table in the morning—everybody was there, whether you worked that day or not. You'd drink coffee until you couldn't swig it down any more. If you had a part in the picture, he'd start telling you about some scenes in the picture, and suddenly a guy over *there* would realize that he was talking about the character *he* was playing—but he'd be talking to you. Now the actor would start using his imagination—I caught wise to this after a year or so—and you could see it, he wasn't listening to the conversation any more, he'd be thinking. This was the way Ford got performances out of people. Some directors will tell you, "Now you pick up the cigarette lighter, and you look at the girl and say, 'You know, I think!'—and then you light the cigarette—'that you and I would make a good team.' Then you close the cigarette lighter." They'd tell them every move, until you might as well have a monkey in there, imitating what this guy is doing. How does he know that *I* would say, "You know I think—" and then light the lighter. I might not do that at all.

LM: What directors used that method?

MILLER: Many of them.

LM: Lubitsch was well-known for acting out scenes for his cast.

MILLER: Lubitsch's pictures, if you look at them, you'll see they are the most old-fashioned pictures in technique. He never advanced his technique. He still would cut, close-up here, cut, close-up for the laugh. He was a nice guy—I did two pictures which he produced; Preminger directed one, and Mankiewicz directed the other.

LM: One thinks of Mankiewicz as a literary type of man; did he have a visual sense as well?

MILLER: I don't think that he knew the visual like Ford, who started before talkies, and *had* to tell his story visually.

LM: What about Fritz Lang?

MILLER: A great director. He talks my language. I met Fritz Lang very curiously. He'd done two pictures at Fox, WESTERN UNION and THE RETURN OF FRANK JAMES; he had two different cameramen. I had been assigned to do this picture with Fritz Lang, and I never made my mind up about a director until I started working with him. So I was called into the office to meet him; he wore those thick glasses, and he said, "Oh, I'm so glad to meet you." I said, "Fine; I hope it's that way when we finish." So he says, "You must come to lunch," and as we're walking through the restaurant, right at the door a guy pulled my trouser leg—it was a cameraman who had photographed one of the pictures with Lang. He said, "You work with this guy

On the set of HOW GREEN WAS MY VALLEY (1941): *John Ford with pipe and dark glasses, then (moving right) Roddy McDowall, Donald Crisp, Sara Allgood, Miller, and Rhys Williams. Sound man Gene Grossman stands to the left of Ford and assistant director Eddie O'Feeney is kneeling at the right.*

three days and you'll want to wrap the tripod around his neck." I said, "Is he that bad?" and he said, "Oh, Christ!" And the other guy chirped in with, "That goddamned sonofabitch!" So I went in to sit down and have lunch with Fritz Lang. Maybe you know this by now, I'm a very ordinary, free-speaking guy. And he said, "I suppose they told you the story about me in Kanab, Utah?" I said, "No, what's that story?" He said, "Yes, I got all the cattle gathered from all over the country, and then on the morning when we went to shoot I said, 'Give me all the ones with white faces in the foreground.' They didn't tell you that?" I said, "No, they didn't tell me that." He said, "Did they tell you when I lined up the telegraph poles, and the next morning came over and ordered the camera put so they were one right behind the other?" I said, "No, they didn't tell me that." Then I said, "Well, what gives you such a terrible reputation? Everybody I talk to can't stand you. I have news for you, Mr. Lang: they talk about me the same way. And if they think you're a sonofabitch, you have never seen one until you work with me. We're going to have a jolly good time." He didn't quite know what to think of me. So we started to work, and the first shot—the picture was MAN HUNT—is a

camera up high over some pine trees, comes down through the pine trees onto the footprint of a man. Then a big German boot steps in. So I figured this all out before Fritz got there; I figured instead of coming down through those trees I'd do it in reverse, so you won't have to come down and fish around on a boom. He said, "I want to come down and ..." And I said, "Fritz, would you mind if we did it in reverse?" He said, "What's the reverse?" I said, "The camera will start down here and move up; I've got black threads on the branches so I can move it gently so we don't break the forest coming down." He said, "Yes, but how are you going to do the foot?" I said, "You'll have the man's footprint in—but you don't want a mark of this boot that steps in there, so I've got some little stones. When the man's foot steps in he's going to rest on those little stones, so you won't have an imprint of his foot. When his foot moves out, I'm going to count one, two, then we're going to start up." He said, "You can time this close?" I said, "I think so." Now, this is a complicated thing to tell a director who doesn't know what you're doing. But he knew exactly what I was talking about. We got the camera all set, the guy took his foot out, the other guy's foot went out; there was the footprint, and we went up. He said to me, "You think it was timed right?" I asked the operator, and he said, "I think we got it." He says, "Well, we won't play more with it; we'll see how good this one is." And we moved. I got along with this man so wonderfully all through the picture. I think this man is one of the great directors of the business. But everybody's against him, what a bastard—he never did anything to me. Oh—there was another thing in the picture. There's a guy in a cave, and he has a little arrow out of a girl's hat on a rubber band, and he's going to try to coax this other guy to look through a cave hole and shoot him with the arrow. So I set the camera up and took about four hundred feet of film with the focus in the tunnel, in the thickness of the rocks, and lit them with cross-lights and baby spots. He didn't say anything about "What are you doing?" We reversed the film, and I made an exposure on this. I had the film up in the camera, and I said, "OK, Fritz, we're ready." He said, "Could you tell me, what was this you were doing?" He wanted to learn. I said, "When the guy's face shows in there, I want his face sharp, but he's looking through a thickness of the wall, so I want that sharp too." So I just photographed it very sharp, focused on it, and had a piece of black velvet in the wall. Now, I took the velvet down, and killed the lights that were on the tunnel, and the guy's face came out, and played the scene. When he saw this on the screen, he thought this was the greatest thing that ever happened in the movies.

LM: Was it a double-exposure then?

MILLER: No—I just took one half of it first, the tunnel, and then the face, on the next exposure. So it wasn't one exposure on top of the other, but it was two exposures in the one scene. He realized then that I was for him, and I could do no wrong for this man. We'd finish at four o'clock in the afternoon. He'd say, "What should we do?" I'd say, "What should we do? We should go home, Fritz. We got a damn good day's work." That picture cost $500,000, when they were spending $2 million [on others]. It was unheard-of. Then they gave him the roust, I don't know why. If I were to do a picture there's two guys I'd hire, and they're opposites. One is Ford, the other is Fritz Lang. Because they save you money. If you give Ford a picture to do, say, "Here's the script," let him shoot it the way he wants to make it, and leave him alone. On THIS ABOVE ALL, one of these things I shot, we used almost a half million feet of negative. I always kept track of the cost of photographing a picture, so the amount of film you used was part of that cost. After we finished HOW GREEN WAS MY VALLEY, I went checking; I went into the camera room where you draw the film and asked them how much film we drew. It was less than 100,000 feet. I said, "You've made a mistake somewhere." They did it again and came up with the same figure. So I went over to the laboratory and asked them how much footage they developed; they came up with the same amount. Less than 100,000 feet. Do you know how much money this saves? All you've got to do is let him alone. If you interfere with him, boy, he can screw you up but good. He knows what he's doing, and he doesn't want anybody to interfere with him.

LM: Would you say that that's the formula for a good cameraman-director relationship, that both men know what they're doing?

MILLER: You never have any trouble. There's a language you use; I don't think that making a picture with Ford I

would speak to him more than, oh, fifty words in a day. He'd be looking at something and I knew what he was looking for. I'd pick up the camera and come over. On HOW GREEN WAS MY VALLEY you look: there's no boom shots, there's no dolly shots. The camera just pans occasionally; when a person is moving from here, I pan, when they get to here they're in close-up. I change size when they're moving. He knew his business; I learned a lot from this man.

LM: But you knew your business too, and that's the point.

MILLER: Yes, I pleased him, I think, because I wasn't a nuisance to him. I allowed him to do his thinking without a lot of "Would you like to look in here?" or "What do you think of this?"

LM: Mutual trust and respect.

MILLER: Yes.

THE FILMS OF ARTHUR MILLER

A complete list of Mr. Miller's short films, from the time he started making movies in 1908 to the time of his first feature film in 1915, would probably be impossible, although Miller recounted a large number of them in his book *One Reel a Week*. Therefore, what follows is a list of his feature films, compiled with Mr. Miller's assistance at the time of our interview. It does not include his work in serials, which provided him with one of his most famous credits, THE PERILS OF PAULINE, in 1914. In the index, director's name follows the year.

1. AT BAY—Pathe 1915—George Fitzmaurice
2. NEW YORK—Pathe 1916—George Fitzmaurice
3. FIFTH AVENUE—Pathe 1916—George Fitzmaurice
4. BIG JIM GARRITY—Pathe 1916—George Fitzmaurice
5. ARMS AND THE WOMAN—Pathe 1916—George Fitzmaurice
6. ROMANTIC JOURNEY—Pathe 1916—George Fitzmaurice
7. HUNTING OF THE HAWK—Pathe 1917—George Fitzmaurice
8. RECOIL—Pathe 1917—George Fitzmaurice
9. THE IRON HEART—Pathe 1917—George Fitzmaurice
10. THE MARK OF CAIN—Pathe 1917—George Fitzmaurice
11. SYLVIA OF THE SECRET SERVICE—Pathe 1917—George Fitzmaurice
12. VENGEANCE IS MINE—Pathe 1917—Frank Crane
13. THE NAULAHKA—Pathe 1918—George Fitzmaurice
14. JAPANESE NIGHTINGALE—Pathe 1918—George Fitzmaurice
15. THE NARROW PATH—Pathe 1918—George Fitzmaurice
16. COMMON CLAY—Pathe 1919—George Fitzmaurice
17. THE PROFITEERS—Pathe 1919—George Fitzmaurice
18. AVALANCHE—Pathe 1919—George Fitzmaurice
19. OUR BETTER SELVES—Pathe 1919—George Fitzmaurice
20. A SOCIETY EXILE—Paramount 1919—George Fitzmaurice
21. WITNESS FOR THE DEFENSE—Paramount 1919—George Fitzmaurice

Miller and Irene Dunne on the set of ANNA AND THE KING OF SIAM *(1946).*

22. COUNTERFEIT—Paramount 1919—George Fitzmaurice
23. ON WITH THE DANCE—Paramount 1920—George Fitzmaurice
24. HIS HOUSE IN ORDER—Paramount 1920—Hugh Ford
25. THE RIGHT TO LOVE—Paramount 1920—George Fitzmaurice
26. LADY ROSE'S DAUGHTER—Paramount 1920—Hugh Ford
27. IDOLS OF CLAY—Paramount 1920—Roy William Neill
28. PAYING THE PIPER—Paramount 1921—George Fitzmaurice
29. EXPERIENCE—Paramount 1921—George Fitzmaurice
30. FOREVER—Paramount 1921—George Fitzmaurice
31. THREE LIVE GHOSTS—Paramount 1922—George Fitzmaurice
32. THE MAN FROM HOME—Paramount 1922—George Fitzmaurice
33. TO HAVE AND TO HOLD—Paramount 1922—George Fitzmaurice
34. BELLA DONNA—Paramount 1923—George Fitzmaurice
35. THE CHEAT—Paramount 1923—George Fitzmaurice
36. KICK IN—Paramount 1923—George Fitzmaurice
37. THE ETERNAL CITY—First National 1923—George Fitzmaurice
38. CYTHEREA—First National 1924—George Fitzmaurice—Color sequences
39. TARNISH—First National 1924—George Fitzmaurice—Collaboration with William Tuers
40. IN HOLLYWOOD WITH POTASH AND PERLMUTTER—First National 1924—Al Green—Collaboration with Harry Hallenberger
41. A THIEF IN PARADISE—First National 1925—George Fitzmaurice
42. HIS SUPREME MOMENT—First National 1925—George Fitzmaurice
43. THE COMING OF AMOS—Producers Distributing Corporation (PDC) 1925—Paul Sloane
44. MADE FOR LOVE—PDC 1926—Paul Sloane
45. EVE'S LEAVES—PDC 1926—Paul Sloane
46. THE VOLGA BOATMAN—PDC 1926—Cecil B. DeMille—Collaboration with J. Peverell Marley, Fred Westerberg
47. THE CLINGING VINE—PDC 1926—Paul Sloane
48. FOR ALIMONY ONLY—PDC 1926—William DeMille
49. NOBODY'S WIDOW—PDC 1927—Donald Crisp
50. VANITY—PDC 1927—Donald Crisp

51. THE FIGHTING EAGLE—Pathe 1927—Donald Crisp
52. THE ANGEL OF BROADWAY—Pathe 1927—Lois Weber
53. BLUE DANUBE—Pathe 1928—Paul Sloane
54. HOLD 'EM, YALE—Pathe 1928—Edward H. Griffith
55. THE COP—Pathe 1928—Donald Crisp
56. ANNAPOLIS—Pathe 1928—Christy Cabanne
57. THE SPIELER—Pathe 1928—Tay Garnett
58. THE BELLAMY TRIAL—MGM 1929—Monta Bell
59. STRANGE CARGO—Pathe 1929—Benjamin Glazer and Arthur Gregor
60. BIG NEWS—Pathe 1929—Gregory LaCava
61. THE FLYING FOOL—Pathe 1929—Tay Garnett
62. SAILOR'S HOLIDAY—Pathe 1929—Fred Newmeyer
63. OH YEAH!—Pathe 1929—Tay Garnett
64. HIS FIRST COMMAND—Pathe 1930—Gregory La-Cava—Collaboration with John J. Mescall
65. LADY OF SCANDAL—MGM 1930—Sidney Franklin—Collaboration with Oliver T. Marsh
66. OFFICER O'BRIEN—Pathe 1930—Tay Garnett
67. SEE AMERICA THIRST—Universal 1930—William James Craft—Collaboration with Allyn Jones
68. FATHER'S SON—Warner Brothers 1930—William Beaudine
69. THE TRUTH ABOUT YOUTH—First National 1930—William Seiter
70. BAD COMPANY—Pathe 1931—Tay Garnett
71. PANAMA FLO—RKO 1932—Ralph Murphy
72. BIG SHOT—RKO 1932—Ralph Murphy
73. YOUNG BRIDE—RKO 1932—William Seiter
74. OKAY, AMERICA—Universal 1932—Tay Garnett
75. BREACH OF PROMISE—World Wide 1932—Paul Stein
76. ME AND MY GAL—Fox 1932—Raoul Walsh
77. SAILOR'S LUCK—Fox 1933—Raoul Walsh
78. HOLD ME TIGHT—Fox 1933—David Butler
79. THE MAN WHO DARED—Fox 1933—Hamilton MacFadden
80. THE LAST TRAIL—Fox 1933—James Tinling
81. THE MAD GAME—Fox 1933—Irving Cummings
82. MY WEAKNESS—Fox 1933—David Butler
83. BOTTOMS UP—Fox 1934—David Butler
84. EVER SINCE EVE—Fox 1934—George Marshall
85. HANDY ANDY—Fox 1934—David Butler
86. LOVE TIME—Fox 1934—James Tinling
87. THE WHITE PARADE—Fox 1934—Irving Cummings
88. BRIGHT EYES—Fox 1934—David Butler
89. THE LITTLE COLONEL—Fox 1935—David Butler
90. IT'S A SMALL WORLD—Fox 1935—Irving Cummings
91. BLACK SHEEP—Fox 1935—Allan Dwan
92. WELCOME HOME—Fox 1935—James Tinling
93. PADDY O'DAY—Fox 1935—Lewis Seiler
94. WHITE FANG—20th Century Fox 1936—David Butler
95. 36 HOURS TO KILL—20th Century Fox 1936—Eugene Forde
96. PIGSKIN PARADE—20th Century Fox 1936—David Butler
97. STOWAWAY—20th Century Fox 1936—William Seiter
98. WEE WILLIE WINKIE—20th Century Fox 1937—John Ford
99. HEIDI—20th Century Fox 1937—Allan Dwan
100. THE BARONESS AND THE BUTLER—20th Century Fox 1938—Walter Lang
101. REBECCA OF SUNNYBROOK FARM—20th Century Fox 1938—Allan Dwan
102. LITTLE MISS BROADWAY—20th Century Fox 1938—Irving Cummings
103. SUBMARINE PATROL—20th Century Fox 1938—John Ford
104. THE LITTLE PRINCESS—20th Century Fox 1939—Walter Lang—Color
105. SUSANNAH OF THE MOUNTIES—20th Century Fox 1939—William Seiter
106. THE RAINS CAME—20th Century Fox 1939—Clarence Brown
107. HERE I AM A STRANGER—20th Century Fox 1939—Roy Del Ruth
108. THE BLUEBIRD—20th Century Fox 1940—Walter Lang—Color
109. JOHNNY APOLLO—20th Century Fox 1940—Henry Hathaway
110. ON THEIR OWN—20th Century Fox 1940—Otto Brower
111. THE MARK OF ZORRO—20th Century Fox 1940—Rouben Mamoulian
112. BRIGHAM YOUNG, FRONTIERSMAN—20th Century Fox 1940—Henry Hathaway
113. TOBACCO ROAD—20th Century Fox 1941—John Ford
114. MAN HUNT—20th Century Fox 1941—Fritz Lang
115. THE MEN IN HER LIFE—20th Century Fox 1941—Gregory Ratoff
116. HOW GREEN WAS MY VALLEY—20th Century Fox 1941—John Ford—Won Miller his first Academy Award
117. THIS ABOVE ALL—20th Century Fox 1942—Anatole Litvak
118. ICELAND—20th Century Fox 1942—Bruce Humberstone
119. THE MOON IS DOWN—20th Century Fox 1943—Irving Pichel
120. THE IMMORTAL SERGEANT—20th Century Fox 1943—John M. Stahl—Collaboration with Clyde DeVinna
121. THE OX-BOW INCIDENT—20th Century Fox 1943—William Wellman
122. THE SONG OF BERNADETTE—20th Century Fox 1943—Henry King—Won Miller his second Academy Award
123. THE PURPLE HEART—20th Century Fox 1944—Lewis Milestone
124. KEYS OF THE KINGDOM—20th Century Fox 1944—Henry King
125. A ROYAL SCANDAL—20th Century Fox 1945—Started by Ernst Lubitsch, completed by Otto Preminger
126. DRAGONWYCK—20th Century Fox 1946—Joseph L. Mankiewicz
127. ANNA AND THE KING OF SIAM—20th Century Fox 1946—John Cromwell—Won Miller his third Academy Award
128. THE RAZOR'S EDGE—20th Century Fox 1946—Edmund Goulding
129. GENTLEMEN'S AGREEMENT—20th Century Fox 1947—Elia Kazan
130. THE WALLS OF JERICHO—20th Century Fox 1948—John M. Stahl
131. WHIRLPOOL—20th Century Fox 1949—Otto Preminger
132. THE GUNFIGHTER—20th Century Fox 1950—Henry King
133. THE PROWLER—Universal 1951—Joseph Losey

Interview with HAL MOHR

Hal Mohr is another outstanding cinematographer whose interest in the field developed at an early age. As his conversation indicates, he had a wide variety of jobs in the motion picture business before deciding to remain a cameraman. This gave him an unusually fine background and provided him with the knowledge he was able to use for so many years thereafter in developing ideas and technical devices. Having won two Academy Awards, for A MIDSUMMER NIGHT'S DREAM and THE PHANTOM OF THE OPERA, Mohr did not rest on his laurels, and continued to *create* as a cameraman through the 1950s, in television commercials as well as feature films. Although he shot several TV series, he is the first to admit that the medium does not permit cameramen to display their artistic talents to any great degree. Increasingly inactive in the 1960s, Mohr reaffirmed his great skill and imagination in 1969 when he was hired as photographic consultant on Alfred Hitchcock's TOPAZ, one of the year's most visually striking films.

Happily married since 1934 to Evelyn Venable, the leading lady he photographed in DAVID HARUM, Mohr provided us with one of our most detailed interviews, covering his long and illustrious career.

LM: How did you get started in the motion picture business?

MOHR: In my youth, in San Francisco—at the time of the San Francisco earthquake and fire, I think I was eleven years old. I had never seen a motion picture; they were very rare articles at that time. As a kid I used to play around with lantern slides, the so-called Magic Lantern, and my fingers explored anything that was new or worth looking at. Shortly after the earthquake and fire, little vaudeville and variety houses sprang up all over the city, in former stores or basements, or burned-out buildings. They introduced this motion picture novelty; at break during the show they'd run a piece of motion picture film. And the first motion picture I ever saw was in one of these little houses; they'd set up a camera alongside a railroad track, and a train came from the distance and passed by the camera—that's all there was to the thing. And I was intrigued with this darn thing, that from that moment on, that was the only thing I wanted to do—I wanted to find out what made that train go through the audience, and not run over anybody. We were an upper-middle-class family in San Francisco, and I had things pretty much the way I wanted them, as a kid. I finished my grammar school, and then in high school I went to Poly, and in my second year at Polytechnic I got a side job—I cut school for about the last year, and never finished high school. I got a job in the film exchange,

splicing film and inspecting films that would come back from the movie theaters. We'd run it on reels through our fingers to catch the breaks, and then splice them. And in the junk of this place I found a little old, almost a toy, projection machine. It was called an optigraph, the forerunner of the motiograph, which became the projector of its time. I asked my boss if I could have it, he said yes, and I took this thing home. I had little scraps of film that I'd run on it; there was no lamp, it was just the head of the thing—it had a two-inch projection lens on it. I began fooling around and I put it in a dark box and made a camera out of it. I'd get little scraps of film—short ends, thirty feet, forty feet, fifty feet, whatever I could manage to scrape enough nickels to buy, and experimented with this thing. I actually made motion pictures with this little machine. I had to load it in the dark—I didn't have magazines for the film—closed it up tight, and the only lens I had was this projection lens. I went around San Francisco with the thing. I made a sort of tripod, and devised a pan head for it, if you please. I got this worm gear, and a spiral gear, and put this thing together so I could pan the camera around, because I couldn't tilt it. But I did use it; I photographed news events around San Francisco, as a youngster; I'd go to the Algin Theater, and Sid Grauman's father had a theater called the Empress. And they were still using motion pictures at the intermission break, or in the case of the Empress Theater, where they had more than one show a day, they'd use the motion picture as the chaser to get the people out of the theater so they'd get the new audience in for the next show. And I used to photograph local news events with this thing, very badly, and I used the camera to make prints. I had to fix up a little developing room in my basement; I'd develop the negative in these tanks that I'd had built, wrapped them on a rack, and then I'd use the camera as a printing machine. I'd get maybe ten bucks or twenty bucks from the Orpheum or the Empress. Now during this period, there existed the so-called Patents Company, and if you know anything about motion picture history you know about the Patents Company. They had the patent rights to the intermittency of the camera, and any device that pulled down film and allowed a slack loop space for the film to be carried before the next pull-down, while the exposure was being made, was an infringement on their patents. The only camera that was built that was not an infringement on their patents I knew as the Gaumont camera; I think it had another name. They used what they called a beater-type movement. The film was pulled down continuously by a sprocket and a finger on a cam would come and knock the film down, and while the slack was being taken up to pull it down again by the single sprocket, the exposure was made. And that did circumvent the

Erich von Stroheim, director and star of THE WEDDING MARCH (1928), *with Hal Mohr and Mohr's first wife.*

Patents Company's patent, so what few independent operators who were within the law—and there were damn few of them, believe me—used the Gaumont camera. I'd been doing quite a bit of work in and around San Francisco, I'd been seen around with this camera. I'd quit school in the meantime, and taken this as a full-time occupation.

LM: How old were you then?

MOHR: By this time I suppose I was fifteen. There was an oilman at this time named Griffin, who owned the cattle interest down in the Salinas Valley, and had a big interest in oil properties. He wanted to make a film, I don't know what the purpose of it was, and wanted to get some motion pictures of the oil wells around Bakersfield. He got in contact with me, and that turned out to be a fairly good job; I began to get into the serious factors of making motion pictures. So when this thing became known, the Patents Company sent their detectives to track me down, and find out what the hell I was doing. The reason I'm going into such detail is that I think this is the most interesting part of my whole career. They trailed me around for days, and I had a big, husky kid who'd been a truck driver, who used to go with me as an assistant of mine. His specific job while I was photographing stuff was

to keep people away from the camera, while I was operating, so they couldn't get a look at the thing and see what I was doing. But these two detectives approached me on another job, and I like a damn fool, to prove to them that I could do what I claimed to do, showed them my camera; that's all they needed—they had an injunction served on me. My father was a property holder, and in business in San Francisco; we didn't want to get involved in a lot of nonsense, so he said, "Well, you'd better give them the camera and forget about it." The family was against my doing motion picture work anyhow. So I went down to this attorney in San Francisco, and brought the camera in to him. He said he had to have it, and I said, "Well, you may get it, but you're not going to get it as a camera," and I threw the thing down on the floor—it flew out in all directions. I said, "There's the camera if you want it." But that didn't stop me; I went to work for other people who had heard of me, the Miles Brothers in San Francisco, and Sol Lesser, when he put together a little film outfit called the Progressive Film Company, in which we did all sorts of documentary films, made films for different commercial outfits. One of the things I did for Sol, was in 1913, when San Francisco had bid to get the Panama Pacific International Exposition to be given there in 1915. Well, San Francisco, as you undoubtedly know, was almost as notorious as the cities are becoming today. There was one area of San Francisco known as the Barbary Coast; it was about eight square blocks, with over 20,000 prostitutes living there. There used to be people going there who'd never come out alive. But the City Fathers decided that before the exposition could be given they'd have to clean up the morals of the city, so they announced that on a certain night the Barbary Coast would be closed, it would be the end of the Barbary Coast, and they meant it quite seriously. All these little back alleys through the Chinatown area, Washington Avenue, Bartlett Avenue, Jackson Street, all these little streets in that area were where these whorehouses were, and they were all to be thrown out of town. Of course, there was a more fashionable area downtown, the Tenderloin, down around Mason Street; they weren't going to bother that, because that was conducted on a more ladylike and gentlemanly-like basis. But this Barbary Coast was a bawdy, wild, murderous neighborhood, so Efe Asher and Sid Grauman were young fellows, boys around town and pretty wild kids. They were working with Sol, and someone got the idea to make a film of the last night of the Barbary Coast. They used to have street lights, and I'd have to photograph this thing at night; they used to have a series of alternating-current arc lights, eight or ten of them running down a street, and they'd flicker all over the place. To improvise some light, so I could photograph at night—I don't know how the hell I got all this knowledge —I went down to the Public Works company and got some of these old broken-down arc lights, fixed them up on wooden stands, and I had two of these things. I'd just run my hook off of the meters, or wherever I could get a.c. current, hook it onto these things, and use them to photograph. At any rate, we made a two-reel subject called THE LAST NIGHT OF THE BARBARY COAST. I was the one-man band: photographer, director, laboratory man, editor, salesman, chauffeur, propman, everything. Very much like the young filmmakers of today; I was really a filmmaker in those days. I made these prints myself; we sold it on a state's rights basis, where we distributed it to territories for exclusive sale, and I made over three hundred prints of that thing. I must have made a hell of a lot of money on it, because I was getting $35 a week at that time to be the factor factotum of the whole thing. Other film companies began developing in San Francisco, and I worked for most of them. A man came up named Jim Keene, built the Kennograph Studio up in Fairfax, and made a picture called MONEY, which he sold to the World Film people. I did the finishing photography and editing on that. Then there was an outfit up in San Rafael called the California Motion Picture Company, which was headed by George Middleton and Alexander Bifus. Middleton was married to an opera singer by the name of Beatrice Licinina; she was the star of some of the films. I photographed a lot of their films, and edited a lot. In those days you did whatever there was to be done; you might be a photographer, or director, actor, *anything*—which was great training. It's too bad you don't have some of that kind of training today. Then I built my own studio over in Berkeley, on Telegraph Avenue. I took over what had been a store on the corner, plus quite a bit of lot area, and a barn, down about a hundred feet from the store area. By this time war had broken out, the First World War in Europe, and it was 1914. Up until that time all of

our really good films, the best grade technical films, actually did come out of Europe, although we did have Biograph, and Vitagraph, Lubin, and all those people, who made exciting American films. But the really well-made films all came out of Europe, and they had a certain flavor. But with the beginning of the war in Europe, that source of supply was cut off; there wasn't much film made in Europe. I think the last film to come out of there was CABIRIA; it was made by an Italian film company, and it was a spectacular film, about the last days of Pompeii. It had the eruption of volcanoes, and palaces tumbling, and all that. And in this they had a shot in which the camera traveled through this tremendous palace—it looked like it was floating on air. I couldn't figure out how the hell they'd done this, but I made up my mind that in my next picture I was going to do this. To get back to the thread of the story, I got the idea that since there was a big Italian colony in San Francisco, and these films had been cut off completely from Europe, there's a market, a gap to fill. So I went to the Italian colony and there was a man named Johnny DiMaria, who owned most of the real estate in the Barbary Coast; he was like a Little Caesar type of character. And I got to Johnny, talked to him, and promoted. He said, "Well, what are you going to put into this thing?" So I talked my dad into giving me $500 as my investment in it. We sold stock among the Italians and raised $4,000 to $5,000, and Johnny said he could put up the rest of the money to complete this project. The project was this: I built a studio, rented this ground on Telegraph Avenue, converted the old store into offices, prop rooms, and dressing rooms. I built an open stage next to the barn; the barn was the shop and loft, where we built the scenery. Half of the stage I covered with a solid roof, the other half I left out in the daylight. I read a thousand books, finally found a book that I liked the theme of, and I literally plagiarized this book, a book by Amelia Reeves, and wrote a motion picture script. I couldn't typewrite very well, so I didn't bother spelling everything out; I abbreviated everything. The whole script was an abbreviation. One line would cover a minute and a half! It was an Italian story, a period thing; our scenery in and around San Francisco lent itself very nicely to the scenery of Italy. I bought a Model T Ford, a Pathe camera, which was *the* camera of the period (the Patents Company was through, by now), and we built an Old Italian street set on this lot. I'd gone to a booking agency in San Francisco and hired an actor and actress, and I had an Italian girl, who was the daughter of one of the investors, who was a fine-looking girl. I used to load the leading man, a valet who was a damn good little actor, and a dog who worked in the picture—I would load the whole company, including this same truck driver who used to be my strong-arm man (he became my cameraman), into this Model T Ford, including the camera and one or two oilcloth reflectors that I put up on sticks. We were all in this Model T Ford and off we'd go behind the hills in Berkeley or up toward Raccoon Straits near the San Pablo Bay area, and we made this picture. I took over this laboratory that had fallen all to pieces in Berkeley, and I fixed it up. I'd be shooting all day, I'd come to the lab that evening, roll up the negative and put it up on the drums, get two or three hours' sleep, then come back and make a positive— develop it and put it on the drums, then go to the studio and we'd go out on location again, or shoot in the studio. Getting back to the CABIRIA thing, I devised this dolly and

I sincerely believe—it may be not true, of course—but I honestly believe it was the first time a camera was ever moved on wheels in a motion picture in America. I made a track, and got little car wheels, put this platform on the car wheels and set the camera on the tripod atop it. We'd built the set with a broken wall, so you could travel from one room to another, and tracked the camera across this thing. That was my interpretation of what I'd seen in CABIRIA. I may be wrong, but to my knowledge it was the first time a camera had rolled on set—they'd had them in automobiles and trains before.

LM: Was that how they'd done it in CABIRIA?

MOHR: No, they'd had an elaborate overhead crane; they went over platforms and down stairs and everything else. They had this thing, as I later learned, on an overhead trolley; the camera hung down from this. That apparatus would have cost more money than my whole damn picture cost! Before we finished our picture—I'll round this story out so I don't leave it up in the air—we ran out of money, and I put the picture together as best I could. DiMaria had something up his sleeve, because he had a contract with me; if I had made a successful picture and sold it, he was going to finance all future products. I had a two-year contract for $100 a week, plus I think twenty or twenty-five percent of the company. So Johnny saw no reason why I should get all this money, I guess; I took the picture, which was incompletely cut, to New York, and showed it to William F. Brady, who was the head of the World Film Company, because they had a distribution company for independent films, called the Greater New York Film Exchange. They played Ping-Pong with it while I was staying in a little cheap hotel at Washington Square, and in the meantime there were several hundred dollars' worth of bills back here, and Johnny put the outfit through bankruptcy while I was in New York, so I was out on my can. I went back to California, and I don't know if the picture was ever sold, or released, or what.

LM: What was the name of the film?

MOHR: I called it THE DAUGHTER OF THE GODS. Shortly after that, Herbert Brenon made a picture with Annette Kellermann called THE DAUGHTER OF THE GODS, a different film. So from then on, I came down to Hollywood; this was late 1914. Arthur Rice, a lab man I'd known in San Francisco, had come down to Universal Studios as a director, and he got me a job as a film editor, at $25 a week. They had just moved out to where Universal City is now, from Sunset and Gower. There were nine of us, as I remember, in that cutting room, cutting the product of fifty-four directors. Most of them were one-reel films, but some of them were features. Lois Weber was one of the directors; I later photographed a picture for her. One of the stars was Ruth Stonehouse, and they wanted to make a director out of her, so I helped her direct, and edited her films. Then World War One came along, that is, our involvement in it, and I'd left Universal—I quit or got fired, I forget—and I got a job with the Rolin Film Company. Hal Roach and Dwight Whiting owned a studio up on the top over what was then the Hill Street Tunnel, downtown. They had a little daylight stage, and Snub Pollard, Bebe Daniels, Harold Lloyd, Toto the Clown

were all working for them. So the draft thing had come along, and I had been given an F deferment, so Whiting figured, "Well, here's a young guy who can be a director, and there's no danger of him being taken away into the Army." So I got a job with them directing Harold Lloyd comedies, and by the time I had made two of them, the draft got me, and I was off to the war in 1917. The way we worked was, we had a stock company, and they had a little schoolbus; we'd load the stock company in the bus. Harold had a Chandler touring car, and his chauffeur, Gil Pratt, wanted to become a director, so he would co-direct with me. We had no scripts, but we'd get a story idea, and develop the thing, and talk it out. We only had to make nine minutes of film, so we'd get a running gag going. The first picture I made for them was called THE BIG IDEA, which opened at the Criterion Theater, the opening week that the theater opened. We'd leave all the interiors until after we'd gotten the exteriors, because the running gags depended entirely on what we did exterior; so then we'd spend a day or two on the interiors, and in one week we'd shoot a film. These were seven-day weeks, of course, not like today. And in the meantime, Harold's other director, Alf Goulding, was preparing, getting his ideas together. So the week that we'd finish, and I'd go into the cutting room to cut the film, Alf was out shooting. So as I say, I got to make two pictures; then when I got back after the war, I started all over again in San Francisco. I went to work for the Miles Brothers again, and did some documentary films. Meanwhile, a company had started out in Portland, Oregon; a man named McMonies owned a big biscuit factory in Portland, and he financed this motion picture company. They'd taken over an old stone foundry out on the outskirts of Portland; they'd made a picture, and hadn't completed it, and a friend of mine who'd gone up there as laboratory man got in touch with me, and I went up to Portland, and finished this picture, as photographer and editor; that was around 1920. It was one of Jean Hersholt's first pictures, and I've even forgotten the name of the damn thing.

LM: Was the light different up there?

MOHR: Different climate conditions . . . of course, by this time they had developed some lights, which were better than what I had had. They were arc lights.

LM: Did you find that the natural light in Portland was different from here?

MOHR: Oh yes; there wasn't as much light. . . . There were very few sunny days, and the film was so slow in those days that if it was an overcast day, you wouldn't get decent photography. I stayed up there about a year or so, then I came back down here, and I've been going ever since.

LM: Did you then decide to concentrate on photography?

MOHR: Yes, I realized that was what I liked. As I say, I'd done everything, and even at that time, directing was still for the birds. It still had no connotation of being anything creative; all a director would do was say, "All right, you come out the door, and you meet her over here, and you turn her around, do this to her, and get on your horse and ride." That was the director's function; the cameraman was the one who actually made the pictures. Not that I'm talking directors down—I think directors have done a

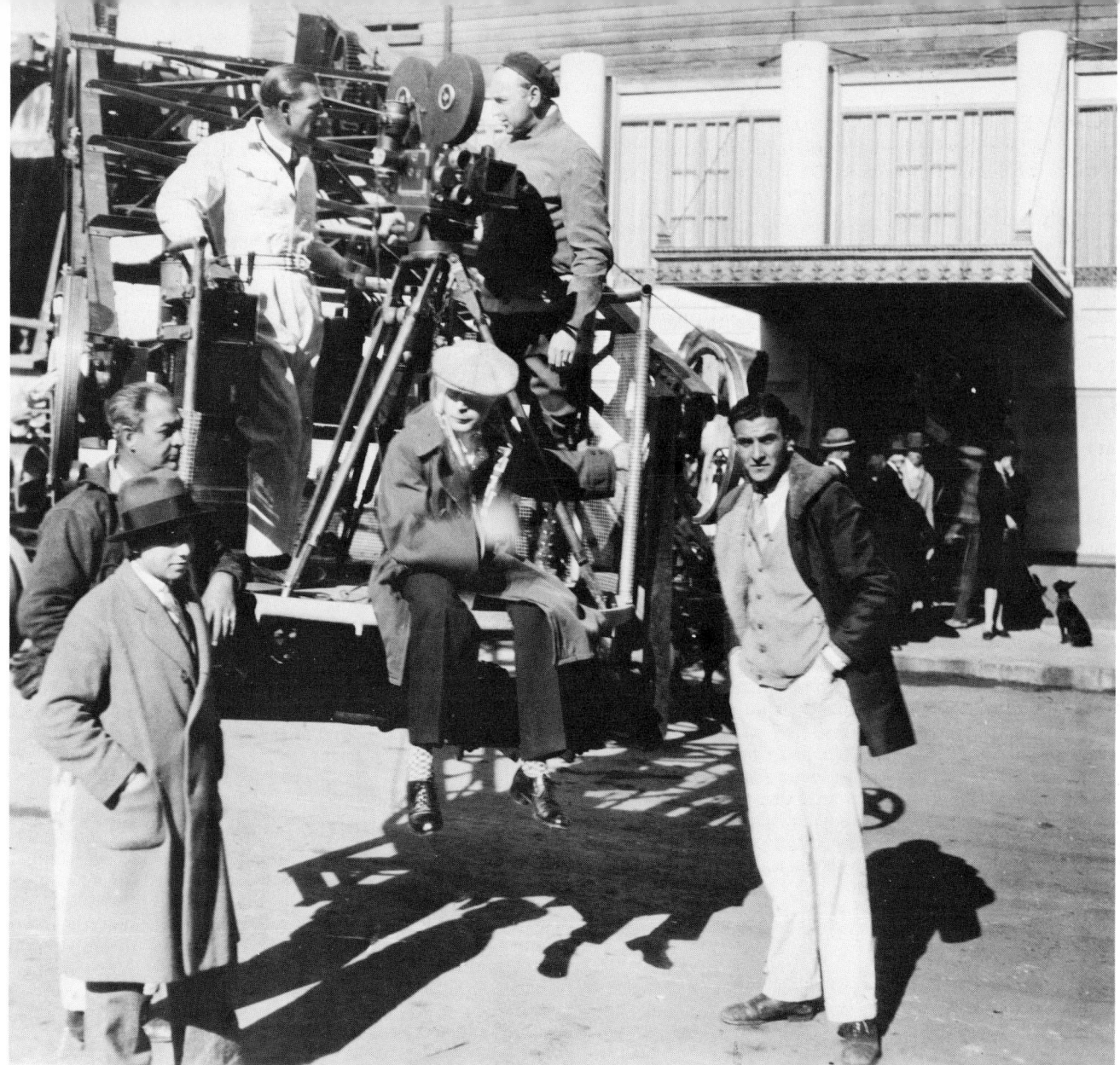

Mohr (with beret) checks on a shot while director Paul Fejos sits on the edge of the famous BROADWAY *crane, and assistant Stanley Cortez (in white pants) waits (ca. 1929).*

magnificent job; I've worked with directors who I look up to as gods. But for my choice, I figured that cinematography was the most creative job, and that was what I wanted to do.

LM: Starting from scratch, as you were—as the whole industry was—how did you learn?

MOHR: There was nobody to show me anything—no American Film Institute to teach me. It was trial and error, but you couldn't afford to make too many errors, because it was too expensive, but mistakes could get by, if it wasn't too tragic a mistake. If you managed to get a picture on the film that you could see, it was all right. Many of the experimental ventures we went into, looking for effects, were just about that. We'd say, "Well, we can get away with it, but the next time we'll do it different." But it was all trial and error; there was nobody to teach

you, and those who had knowledge were very jealous of that knowlege, and they wouldn't show you. There was no exchange of ideas, and that went for everyone in the business; but it was evolutionary, and eventually in the golden era of motion pictures, we reached the point where there was an exchange of ideas. I as a cameraman might call, say, Bill Daniels, and say, "Bill, I've got a thing coming up in a picture. How did you do so-and-so in such-and-such a picture?" Or somebody would call me. And the result was a rash of spectacular motion pictures made, because it was a concerted effort; today they're going to the point where it's a one-man effort.

LM: Did being an editor help you as a cameraman?

MOHR: It helped me a lot. Script girls used to get kind of mad at me, because they'd never have a chance; I'd put pictures together, so I knew instinctively that the man had gotten off the horse and gone into the saloon on camera left so he had to come in the next scene from camera right, or from center down. So I'd set up accordingly. I think the editing is the best source for learning the mechanical putting-together of a motion picture. It has become a highly skilled profession. Even in the days when I was cutting silent pictures, I used to change the whole story through editing. If we had an actor, a leading man, who was not too good, and we could possibly switch him around and make him the heavy, and make the heavy the leading man, we'd do it—of course, with titles you could put whatever words you wanted to into the actor's mouth. Of course, they don't do that today, but that's the kind of thing a film editor has in his hands.

LM: One of the first pictures I have credited for you is a Richard Talmadge vehicle called WATCH HIM STEP.

MOHR: That was made on Poverty Row, it was the first picture that Richard Talmadge ever made. Morris Schlank was quite a character, and he had money, and he financed it. We made it in what was the old Francis Ford–Grace Cunard studio, which was across the street from what is now the Columbia Publicity Department building, on the corner of Sunset and Beechwood. Dick Talmadge, as you know, was Douglas Fairbanks' double; anything that was really hazardous, Dick did. His real name was Sylvester Matsetti; he was one of a family of Italian acrobats . . . there were five or six of them, and they were just wonderful. They could do anything. Syl had done doubling for Doug Fairbanks, and Schlank got the idea, and a damn good idea, to give him a different name and make a star out of him in action pictures. So they gave him the name of Richard Talmadge, which was a good name in those days. Their first picture was done on location, and I photographed it for them.

LM: I suppose the idea was to get as much in as possible on each stunt.

MOHR: Oh yes, you had to show the authenticity of each stunt. For example, there was one shot we made down in what is now Azusa—it was just a crossroad at that time. It was a chase, and why he had to run up the telegraph pole I don't know, but during the chase he went up the pole—one of these high-tension line things, which was a damn dangerous thing for him to do, and we had no precautionary measures. So I got this long-shot—I started off in close-up to identify him, of course—then we moved back to get the whole thing, the whole geography in the picture. So as the heavies start up the pole after him, down on the street comes this wagon, and in the bed of the wagon were straw and blankets—one of the other brothers was driving the thing, so they would time it right. And Syl jumped off the top of this damn pole just before the guys got there, lands in the wagon, bounces off and takes off running down the street. This was all done without a cut; it had to be him, and he did it. I think that's the only one I did with him; it was a great experience.

LM: Next I have something called THE UNFOLDMENT . . .

MOHR: With Florence Lawrence . . . you're really going back into history. It was made by a man by the name of George Kern. It was made at the old Hollywood Studios, which is now the General Service Studios, and at that time

there was nothing on Santa Monica Boulevard but the studio itself.

LM: What were working methods like on Poverty Row, as compared to more prominent studios?

MOHR: It was just what the name implies; if a guy had three dollars and good credit, he'd make a picture. If I could collect all the money I never collected on salary, and my salary was small, I'd have a small fortune. If I got $125 a week, I was getting a hell of a lot of money, and for that I would supply a camera and an automobile to haul the camera around in, and in many cases I would supply my own assistant.

LM: Were you still working in the lab at this time?

MOHR: By this time the laboratory had moved on; we still cooperated. In those days, the cameraman had to be a photographer. He had to be able to read his own negatives and know what the hell it was about. For example, even up to the time that I was doing THE JAZZ SINGER, I'd get there a half-hour ahead of time and go to the laboratory. At that time we made tests of every setup, and the negative developer had all my test strips lying on a light-box. I'd go through with the lab man, and they'd all be developed to a certain time. There were many cases where you deliberately overexposed a scene for a certain effect, or you deliberately underexposed a scene. When you'd over expose, the purpose was that they'd short-develop it, to get a soft, flat effect; where you'd underexpose, the purpose would be that they'd force development, to build up contrast. So we'd go through the tests, and he'd know what I had in mind—he'd know they weren't just mistakes that I'd made. And when I did make mistakes, we'd get together and figure out how we could save them. The really great cameramen, men like Arthur Miller, Ernie Palmer, Charlie Rosher, Arthur Edeson, Hal Mohr—the old school of men who came up the hard way—were all fine photographers. Karl Struss is one of the finest still photographers who ever lived. We *had* to know photography—that was our job.

LM: We're into the 1920s now; was working then a collaborative effort?

MOHR: Oh yes. You see, like with Alan Crosland, we did many pictures together—we were in France together in World War One, in the same outfit. We would set up a production unit, and I'd just do Alan's pictures. I'd be on salary, and we'd be preparing a story, go somewhere to talk it over, and it was a combined effort, so when we got to making the picture everybody knew what it was all about.

LM: So you were involved from the start?

MOHR: From the very beginning, you were involved in the making of the film, and up to the time of the preview, because you'd look at the editing. If there were something he didn't like you'd discuss it with him. I don't mean that we intruded on each other's authority—I didn't direct his picture, nor did he direct the photography—but we helped each other. He'd say, "Gee, Hal, this would be a great place to get an effect, something like this," you'd discuss the thing and work it out. You'd work it out in your own photographic way. And the thing we didn't do that they're doing tremendously now, is that if we moved the camera or put an obstacle in the way of the camera, it was for a definite purpose, to state something. I saw a show the other night, one of these detective things, where they kept on shooting through curtains, and windows—what is happening? If the director's purpose was to confuse the audience—and maybe that's what it was—he was certainly successful. I think the new techniques, a lot of them are magnificent, don't misunderstand me, and when I started making commercials a lot of the effects that I made have now been taken over by the industry—this stuff of shooting into the sun, etc. I think that properly used, to get the effect to say what you want it to say, is just magnificent, but to do it just to have smears go across the camera, I don't think means a damn thing.

LM: Were some directors more important in visual contributions than others?

MOHR: Oh yes. Bill Dieterle, for example; he'd like to know what the hell you're doing. He'd have ideas, but not as much as Mike Curtiz. And Fritz Lang was very interested in what you were getting photographically, and rightly so. I think a director should know what's going on that film.

LM: When you did the Mary Pickford pictures you were collaborating, weren't you?

MOHR: On LITTLE ANNIE ROONEY, which was the first one, I worked with Charlie Rosher. Charlie was the director of photography, and I was second—I handled the second unit. Then the next picture was SPARROWS and I took Charlie's place, and Karl Struss took my place, so to speak.

LM: How did you divide your responsibilities?

MOHR: Struss shot stuff on his own, and I shot stuff on my own. Sometimes we worked together, but most of the time we were working separately. Same thing on LITTLE ANNIE ROONEY.

LM: Were you both going for the same visual concept?

MOHR: Oh yes, I had made my photography conform with Charlie's and Struss would make his photography conform with what I was doing. Which was the proper thing; you can only have one general, you can't have an army of generals, and no privates.

LM: SPARROWS is a beautiful movie.

MOHR: It was a very good movie, and I had some very effective stuff in it, damned effective stuff. Karl was responsible for a lot of it—I don't want to take any of the glory away from him. Mary was one of the most adorable people I've ever known. There was only one thing you had to watch out for with Mary: she only had one side of a face. I forget if it was the right side or the left side—let us assume it was the left side. Now if I'm doing a close-up where she's working opposite me, and the master scene was done from the right, to carry the continuity she has to look from left to right. So she would keep the left side of her face to the camera, but the eyes going to the continuity, where it belongs. The other thing you had to watch for was to keep her looking small, looking tiny, and you usually did that by comparatively high setups and tall actors, and so on.

LM: Did you back-light her hair a lot?

MOHR: Oh, that was the mode, not just for Mary, but everybody. We used to put back-lights on them looking like MIDSUMMER NIGHT'S DREAM. We had back-lights on some people where they would just radiate. I remember the old Mae Murray pictures; Bill Daniels and Ollie Marsh used to light her with back-lights where you couldn't see her face!

LM: Do you remember a scene in SPARROWS where a barn door dissolves into a pastoral scene of Christ, which Mary Pickford envisions? How was that done?

MOHR: It was done in the barn, with the pastoral scene in the background. It was actually photographed right there. I don't think we did any location work at all, it was all photographed right in the studio. Even the chase, at the end, was all done right there. And we did miniatures. The art director on that film was Harry Oliver; he was the art director on Mary Pickford's pictures, and he was a nut. He had the craziest damn ideas—he and I got along great. The SPARROWS set, for example, was a dilapidated, run-down sort of thing. He'd be driving along, and pass by a refuse dump; if he'd see a piece of wood that would intrigue him, he'd stop and put it in the car, bring it into the studio. He'd sit there and burn a piece of wood to a certain point, brush it off and use it. He was nuts, but nuts to create. A very creative guy.

LM: What kind of lighting problems did you have with the swamp scenes?

MOHR: We did that with diffusions, and exposures. I talked about controlling exposures. A man named Aller had Consolidated Film Labs, before they were called that. And Charlie Rosher was responsible for this. We used to develop our negative at that time from what was known as the ABC Pyro developing system. It was a very short-lived developing agent—you had to mix a fresh batch for each drumful of film—but it had the capacity of giving you a magnificent negative. It put a lot of color in the base—brownish tones to the background. Charlie developed a method for shooting this (this is all black and white I'm talking about—you can't do these tricks with color). We'd go into a situation where you'd be shooting, let us say, into a terrific back-light, a lot of reflected light coming in, and so on. It would call for, in those days, an f.8 stop—well, we'd photograph it at 4, or 4.5, and that's several stops overexposed. Then Aller would skin-develop it; as soon as the image would show through, it was stopped. If it had been developed to its entirety it would have been just a black contrasty nothing. But that's how we got this soft, ethereal, foggy look. Of course, we used a lot of fog machines, also. But the overall photography was controlled by the director of photography in connection with the effect he wanted to get, and with the complete cooperation of the laboratory.

LM: Now let's get to Michael Curtiz; you worked with him quite a bit.

MOHR: That's right. You know, he was a refugee from World War One, and Mr. Warner took full advantage of the circumstances, with a master powerful grip over the man, with the threat that he would be deported to Hungary if he didn't concur with Warner. Mike had been a cameraman in Hungary, and a director, a wrestler, strong-man—I don't know if Mike had done any acting, I suppose he did some of that too. But THE THIRD DEGREE was his first picture in this country, and I was assigned to make it with him. I enjoyed Mike very much; he was a brutal sonofabitch. He had no consideration for anybody's feelings, but still a very kindly guy. He was generous to a fault. But cruel—if a man was to fall off a horse into a bed of cactus, he had to fall off a horse into a bed of cactus, and if a baby had to cry ... That was a time I damn near did battle with Mike, on location in Pasadena. We had a darling little baby in a picture called A MILLION BID, and the baby was supposed to cry. So Mike would go up to say something to the woman who was holding the baby, and he'd fuss around, adjusting the diaper or something. The baby would start to cry, and he'd turn on the camera. I took about four or five takes before I caught on to what the sonofabitch was doing: he was pinching the baby to make it cry. Well, I don't go for that; I don't go for people killing animals, just for an effect in a film, or hurting people. I say that you can get the same effect if you know what you're doing without jeopardizing anybody. You don't have to be a sonofabitch about it, or be cruel, and Mike had that faculty. With all the love and admiration I had for Mike, he had that faculty, and it was finally what broke us up. But he was a creative man; he'd work right with you, with an old-fashioned finder. Actually, the finder he was working with was a camouflage, because he would never call lunch. He'd always have a sandwich stuck in the goddamn finder, which he'd be chewing on while looking for the next setup! It finally reached the point in my relation with Mike that at one thirty or two o'clock I'd just turn to the head electrician and say, "Kill 'em, we're going to lunch." And Mike would hate me for it, but nevertheless, he knew that I was calling his bluff. But he'd work alongside the camera; he'd pick an angle, and he wouldn't say, "Now, we're going to use a 25mm lens, and we'll do this and do that," but he'd give me an idea of what he had in mind, and I'd compose the picture, pick the lens to do it with, and so on. Mike would look through, and we'd talk about it. He had a great artistic instinct. And THE THIRD DEGREE I saw recently, and I was really pleasantly surprised at the beauty of some of the shots we got. And the main feature of it was the multi-exposure photography, the overlays and everything. That was all done in the camera; there was no such thing as optical printing in those days. That film would go through the camera time after time after time. I had film for that picture—they cut some of it out—that went through the camera eighty-odd times, forwards and backwards. We'd reverse it after we'd expose, reverse it to the the starting point before we'd can it. Then we had charts all made out as to what they were supposed to do.

LM: What kind of stoppage would you use for the different exposures?

MOHR: You'd expose for each exposure; because you didn't expose the entire layer of film, you'd expose certain areas of it. All that placement was done in the camera itself, by means of black mattes in front of the camera. You had to know what you were doing.

LM: IN OLD SAN FRANCISCO harked back to your youth ...

MOHR: Yes indeed. That was with Alan Crosland direct-ing. We had miniature, of course, in that—but I did a trick on that thing that I think was pretty damn good, on the earthquake scene, and the earthquake scenes were more effective, I think, than they were in the later MGM film SAN FRANCISCO, where they destroyed whole sets. I did a gag on that; I think it was the first time it was done, maybe the only time. But it worked so damned effectively. On the front of the camera I had a control box made. I took a square reducing-glass—it was quite a heavy reduction element. I set that on very soft sponge rubber, and placed it on iris arms in front on the camera, and I'd photograph the scene through that ... you'd have to refocus, you couldn't use the regular focal scale. We'd be doing the scene, and when the earthquake was to happen, I'd just gently tap this reduction element—and of course, there were certain mechanical elements happening on the set, like a thing would fall or a dump box would dump from the top of this set. But by tapping on this frame that held the reduction element, it would make the reduction element jump and quiver, and the result was that you got a distorted picture—it looked as if the buildings were rolling. We used that through all the earthquake scenes; it was very effective, but done in a very easy way.

LM: Now we come to THE JAZZ SINGER.

MOHR: THE JAZZ SINGER was of course the first major talking picture; of course it was not a complete talking picture, a lot of scenes were silent. But there were some amusing things that happened on that that will bear repeating. We started the picture shooting silent, because the Vitaphone thing had not yet been perfected; we didn't know what kind of lights we were going to have to use, because we were going to have dialogue, and the panchromatic film was so bad in those days that we didn't want to use it generally throughout the picture. We'd use the orthochromatic film on everything that we could, and then wait and use the panchromatic film under circumstances where we had to use it. And the reason we had to use it was that we couldn't use any arc lights, which we used on the orthochromatic film; we had to use incandescent lights for the red end of the spectrum, to which the pan film was supposed to be sensitive. And there was an unbearable heat condition with those damn things, you had to use so much of them to get an exposure. So one of the things that happened was that we had May McAvoy as the leading lady, and May had red hair. We did the silent scenes first, and shot them all with arc lights on ortho-chromatic film, and orthochromatic film was not sensitive to red. So the result was that May was a brunette in all these scenes. And you know, it wasn't until after I'd seen the picture two or three times that I noticed this, but she walked from an exterior into the interior of the home, and she had some dialogue with Al Jolson, then when she walked from the outer room into the bedroom she suddenly became a blonde! And throughout the picture, in all the dialogue scenes, her hair was about eight shades lighter than it was in the silent scenes. But nobody noticed it while we were making the picture.

LM: How confining was it working with the new sound equipment?

MOHR: Oh, it was terrible. When they went to talking pictures, what happened is what so often happens when there's an innovation: the man with the new idea becomes the lord and master of the set. The technicians from

AT&T, the soundmen, said, "Look, you're going to make talking pictures, you're going to do it the way I say it can be done, regardless of what you've been doing." So the restrictions they placed on us in the placement of microphones, that sort of thing, and the fact that we couldn't edit—it had to be shot as a continuous scene, with multiple cameras—was really something. The sound was being put on wax disks, and they had no way of editing those disks; in other words, we could construct a scene so the entire scene would be photographed at once. Sometimes it would fill a disk, two or three minutes, and sometimes it would only use a little bit of the disk. But you had to cover all of your close-ups, and everything, all with one setup. We used the techniques then that they started using in live television later. The only difference then was that we had cameras that sounded like McCormick harvesters, and we didn't have any blimps for them—we had iceboxes. The icebox was about six feet square, with a piece of optical glass in front; the operator and assistant could be in there, and the poor guys would die for lack of oxygen, and the heat. Well, with four or five of them

around, where would you put your lights, with all these iceboxes fencing you in? That was bad enough, but then the soundman would say, "I've got to have the microphone right here"—they didn't swing the mikes back and forth—and it was never above the head, always they wanted to get it so you would talk directly into it. Well, that soon proved itself impossible, because you had to see the actor, and if you were working over a table, and there was a vase of flowers on the table, or a water pitcher, that would be the receptacle for holding the microphone, but in the longer scenes where we had to have head room above the person, and the microphone had to be above the head, it was a case of either putting the frame of the picture on top of their heads, which you couldn't do, and have all floor down below—or in many cases we introduced a piece of glass in front of the camera, on stationary shots, had the man put the microphone where he wanted to, and then have the assistant with a piece of chalk put a dot on the glass where the microphone was. Then I'd have a scenic artist come in and paint a little picture on that glass, which would in effect be hanging on

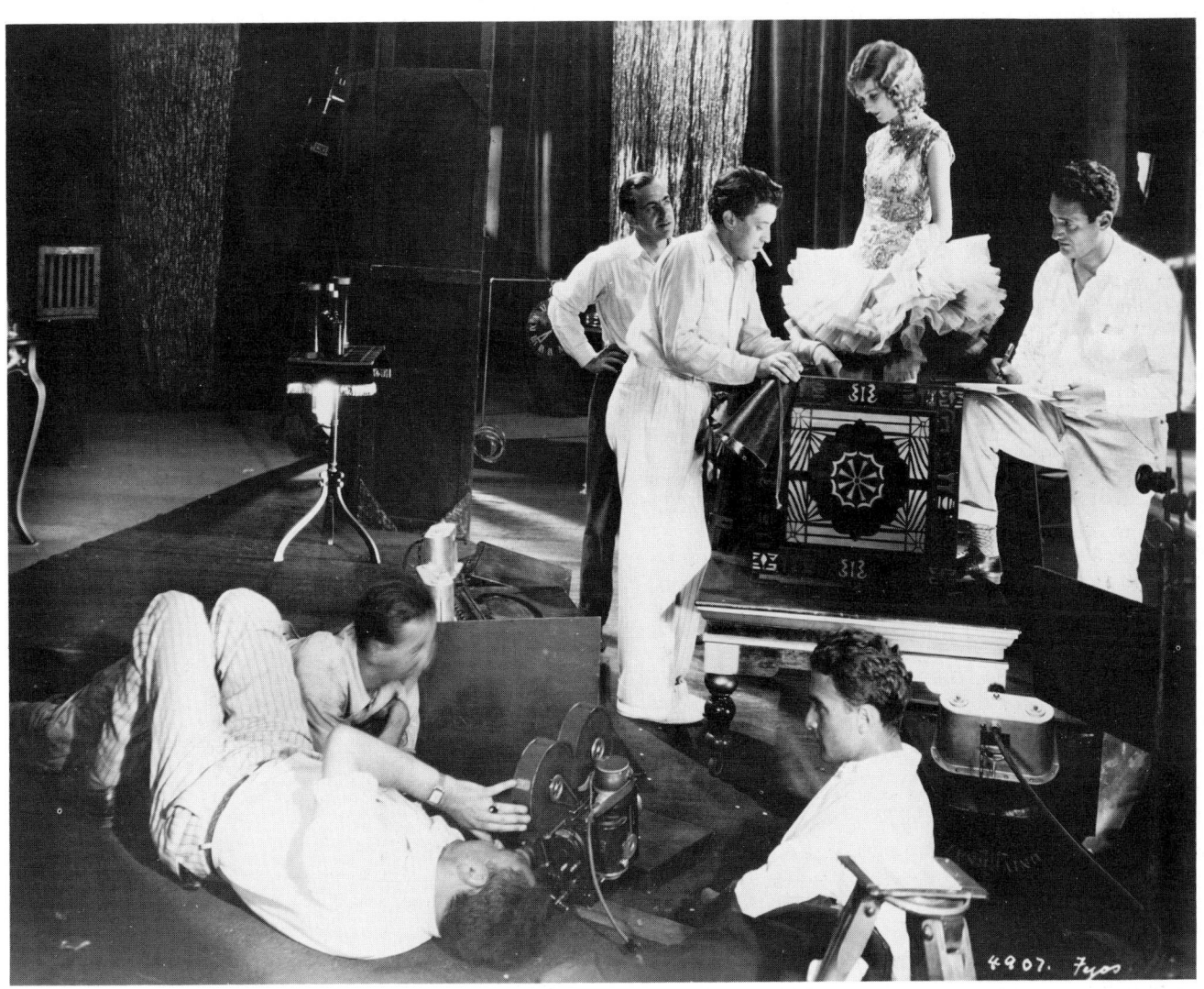

Mohr lines up a low-angle shot for THE LAST PERFORMANCE (1929) *while director Paul Fejos (with megaphone) adjusts a prop for star Mary Philbin.*

the wall behind the actor. And that painting on the glass was camouflaging the microphone, which would have gotten in the scene otherwise. We had to resort to that several times. But it wasn't too long before we reached the point with the directors, the producers, and cameramen, and we just said, "Now look, this is the best we can do for you; you get your microphone wherever you can get it."

LM: I've just seen THE WEDDING MARCH recently, and there again is a beautiful film.

MOHR: I took that over, you know; they had been about six weeks on that thing. I don't know what the credits read on it, but I took it over as they were about to wrap it up. Stroheim was a difficult man, but he was an exacting man. I don't know what the trouble was, but I went out and took that over from Harry Thorpe and Bill McGann, and I think we retook everything they had made, I think that was the way Stroheim worked. I was eight or ten weeks on the thing, and had a very exciting experience. I worked like a dog; we worked day and night, and there were days I never left the studio. . . . I'd sleep there on the set, send one of my assistants out to get me a sandwich and a cup of coffee. That includes Sundays and everything else. . . . oh Jesus, that was a difficult picture to do. But it was a great opportunity to make a beautiful display of photography, I thought. So much I shot I knew they couldn't use in the picture. For example, there was one sequence, when Fay Wray goes to the confessional, I did a thing leading up to that—now whether any of this is in the picture or not, I don't know—but I did a nine-minute lead-in to that confessional scene, of just things inside the cathedral: the dripping wax, the candle flame, the window, the statues, just a series of artistic orgasms, that's what it was. They were all dissolves, but we only had four-hundred-foot rolls of film, so I had to time it and figure the thing, so that when I had to reload the camera, and put a new magazine in the camera, it would be on a static moment, so we could cut to that static moment and then go on. So the result was we had a nine- or ten-minute continuous film that was just dissolve after dissolve—some superimpositions. I think it's the loveliest thing I've ever done, from an aesthetic point of view—completely useless insofar as telling the story is concerned. He said to make it, make an atmosphere for this girl to come to the cathedral.

LM: That was originally a two-part picture, wasn't it?

MOHR: Yes, there was THE WEDDING MARCH and then THE HONEYMOON. I finished THE WEDDING MARCH, and I got about halfway through THE HONEYMOON when the bomb burst, insofar as Von and I were concerned. I just picked up my camera, walked off the set and went home, and that was the end of it. I don't know who he got to finish it.

LM: Did you do the color sequence?

MOHR: I'm pretty sure I must have, if it was part of THE WEDDING MARCH. It was two-color; I'm sure I supervised that. They had a Technicolor cameraman to do that, but I'm sure I supervised that.

LM: They've restored that sequence, and the hues are surprisingly rich and vivid.

MOHR: In the two-color process the blues were not true and the yellows were not true; blues were green, and the yellows were orange, but other than that, two-color Technicolor wasn't bad.

LM: The flesh tones are very good.

MOHR: In my more recent pictures in color, where I could, I would not put makeup on the people; I'd photograph them without makeup, just to get away from the ridiculous color they come through with. I'd tell a woman to just put on a nice street makeup, "Put on the makeup you'd wear if you were going to a party, but don't put on motion picture makeup." Of course, makeup men hated me for that.

LM: Let's go back again, to NOAH'S ARK.

MOHR: NOAH'S ARK is where I split with Mike Curtiz. We were doing NOAH'S ARK, and we really went all-out on the thing. We had tremendous sets—if you saw the picture, you know what was involved with it. When we got to the flood sequence, we built a number of sets, tremendous sets, going up fifty feet in the air and that sort of thing. In one sequence we had sixteen cameras going at once . . . Mike had worked it all out. It was a big venture to do, and it had been awfully hard work. So we got to the point where the flood was to topple these temples, and columns would fall on people, and that sort of thing. And we had possibly forty or fifty stunt men and women who had been engaged; I have no particular sympathy for them—I mean, if they know their job, and they know what they're doing, they can protect themselves. But we had thousands of extra people on the sets, and they would do anything you'd tell them, just to get the day's work, but they had no idea what the hell was going to happen. So we'd gone around to plot how we were going to handle these collapsing sets, and there was a man there at the studio at that time named Fred Jackman, who had a blue-backing process that was very effective, where you could superimpose solid things over other things. I knew damn well that we could have these people on the set, and drop a certain amount of water on them, and maybe a few pumice and balsa-wood sections on them, and they wouldn't get hurt, and I knew that over that, Jackman could take a miniature of a tremendous amount of water, and tremendous columns collapsing, and blue-backing them over this action, make it look as if it was a one-piece film. So I assumed we were going to do this in a trick way, but when we were looking at these sets I talked to Mike, and Darryl Zanuck, who was producing it, was with us, and I said, "Well, we'll have to make provisions for Jackman to overlay his miniature stuff . . ." and he said, "No, we're not going to use Jackman on this." I said, "What do you mean?" He said, "We're going to actually have these columns collapse," and they had these spillways built on top of the columns that held tons of water, and they would come whooshing down onto the set. I said, "Jesus, what are you going to do about the extra people?" He said, "Oh, they're going to have to take their chances." I said, "Not as far as I'm concerned, I'll never have anything to do with a thing like that," and I went through this very carefully with Jackman, and explained how they could have a few stunt people and he could lay in the other extras, and it would be just as realistic, just as effective, but without killing anybody. They insisted they were going to do it the way they wanted to do it, so I told them to shove the picture, and walked off the set. Then the boy who had been my assistant took over the picture to finish, he and Chick McGill. They modified their extremities to some degree, but one man lost a leg, a couple of people were injured to the point that they never did recover. The goddamned murderous bastards never should have permitted a thing like that to happen. So that was the last thing I did with Mike.

LM: Can you explain about the different film stocks at this time?

MOHR: In the orthochromatic stages, before panchromatic film became the thing to use, because of sound, there was a competitive film made by the Dupont film. It was a true orthochromatic film, and by being true orthochromatic it did have yellow sensitivity, and certain qualities that the so-called orthochromatic that Eastman made did not have. In my opinion, it was a superior film. I had had such good success using Dupont film, where I could use it, that I had a preference for it. Warner Brothers had a financial tie-up with Brulatour, who was the distributor for Eastman film at that time, so they were committed to Eastman film. The Eastman film was a damn good film, don't misunderstand me, but I had a leaning to the Dupont, which was finer quality. Now the panchromatic film that Eastman was making at this time was deplorable. Brulatour had died, and Bill German was now the distributor for Eastman film out here, and I told Warner Brothers, "Look, if we're going to do NOAH'S ARK the way we have it set up, to meet these requirements, I want to do it on Dupont film. If I have to use Eastman panchromatic film, I know that I can't handle sets of this size and get the quality that we want to get into it. I think that I can possibly get it on the Dupont, and I'll make comparative tests to prove it." So they reported that to Eastman, who threw his arms up—"There's a revolution!" But Bill German was a smart little guy, and a pretty good friend of mine; we sat down and had a talk about it. I said, "Bill, it's reached the point where if I'm going to photograph NOAH'S ARK, and maybe I won't as a result of this, I cannot do it on your panchromatic film." So he got on the phone to Rochester, and they went back and forth, and made an experimental emulsion panchromatic film, and came out with what is known as Type 2 panchromatic negative. I made tests with it and found that I could do with that what would be required. It wasn't what the final black and white films are, the double and triple x, which are exquisite films, but by beating them over the head hard enough, they did come out with this Type 2 negative that had the sensitivity and not the degree of contrast the old panchromatic film had. So I've always felt in a sense responsible for bringing out that film, which was the beginning of the evolutionary stage of panchromatic film.

LM: They wanted you to use Eastman panchromatic, you wanted to use Dupont ortho. What about Eastman ortho at the time?

MOHR: Eastman ortho was not ortho. It was a black and white film, but it had no sensitivity at the yellow end of the spectrum. I don't know what you'd call it. On the old orthochromatic film, if you were to put a red filter on it to try to control sky, you got nothing. But on the Dupont I could use a K-3 filter or something, and get blue sky held down, and the white clouds would come through. K-3 was a very heavy amber filter.

LM: When you got into 3-strip Technicolor, the blue strip was orthochromatic film, wasn't it?

MOHR: Yes, that's right.

LM: Did you have to start using arc lights again?

MOHR: No, we had to use a hell of a lot of light, but the blue record was the worst record of the three. I think the blue record was behind, the back negative, and that was just to get a record that would throw blue in—it wasn't for resolution purposes. I think we used to get our black and white prints off the green negative, or the red. But the requirement of the ortho strip in the three-strip camera was not too great.

LM: When you worked in 3-strip, you had a lot of latitude with color control, didn't you, depending on how dark the black and white image was, and whether you took it from the red or the green?

MOHR: That's right ... if you were doing a night scene, for example, it could all be handled by the color control in the laboratory. It was actually a lithographing process, and they'd make the matrix off the original negative, and then print these dye surfaces on—they could intensify the amount of the matrix in any color that they wanted to, or intensify the black and white image. They had infinitely more control, but it was subject to a lot of error, too. And it was a very expensive process; a good matrix was only good for possibly fifteen or twenty prints.

LM: Going back again ... what are your memories of BROADWAY?

MOHR: That was directed by Doc Fejos, Paul Fejos, who was quite a character. He was actually a doctor of biology, married to a woman who was a doctor too. He came into the industry on the strength of one film. He wanted to get into the motion picture business, so he got money together and made a picture called THE LAST MOMENT. Its premise was a good one; he took a person who was drowning, and during that moment just before his death he reviewed this person's entire life. On the strength of this he did get a deal with Laemmle at Universal, and I think Carl, Jr., who was just a kid, was a great fan of Fejos, and he was responsible for it. I did several pictures with Paul. The final thing Paul did at Universal, that we started, was LA MARSEILLAISE. I think what really happened, and this is pure conjecture on my part, was that the picture got out of hand—it got too big for him. So we went to lunch one day; we'd been set up on top of the HUNCHBACK set, and I think he wanted to get out of it. I surmise that—I don't make it as a statement. Anyway, we went to lunch, and he was the last one to leave the set, and they found him lying at the foot of these stairs. He had seemingly fallen all the way down these stairs and was lying there in a semiconscious condition. They called an ambulance and carted him off to the hospital. His recovery was very slow. The reason I say "seemingly" is that a hell of a lot could be simulated. I think he wanted to bow out of the picture, and this was his way of bowing out. I forget who took it over for him. But getting back to BROADWAY, the premise of the original story never lent itself to the motion picture. The premise was that this little guy working in a honky-tonk basement cabaret had one ambition, to get a better job so he could get out of that place. Well, that was the day of the big musicals, you know, so Doc's premise was that in order to make a successful picture, you couldn't play in a depressing little honky-tonk area, it had to be a spectacular picture. So we designed this set—it was like Grand Central Station—it was the biggest interior set that had ever been built. It was so big that it was almost impossible. So that led to a chain of events. He also wanted to build a crane, a camera crane, and we built the so-called BROADWAY crane for that picture. Doc and I designed it, and it was built by the Llewellyn Iron Works. I'll tell you a follow-up story on that. We used to go down there two or three times a week to watch the construction of this thing going on. It was really a great piece of engineering equipment. It was the first really great motion picture crane. And when we got this thing finished, they didn't have a stage at Universal that could accommodate this crane, it was such a huge thing. The stages were only thirty or forty feet high, and just the arm of this thing was forty or fifty feet long—I'm not sure exactly how long. So they built the BROADWAY stage, Stage 12, to accommodate this crane. We went all out and had the BROADWAY set fill the whole goddamned stage, so that this little honky-tonk that Tryon was trying to work his way out of turned out to be something like you've never known in your entire life. It wasn't a bad picture, as I recall it, but the premise was really idiotic. Here he wanted to get to play the Palace—well that nightclub could have taken the Palace, the Winter Garden, and the Hippodrome all in one! But that boom was some piece of equipment; we used that subsequently on everything we made. We used it on KING OF JAZZ, every picture that I made there. Incidentally, I'd lost all contact with that crane; I knew that they'd been using it as a rigging device, to haul equipment up to the roof of the stages, and so on, and it had not been taken care of, which I think is a sin. When I was doing TOPAZ, I had occasion to go to the back lot on location, and I saw this familiar-looking steel structure standing over in a junkyard behind some sheds. I drove over there and here was this BROADWAY crane. It was one of the most tragic things I've ever experienced. I damn near wept when I saw that thing standing there; a lot of my hard blood went into that thing, and a lot of Doc Fejos'.

LM: I read that it cost $40,000 to build.

MOUR: It cost $50,000, and we knew it was going to cost a lot of money when we went to build it, but that thing could do everything but bake beans. It had a trailer that could hook onto the thing that was its own generator, to generate the electricity that operated the thing. It could drive itself—you could steer it; you could swing the arm in any direction. And on the camera platform, which was a circular platform, there were controls, like a motorman's controls on an old electric streetcar, and the crane operator rode on that platform with the cameraman. We'd set up either on a high-hat, or a tripod on the platform, which had a little rail around it. This platform could revolve 360 degrees continuously in either direction. The crane could go from the ground and do a complete turnover to the ground over *there;* it could do 360-degree turns, stopping any place you want to. You had absolutely complete control—more so than you have on the traveling booms today. The traveling boom has its limitations, because it can only go to certain places in relation to the chassis. With this thing you could swing around a full 360 degrees, in any position, and rotate the camera platform at the

same time. The result was, we made shots in BROADWAY where it was an exposé of the abilities of this crane; it was pretty exciting.

LM: It was very well directed, too; all the people in the scenes are doing interesting things.

MOHR: That's right—well, Doc was not a bad director.

LM: KING OF JAZZ is one of the greatest movies I've ever seen.

MOHR: KING OF JAZZ was a hell of a picture. That was such a big thing that we broke that up into several areas. I had Ray Rennahan working with me on that; he was the Technicolor cameraman. I was the director of photography, of course, but Ray did a hell of a lot of the work. I was away doing a lot of trick stuff while Ray would be on the set, so I was in and out of the set, all over the place. Some of the things we did in that I don't think have ever been equalled by anybody, even the Busby Berkeley miracle films.

LM: How much were you involved in the color?

MOHR: Of course, I was greatly involved. Ray Rennahan was my consultant, naturally, and we had an army of Technicolor consultants, Natalie Kalmus and all of her concubines, constantly on the set, advising us as to what colors we could use and couldn't use. Rennahan knew the light requirements for the process, and Jesus, we even warped the top of some of the pianos from the amount of heat coming out of those lights. These were incandescent lights. You had to use more light on two-strip than on three-strip; we used as high as 1,200- to 1,400-foot candles, I think up to 2,000-foot candles on some of the shots.

LM: You've said that you were specially proud of your work on OUTWARD BOUND.

MOHR: Yes, that was made by Robert Milton. You know the story, of course. Bob Milton had directed the play on the stage, and he came out to Warner Brothers to make the film. I enjoyed so much working with people who knew their stage techniques and didn't know a damn thing about making pictures, and would say, "Hal, what do I do here?" On WATCH ON THE RHINE I had the same thing with Herman Shumlin; he had never made a picture. Let me just jump ahead for a moment. Herman came out here to make WATCH ON THE RHINE for Warner Brothers, and he got into a lot of trouble because he wasn't getting the kind of help he should have had. The creative film people were each trying to do something for their own glory, and so he got into a lot of trouble. He was going to quit the film and go back to New York, and Wallis and Bill Koenig prevailed on me to come out and take the picture over. I don't like to take another cameraman's picture over—I just don't like to do that. If I can help pull him out of the mud, I'll do it, and I've done that on many occasions, but it's happened where I've had to take the other man's picture over—THE FRONT PAGE was the same thing with Tony Gaudio. So Herman would rehearse the scene as though it were on the stage. Then he'd go up to his office, I'd take the stand-ins and plot out the mechanics of how we'd shoot this sequence—how I would suggest we'd shoot it. The script girl would take notes on the thing, and it would take three quarters of an hour. Then we'd call him back down, and I'd show him with the stand-ins, and if he didn't like what we had done, he'd make suggestions, he'd make changes, and so on. But I laid it out according to the ramifications of the camera. And that's how we made WATCH ON THE RHINE, and I think it was a pretty good picture. Shumlin was very appreciative. I was having a feud with Warner Brothers at this time; the only time they'd call me in to do a picture was if they were in so much trouble they couldn't get out of it. It happened on several pictures I did for them. Getting back to OUTWARD BOUND, I had the same production situation on that. We were out of the iceboxes by this time; we were using celluloid blimps on the cameras, and we had a little more mobility. So Bob Milton would rehearse the scenes, and I'd lay them out for them. But I conceived a method of handling the thing photographically that he went for immediately, and I think it helped the picture a lot. The play was in three acts; in the first act it's all material, realistic; in the second act this boat is a doubtful entity; and in the third act it is a nothing, it's out beyond. So physically I got the idea of treating it in just that matter. I had the boat set built all realistically, and then for the second act—although it was not done in acts, per se—I had the whole set fogged with a kind of an umber, and even the high detail points of the furniture were umbered over to a degree. So it became a kind of half-unrealistic thing. And then for the third act, I had everything on the set sprayed a light gray, so all the detail of the set was lost almost completely. And on top of that I used heavy gauze to photograph through, and used the fog machines on the set. So by the time they're reaching the point of death it was really something—and then when they're brought back to reality it was like *snap!* I was very proud of that, but the picture was never a success.

LM: You mentioned a picture I didn't know you'd done, THE FRONT PAGE.

MOHR: Yes, I did THE FRONT PAGE, I took that over, did that with Lewis Milestone for Howard Hughes; that was how I met Howard Hughes.

LM: Milestone's films always had a lot of camera movement.

MOHR: Lewis is a strange guy; I've never been a fan of his, but he's a nice guy. He had a lot of good ideas—you recall in the press room, where the camera went around the inside of the press table, following all the faces of the guys—we hung it from an overhead thing. That was his idea. THE FRONT PAGE I took over from poor Tony Gaudio; Tony and Lewis just didn't get along. A lot of these things where cameramen get fired off of pictures is lack of compatibility with the director.

LM: One striking thing about the 1933 STATE FAIR was that it seemed to me that the cast never set foot outside the studio to film it.

MOHR: Oh, we did a little outside; we went out to what is now Mandeville Canyon, and the main entrance of Bel Air was then just the top of a glen—it was all done in the local area. There was a hell of a lot of process in that. That was a problem, because old Henry King—another guy who I love—doesn't know a thing about photography, or what a camera can do, but he thinks he knows every-

thing about it. I don't say that disparagingly, because I think Henry is one of our great directors, but on pre-production he went back to Kansas, to the state fair, and did all of his process plates while he was back there. Now there are certain things you do and don't do for process plates, and there are damn good reasons. Your foreground perspective is married to the perspective that you have on your plate; if you're going to have a set built in front of a plate, the set has to be photographed with the same focal-length lens that you shot the plate with—otherwise your vanishing points vary. So Henry went back there, and he would always say, "You know, someday I'm going to build a camera, and I'm going to have two lenses: a twenty-five, and a four-inch." He had this phobia, and anything more than a close-up he shot with a 25mm lens, which was the widest lens that we had at this time. He shot all of these plates back there: livestock halls, and livestock, and everything, with a 25mm lens, in order to get scope. When it came to building the interiors that had to go against those plates, I had to resort to building them in false perspective. In other words, a hog pen tapered back incredibly, in order to meet the perspective of the 25mm lens. That was a hell of a problem on a lot of that film, for that reason.

LM: Wouldn't it have been easier to just shoot it on location?

MOHR: Oh yes. But as I remember it turned out to be a pretty good picture.

LM: So then you were with Fox for a while.

MOHR: I was with Fox for several years, before it became 20th Century Fox, when Bill Fox had it and Wini Sheehan was the head of production.

LM: I presume DAVID HARUM was where you met your wife.

MOHR: That's where I met Evelyn. I did that picture with Jimmy Cruze, one of my favorite human beings. And old Will Rogers, he was wonderful. He autographed a picture to me as Cupid—he thought he was the matchmaker with us.

LM: In the mid-1930s you moved from Fox to Warner Brothers. It seems sometimes that you can see a definite style at each studio; did you find this to be true?

MOHR: Well, the different studios would specialize. For instance, the Warner Brothers would specialize in the Buzz Berkeley, the Humphrey Bogart type of thing. 20th Century was hipped on the newspaper headline; that was Zanuck's pet idea of making pictures, from today's headlines. But I think that the style of the various studios was dictated almost entirely by the personnel that made their pictures. If you keep it down to the basics of photography, I carried my style to whatever studio I came to, and I gravitated among most of them. So I think the studio policy could set the type of picture, but I don't think the style of the picture could be set by the studio. Which brings us to one of the most important things, I think, about photography. I think that the photography of a motion picture is most brilliant in its inconspicuousness—taking all in all, I mean MIDSUMMER NIGHT'S DREAM is something else—but I think the photography of a picture should contribute to the telling of the picture by its mood and its style just as much as the story. I don't think there's any such thing as documentary photography or beautiful photography. I think photography is beautiful only insofar as it is absorbed within the production, and I think that a cameraman should be versatile enough to conform to whatever the story would be.

LM: Now we come to the big picture, MIDSUMMER NIGHT'S DREAM.

MOHR: Now there again is a picture that I took over. There was another case where Warner Brothers called me because they had to have me, or thought they had to have me. There they had all these creative people all around them: Reinhardt, Dieterle ... But they got so filled with what Reinhardt was going to do with Shakespeare, their perspective in their thinking got beyond the realm of motion pictures. For example, in an exterior scene, with great expanses of pastoral land, you don't do that within studio stages to any great degree, but there they *had* to do it because it had to be controlled. When the art director built the sets, they were going to make the damnedest forest you'd ever seen. He built a forest set that covered two full stages; it was so realistic you couldn't photograph it. When I say you couldn't photograph it, I mean specifically that there was such beauty, and the trees were so natural and so dense and so huge, that there was no place to get any light through the damn things. Fortunately, MIDSUMMER NIGHT'S DREAM didn't lend itself to reality, so it didn't have to be photographed in that way and therefore didn't have to be that realistic. So this cameraman was a very good cameraman, but he didn't have the guts to say, "You can't photograph it, you've got to do it *this* way." He tried to conform to what the art director had created; I'm not taking away from the art director, because I think he did a tremendous job, but you couldn't photograph it. So they'd been on this thing for about eight weeks, and they were really in a lot of trouble, and the rushes were not the way they wanted them—nothing was coming through the way they wanted it. It was supposed to be an ephemeral kind of thing. So Bill Koenig, who was a very dear friend of mine, and Hal Wallis hit this impasse, and Koenig told Wallis that there was only one thing to do, get somebody to photograph the picture who could control it, take it over and do what was necessary. So Bill called me to come out there, and I said, "Bill, I'll come out and look at some of the film, but I won't talk about doing the picture until I've seen the film and seen what it's all about." So I looked at the film, and said, "Bill, I'm very reluctant to take the picture over, because I can see that they're trying to do something that can't be done, but I'll be happy to work with this man for a few days and try to aim him in the right direction—I won't even charge any salary." He said, "No, it's gone beyond that; we're closing down the picture as of tonight. I want you to take it over." So I said, "Well, under those circumstances I guess the only thing I can do is take it over. But I'll take it over under one condition, that I have absolute control. I can do whatever I want to do as far as photography is concerned. I will conform with the effects that the story calls for, as Mr. Reinhardt and Dieterle and Wallis see it, but my method of doing it is my method of doing it. I don't want any interference from anybody. If I want to change things—for example, I'm going to do a lot of work on these sets—whatever I want to do has to be

considered OK. Otherwise I'm not going to make the picture." He called Hal Wallis, and Bill put it to him plain, and he said OK. That night I got a gang of painters on the set—every painter they could get, with spray guns and pumps, and I had special effects there with cobweb machines. The gaffer was an old friend of mine, and he had worked with me several times before. So I had George [Hilliard] light all the lights down one side of the stage, and the light would filter down through the trees in places, and leave shadows in places. I wanted it to carry the effect of sunlight coming from one side. I told the painters, "Where the light is hitting, spray everything with aluminum paint." Well, he nearly dropped dead, and the art director wanted to commit suicide, because I was spraying all the trees, the foliage, the grass, the shrubs— everything where the light was hitting—with aluminum paint. I said, "Where the light is not hitting, use orange and brown shellac—spray everything on the shadow side with that shellac. So we'll have two tones on the set, bright aluminum where the light is supposed to be, and the deep orange where there is no light." Then I had the special effects men go in with their spray guns and cover the trees, bushes, and everything with this cobwebby material. I sent out and had them bring in several hundred pounds of what you call casket flitters—they are little particles of round, shiny material. They used to scatter this on greeting cards so they would sparkle. I had follow- up men going around after the men with the spray guns, and while the rubber cement was still wet, they'd blow these casket flitters onto the cobwebs, so they would stick to them. The result was that by the time I got done spraying this set with color, and cobwebs, and glitters, it looked almost like a Christmas card. It was like a fairy- land. I stayed up the whole night working with these guys, and nobody from the production stayed there at all. And the next morning, when they walked in and saw what I'd done with their set, they almost dropped dead, because nobody had thought what was going to happen. I figured one of two things would happen: either they'd throw up their hands, walk out, and that would be the end of it, or it was going to be a very successful thing. So they went for it, and the result of course was MIDSUMMER NIGHT'S DREAM. And I even went so far as to take in front of the camera, to carry on this sparkle effect in the fairy-type stuff, I had frames made, and I had very fine steel wires, making a kind of net, and I had this cobweb material sprayed on that, and blew some flitters on. If I kept all the light off of this, it was invisible, you never saw it. But I'd put around the camera little tiny light bulbs that I could control individually, and as they would come on, these flitters would pick up and sparkle, very close to the camera. And on top of that, I photographed through a disk, a piece of glass with an interlaced pattern, which gave an overall diffusion, which I wanted, but these spar- klers would hit the lens, bounce back to the surface of this disk, and then come through and photograph, taking on starlike quality. So you had these radiating stars sparkling on and off all over the screen, and where the actors were going to be I'd just clear out the cobwebs in that little area, but they'd be surrounded by these sparkling things. There is a follow-up to this that I have to tell, although I'll be hated for it. This picture was made shortly after the very tragic 1933 strike, and I had been considered quite a heavy in it, although I worked for the best interests of all the people who had been on strike, and for the best interests of the industry, because I had the strike terminated. So I was a sonofabitch to many people because of that. At that time, the Academy Award nominations were set up by committees, and the pictures to be nominated for cinematography award were to be nominated by a committee of cameramen. This nominating committee refused to consider my picture, because of the personal antipathy they had toward me. So my picture wasn't nominated that year. But there had been a practice in the past that had never been used, whereby you could put a write-in vote on a ballot, in place of voting for any other picture. That had been the practice, but nobody had ever done it. Whether it was due to a campaign on the part of the Warner Brothers studio, or whether it was due to a campaign on the part of the people who saw the picture—I'm pleased to think that that was the reason—it was, let's face it, a spectacular and beautifully photographed picture for its time, and as it turned out it was the only thing in the picture worth looking at. Evelyn and I had been out to Jimmy Cruze's home in Flintridge the night of the Academy Awards; I was unshaved, and in my work clothes, and Evelyn was in slacks. The phone rang, and it was Eddie Blackburn, who was with the Brulatour Company; he was at the Academy Awards at the Biltmore Bowl. He said, "Hal, I can't tell you how I know this, but you have won the Oscar for MIDSUMMER NIGHT'S DREAM. It's going to be presented within an hour." As it is today, nobody knows until they open the envelope—it's the best-kept secret in the world. I don't know how the hell Eddie knew it, but he had gotten in on some previous information that I had had a write-in. I said, "Eddie, you're kidding; it can't be so. There wouldn't be that many people to write in a vote. Forget about it, I don't give a damn about the Academy Award." But he kept working on me and working on me, and finally I said, "Call me back in ten minutes; I want to talk it over with someone." So I talked to Jimmy about it, and I talked to Evelyn about it. I said, "It means that we've got to go on home, we've got to get into dinner clothes, be down at the Biltmore in time for the award, and I don't think I'm going to get it." So Jimmy, who was very proud of me, and loved me about as much as I loved him, said, "Hal, if you never do anything else for me, do this. It will be the best thing that ever happened to you." So we jumped into my car, we raced up to Hollywood, I shaved and threw on a tux, Evelyn put on a face and threw on an evening gown, and raced down to the Biltmore Bowl. If you've been down there, you park your car in a garage next to the Biltmore Hotel, then you go through the lobby and there's this long corridor that goes back to where the ballroom is, the Biltmore Bowl. This was around eleven o'clock in the evening, and Evelyn and I were walking quickly. I could hear Frank Capra, who was the toastmaster, saying, "Now the next award is for cinematography," and we've got a couple of hundred yards to walk yet. He said, "Such-and-such pictures were nominated, but the way it has worked out, none of these pictures has been voted best-photographed picture of the year. The man who has won the award is not here, because he was not nominated, but it is Hal Mohr for MIDSUMMER NIGHT'S DREAM," and just then we stepped on the floor of the place—you'd think it had been rehearsed—and I walked up and Frank handed me the Oscar, and I got a hell of a lot of applause. I'm terribly proud of that. And of course the next thing they did was to immediately cancel the write-in vote; there was never a

write-in vote again. I'm the only one who ever got a write-in vote. So that's the story of MIDSUMMER NIGHT'S DREAM: what else have you got?

LM: Well, I want to try to touch most of the highlights. The next year you did another fine film, THE GREEN PASTURES.

MOHR: That was an interesting film too. Again I had a director who had never made a film, Marc Connelly. Marc didn't do the whole picture; he got about halfway through when they had to take him off and put somebody else on, although Marc produced it. Again, a hell of a fine person, but completely out of touch with motion picture technique—purely a stage director, and mainly a writer. Again we had to have tremendous sets that covered whole stages, and again I had a director who knows nothing about film. He left me alone insofar as photography was concerned, and I did a great deal of lining up of shots for him. But his method of working was, for example, we'd have four or five hundred Negroes on the set, and instead of keeping his mind on the principal action in the foreground and letting his assistants take care of the little black angels who were sitting on clouds at the far end of the stage, he'd run all the way back there and start telling them to sit a certain way, or do a certain thing—and for Christ's sake, you'd never even see it. We got so far behind schedule due to this inattention to the proper things that they finally put Bill Keighley on to finish the picture. It's nothing against Marc, but he just devoted himself to the unnecessary things that he let the major things get away from him. But it was a happy experience; I enjoyed working with these people.

LM: Let's go on to DESTRY RIDES AGAIN.

MOHR: That was a happy picture; a lot of fun.

LM: How did you handle Marlene Dietrich, as far as lighting and glamour treatment were concerned?

MOHR: Well, I took a page out of Joe von Sternberg, out of the way he handled her. I have a lot of respect for Marlene, as a performer, as a professional, far and above that which I have for a great many people in this industry. She knew what was best for her, and she knew a little something from what Joe had taught her. He taught her a lot about where the key light should be in relation to her, and so on. That didn't mean that she told me how to light the thing, but it meant that when I had a key light—well, George Marshall directed the picture, and George would rehearse a scene. I'd watch them rehearse, then I'd put in stand-ins to light them, and I'd get certain key lights here and there, always thinking of what light was good for Marlene. She'd watch while I was lighting the set, and then I'd go through with her, and say, "Now there it is up there for this position, Marlene, and there it is for that position . . ." She was just wonderful. I don't think her performances suffered for it, because she did it instinctively. I didn't use any great diffusion—it wasn't that kind of a picture—as I would have with the other kind of things she was doing with Joe, SHANGHAI EXPRESS, and such. She looked more realistic—she was sharper, in DESTRY. I did use some diffusion, but the lighting was meticulous, and she worked right to the lighting. We did one thing on that picture that was very amusing. There were several scenes

Mohr consults with a script girl while director William K. Howard gives instructions to Aline MacMahon for BACK DOOR TO HEAVEN *(1939).*

played in a small dressing room. I was lighting the set, and she was sitting there. There was a great rapport between us, and she started saying, "Don't you think you ought to so-and-so and so-and-so?" I said, "Look, Marlene, if you want to light the set, you go ahead." I took my blue glass off and handed it to her, and said, "You go right ahead." In those days you could take a little more time. So I sat down, and she started trying to light lights, and she got so involved, she finally said, "For Christ's sake, Hal, go and light the set." So I cured her of that.

LM: Then you won your second Oscar at Universal for PHANTOM OF THE OPERA.

MOHR: That's right. That was color again, three-strip; I had Duke Green working with me, the Technicolor man. He did almost everything I did out there; I always used a

color man with me. Billy Skall worked with me on one thing I did out there, SCHEHERAZADE.

LM: What was his function?

MOHR: He'd watch and see if I was getting in trouble technically; he'd say, "Don't you think we ought to have a little more light here?" He was kind of a follow-up man; he'd go in and measure the light to see if it was up to the Technicolor requirements. He was really very helpful.

LM: Did you prefer working in color or black and white?

MOHR: I had no special feelings, because eventually I had been working with the same color coordinator. I reached the point where I had enough self-assurance and control that I could light it the way I wanted to light it. And I lit for color exactly as I'd lit for black and white. I didn't change the method at all. At first, I would throw more fill light in, but then I realized that that was all crap, that you just light the thing the way it looked best to the eye, and throw enough light on to get the exposure, and that was it.

LM: While you were at Universal, you worked on a number of B pictures; how did working on a programmer change your method of working, or preparation?

MOHR: Well, you didn't have that much time with a B picture, and mostly the B pictures weren't that artistic in their concept, so it was just good, straightforward photography. There was nothing special about the photography, nothing you could be creative about.

LM: What about working with Fritz Lang?

MOHR: I think Fritz is a hell of a good director. I did RANCHO NOTORIOUS with him. He was all right, but I don't like people who abuse people; I guess that's inherent with me, all my life. I've never abused anybody; I'm rough with people, a disciplinarian, but I don't abuse them, use people as a patsy. Fritz was a lovable guy, a nice guy, and Dietrich adored him, but he had the faculty of riding the camera dolly. He had to watch through the finder; he'd hold the operator to one side while he'd be looking through. Hell, an operator has to have complete control of the camera while a scene is being shot. In rehearsal it's all right, but when you're shooting the scene, you have to leave that man alone. I can get behind the camera and see what the operator is doing, I can see if he's getting the scene or not. But with a guy doing what Fritz did you can't do the job. He got very abusive to some of my camera crew. So one day I finally had to have it out with him; it was a very unhappy occasion. But I finished the picture. Howard Welsch was the producer, and I wanted to get off the picture, I wanted to quit. Howard prevailed upon me to stay—and Lang wanted to fire me, he wanted me to get off the picture. So we never talked to each other for a long time, we just went ahead and did the work.

LM: Having gone through one flood experience you then did THE LAST VOYAGE, which was also quite spectacular.

MOHR: I wanted to do the picture; I had known Andy and Virginia Stone—they're one of a kind. I'm very fond of Andy, and of Virginia. But Andy's idea of making films is not my idea of making films. I had one experience with Andy; many many years ago I had done a short with him for Paramount. He had tried several times to get me to make pictures for him, and I'd always found a way not to do them, because I knew his reputation with other cameramen, the number of them he had fired, and that had quit. So when this thing came up, THE LAST VOYAGE, he asked me to come out and talk to him, and I did, and of course he was wooing me. I took a long time to make up my mind that I'd do the picture. And in the meantime people were telling me, "Hal, don't do it; the first day you'll either punch him in the nose, or walk off the set, or something. It's going to be made in Japan, and that's a hell of a place for that to happen. So just don't start the picture." They did this to me so long that I finally said, "Now wait a minute, I've worked with some directors I was warned against—Alan Crosland they told me the same thing about, that I'd never get along with him. With von Stroheim I got along beautifully up until a moment

when a thing happened within a few seconds. I got along beautifully with Fritz until the last moment." So I got along with directors that other cameramen didn't get along with, and they were crazy about me, and I attribute it to the fact that I was doing my job, and I was doing a professional job. So I said, "I'm going to prove something: I'm going to do this picture; I'll do it, and I'll finish it. I won't quit; I don't care what he does." So I took the job, went to Japan, and he was everything that they said he was. But I had perfect control of him. Sometimes I would reach a pretty strenuous point, and Virginia would intercede, and it worked out. It was a tough picture to make; the most difficult picture I've ever made in my life, as far as physical hard work is concerned. And before the picture was finished, he wanted to sign a contract with me, make me a partner. I told him, one day on the boat, weeks before it was finished, "Andy, I love you, and I've proven now that you couldn't beat me down. I'm making this picture, I'm going to finish this picture, but you sonofabitch, I wouldn't work for you again if you had all the money in the world. I want to be good friends with you, but I'll never work for you again."

LM: When you finally sank the boat, there were no retakes, were there?

MOHR: No, no . . . and you know, the only shot we made that was not made on that boat was the final shot of them running up the deck with the boat going under the water; finally the boat goes under the water, they jump overboard, and the camera goes under the water with the boat. I think that's one of the finest shots that's ever been seen in motion pictures. We did that out here at the beach at Santa Monica—because obviously, you couldn't have actors working on a sinking boat. But nobody ever knew it wasn't made on the boat, it was that realistic. But what I wanted to do, if you recall that particular scene, as they dove off the boat, and the water finally overtook them, it also overtook the camera, and the camera submerged; then you saw them climbing into the lifeboat. What I wanted to do was, I wanted to make the camera go under water, as it did, have them disappear, take an air chamber and have this chamber give a terrific burst of air flying in front of the camera, have the camera tilt up and away from that, up to the surface of the water, and you'd see the silhouette of this lifeboat, and see these figures being pulled into the boat. It would have cost some money, and Andy was very bad with money, but what I wanted was in effect a continuous shot. I would have done it in three pieces. But it would have involved getting an underwater camera, and an underwater cameraman; it would have cost a few thousand dollars, and Andy wouldn't go for it. But as it was, it was a hell of an effective shot. But a lousy picture.

LM: When you went to make TOPAZ . . .

MOHR: . . . I didn't make TOPAZ. I want to set the record straight on that. The TOPAZ situation had to do with the unions, and it had to do with my admiration for Hitchcock. I had never worked with Hitchcock, but I had observed his work and I've been a fan for his for years. I think he is a creative genius, and I've always wanted to do something with Hitch. When they got to making TOPAZ, it was being originated here, but it was being photographed mainly in Denmark and Paris. And Hitch had this English

Mohr in 1970 at the Los Angeles County Museum.

credit as photographic consultant. But I did have this association with Hitchcock, which I cherish very much.

LM: Have you done any television?

MOHR: Oh yes, I've done several series. I did some commercials first, and then I did two or three years with Joan Davis, then two or three seasons with Bob Cummings. I did LIFE WITH FATHER, several different series. I enjoyed them; they were quick money, and we made them fast. Of course, you don't do your best work on television shows. Most of the television shows I did were multi-camera operations, like live television.

LM: But I guess you had even more opportunity to be creative in commercials.

MOHR: I've done a hell of a lot of things in commercials that I have subsequently done in features, and I've got a lot of things left that I have done in commercials that I would do in features if I did any more of them. Because we've had traditions to overcome, and that leads us to where we are today in the industry. We've been bound by traditions, and I do have great admiration for technical advancement and change. I have no respect for people who just use it for its own sake. But I've done some of my most creative work in commercials.

LM: Do you have a favorite of all the films you've done?

MOHR: Well, DAVID HARUM, for obvious reasons. But professionally, I would have to say a picture that we didn't talk about, THE WILD ONE. That was a very interesting picture, and it was way ahead of itself, both in my technique as well as the story. I did some things in that, with the motorcycle, that were really quite innovative, and have been used quite often since then.

THE FILMS OF HAL MOHR

Hal Mohr's early career is one of the most difficult to index, since he worked outside of Hollywood for many years on independent productions that often were not only unrecorded in reference books but usually uncopyrighted. Several of these are mentioned in the course of the interview, most notably THE LAST NIGHT OF THE BARBARY COAST, which was produced by Sol Lesser. *Film Daily Yearbook* doesn't list Mohr until its 1923 volume, and from that point on, omissions are quite possible. But with the research at hand, and Mr. Mohr's memory, we are hoping that the following list of feature films is substantially complete from the admittedly late starting date. Mohr also filmed several TV series in the 1950s, notably I MARRIED JOAN, and numerous commercials.

1. WATCH HIM STEP—Goldstone 1922—Jack Nelson
2. THE UNFOLDMENT—Associated Exhibitors 1922—George Kern and Murdock MacQuarrie—Collaboration with Ernest Miller
3. BAG AND BAGGAGE—Selznick 1923—Finis Fox
4. A WOMAN WHO SINNED—FBO 1924—Finis Fox—Collaboration with Jean Smith
5. VANITY'S PRICE—FBO 1924—Roy William Neill
6. HE WHO LAUGHS LAST—Bud Barsky Corp. 1925—Jack Nelson

cameraman, Jack Hildyard, who's a very good cameraman, whom he insisted on using. (English cameramen, by the way, are not like our cameramen—they're lighting directors. They never bother with the camera; they do what the lighting director does in television.) At any rate, Hitchcock wanted this man, and the only way they would allow him to work in this country was if a union man covered Hildyard. Hell, my salary is anything but union scale, but Universal asked me if I would be willing to take the job. I said I would take it over on one condition: I'm not just going to be a card-carrier. I said, "I'm not going to be a featherbed; I don't approve of that. If I can earn my salary on the production, I'll come and cover Hildyard. I can more than pay for my salary in work that I can do in preparing the picture and doing things." So by God, they agreed to pay me my salary, which is about four times scale, and I went there when they got back from Denmark, and I was with them to the very end of the picture. I did do a hell of a lot of the pre-lighting of sets, pre-arranging, making shots, working out shots. I worked out the stuff when the little girl jumps in the car and hurts her leg when they're making their getaway from the department store, and they shot the reflection in the mirror. Well, process shots are tough to do, and I figured out and lined those shots up for them. I did a lot of the picture ... but I didn't photograph it. I think I finally took

7. THE MONSTER—MGM 1925—Roland West
8. PLAYING WITH SOULS—First National 1925—Ralph Ince
9. LITTLE ANNIE ROONEY—UA 1925—William Beaudine, in collaboration with Charles Rosher
10. THE HIGH HAND—Pathe 1926—Leo Maloney
11. THE MARRIAGE CLAUSE—Universal 1926—Lois Weber
12. SPARROWS—UA 1926—William Beaudine—Collaboration with Karl Struss and Charles Rosher
13. THE THIRD DEGREE—Warner Brothers 1926—Michael Curtiz
14. A MILLION BID—Warner Brothers 1927—Michael Curtiz
15. BITTER APPLES—Warner Brothers 1927—Harry Hoyt
16. OLD SAN FRANCISCO—Warner Brothers 1927—Alan Crosland
17. THE HEART OF MARYLAND—Warner Brothers 1927—Lloyd Bacon
18. SLIGHTLY USED—Warner Brothers 1927—Archie Mayo
19. THE JAZZ SINGER—Warner Brothers 1927—Alan Crosland
20. THE GIRL FROM CHICAGO—Warner Brothers 1927—Ray Enright
21. TENDERLOIN—Warner Brothers 1928—Michael Curtiz
22. GLORIOUS BETSY—Warner Brothers 1928—Alan Crosland
23. THE WEDDING MARCH—Paramount 1928—Erich von Stroheim—With Ben Reynolds and B. Sorenson. One sequence was filmed in Technicolor
24. NOAH'S ARK—Warner Brothers 1929—Michael Curtiz—Mohr quit midway through filming, and was replaced by Barney McGill.
25. THE LAST WARNING—Universal 1929—Paul Leni
26. BROADWAY—Universal 1929—Paul Fejos
27. THE LAST PERFORMANCE—Universal 1929—Paul Fejos
28. SHANGHAI LADY—Universal 1929—John S. Robertson
29. KING OF JAZZ—Universal 1930—John Murray Anderson—Filmed in Technicolor, with Ray Rennahan and Jerome Ash
30. CAPTAIN OF THE GUARD—Universal 1930—John S. Robertson and Paul Fejos—Collaboration with Gilbert Warrenton
31. THE CZAR OF BROADWAY—Universal 1930—William James Craft
32. BIG BOY—Warner Brothers 1930—Alan Crosland
33. THE CAT CREEPS—Universal 1930—Rupert Julian
34. THE COHENS AND KELLYS IN AFRICA—Universal 1930—Vin Moore
35. OUTWARD BOUND—Warner Brothers 1930—Robert Milton
36. FREE LOVE—Universal 1931—Hobart Henley
37. THE FRONT PAGE—UA 1931—Lewis Milestone—Mohr replaced Tony Gaudio during filming, and did not receive credit.
38. A WOMAN OF EXPERIENCE—Pathe 1931—Tay Garnett
39. BIG GAMBLE—Pathe 1931—Fred Niblo
40. DEVOTION—Pathe 1931—Robert Milton
41. LADY WITH A PAST—RKO 1932—Edward H. Griffith
42. A WOMAN COMMANDS—RKO 1932—Paul Stein
43. WEEKENDS ONLY—Fox 1932—Alan Crosland

44. FIRST YEAR—Fox 1932—William K. Howard
45. TESS OF THE STORM COUNTRY—Fox 1932—Alfred Santell
46. STATE FAIR—Fox 1933—Henry King
47. WARRIOR'S HUSBAND—Fox 1933—Walter Lang
48. I LOVED YOU WEDNESDAY—Fox 1933—Henry King, William Cameron Menzies
49. THE DEVIL'S IN LOVE—Fox 1933—William Dieterle
50. THE WORST WOMAN IN PARIS—Fox 1933—Monta Bell
51. AS HUSBANDS GO—Fox 1934—Hamilton McFadden
52. CAROLINA—Fox 1934—Henry King
53. DAVID HARUM—Fox 1934—James Cruze
54. CHARLIE CHAN'S COURAGE—Fox 1934—George Hadden
55. SERVANTS' ENTRANCE—Fox 1934—Frank Lloyd
56. UNDER PRESSURE—Fox 1935—Raoul Walsh
57. THE COUNTY CHAIRMAN—Fox 1935—John Blystone
58. A MIDSUMMER NIGHT'S DREAM—Warner Brothers 1935—Max Reinhardt and William Dieterle—Won Mohr his first Academy Award; his assistants were Fred Jackman, Byron Haskin, and H. F. Koenekamp.
59. CAPTAIN BLOOD—Warner Brothers 1935—Michael Curtiz
60. THE WALKING DEAD—Warner Brothers 1936—Michael Curtiz
61. BULLETS OR BALLOTS—Warner Brothers 1936—William Keighley
62. THE GREEN PASTURES—Warner Brothers 1936—William Keighley, Marc Connelly
63. I MET MY LOVE AGAIN—UA 1938—Arthur Ripley, Joshua Logan
64. BACK DOOR TO HEAVEN—Paramount 1939—William K. Howard—Collaboration with Bill Kelly
65. DESTRY RIDES AGAIN—Universal 1939—George Marshall
66. THE UNDER-PUP—Universal 1939—Richard Wallace
67. RIO—Universal 1939—John Brahm
68. WHEN THE DALTONS RODE—Universal 1940—George Marshall
69. CHEERS FOR MISS BISHOP—UA 1941—Tay Garnett
70. POT O'GOLD—UA 1941—George Marshall
71. INTERNATIONAL LADY—UA 1941—Tim Whelan
72. TWIN BEDS—UA 1942—Tim Whelan
73. WATCH ON THE RHINE—Warner Brothers 1943—Herman Shumlin—With Merritt Gerstad
74. THE PHANTOM OF THE OPERA—Universal 1943—Arthur Lubin—Won Mohr his second Academy Award—Color
75. TOP MAN—Universal 1943—Charles Lamont
76. LADIES COURAGEOUS—Universal 1944—John Rawlins
77. THIS IS THE LIFE—Universal 1944—Felix Feist
78. SAN DIEGO, I LOVE YOU—Universal 1944—Reginald LeBorg
79. THE CLIMAX—Universal 1944—George Waggner—Color (Mohr's Technicolor collaborator on all subsequent Universal productions was W. Howard Greene)
80. THE IMPATIENT YEARS—Columbia 1944—Irving Cummings—Color
81. MY GAL LOVES MUSIC—Universal 1944—Edward Lilley
82. ENTER ARSÈNE LUPIN—Universal 1944—Ford Beebe
83. HER LUCKY NIGHT—Universal 1945—Edward Lilley

84. SALOME, WHERE SHE DANCED—Universal 1945—Charles Lamont—Color
85. SHADY LADY—Universal 1945—George Waggner
86. BECAUSE OF HIM—Universal 1946—Richard Wallace
87. A NIGHT IN PARADISE—Universal 1946—Arthur Lubin—Color
88. I'LL BE YOURS—Universal 1947—William Seiter
89. SONG OF SCHEHERAZADE—Universal 1947—Walter Reisch
90. THE LOST MOMENT—Universal 1947—Martin Gabel
91. PIRATE OF MONTEREY—Universal 1947—Alfred Werker
92. ANOTHER PART OF THE FOREST—Universal 1948—Michael Gordon
93. JOHNNY HOLIDAY—UA 1949—Willis Goldbeck
94. WOMAN ON THE RUN—Universal 1950—Norman Foster
95. THE SECOND WOMAN—UA 1951—James V. Kern
96. THE BIG NIGHT—UA 1951—Joseph Losey
97. RANCHO NOTORIOUS—RKO 1952—Fritz Lang—Color
98. THE FOURPOSTER—Columbia 1952—Irving Reis
99. MEMBER OF THE WEDDING—Columbia 1952—Fred Zinnemann
100. THE WILD ONE—Columbia 1954—Laslo Benedek
101. THE BOSS—Allied Artists 1956—Byron Haskin
102. BABY FACE NELSON—UA 1957—Don Siegel
103. THE LINE-UP—Columbia 1958—Don Siegel
104. THE GUN RUNNERS—UA 1958—Don Siegel
105. THE LAST VOYAGE—MGM 1960—Andrew Stone—Color
106. UNDERWORLD U.S.A.—Columbia 1961—Samuel Fuller
107. THE MAN FROM THE DINER'S CLUB—Columbia 1963—Frank Tashlin
108. BAMBOO SAUCER—NTA 1968—Frank Melford—Color
109. TOPAZ—Universal 1969—Alfred Hitchcock—Mohr was billed as photographic consultant; Jack Hildyard was director of photography—Color

Interview with *HAL ROSSON*

Harold (Hal) Rosson boasts a rich family heritage within the motion picture industry. His brother, Arthur Rosson, was a successful director, and several other relatives took varied jobs in the film business in its infancy. It was only natural that he should follow them, and circa 1913, he worked on his first film, settling before too long in the position of cameraman. Although his career spans a great many years, Rosson is most closely identified with his MGM period, during which he photographed some of that studio's most elegant and successful films; indeed, it can be said that he was a major contributor to the renowned MGM polish. His association with the studio was furthered still when he married its biggest star, Jean Harlow, in 1933.

Our interview with Mr. Rosson touched on just a few of the highlights of his career—and hopefully his thoughts about many fine films we were not able to discuss will someday be set down for posterity. This discussion focused more on change and trends in the motion picture business than on specific films; a precise man, Mr. Rosson strove to provide precise answers to our questions.

LM: What was the first film you ever shot, and how did it come about?

ROSSON: I would almost have to get out papers to answer a question like that. I do remember it was for a company known as the Metro Pictures Corporation, many years ago. I came to California from the East, prior to the First World War—I'll guess now and say 1912—and many members of my family were already in the motion picture business out here on the West Coast, so I was anxious to join up in the same business. I knew some people at the Metro Pictures Corporation here, and I made an arrangement with them, and from there I got into the business. I was everybody's assistant. I was an assistant cameraman, and if there is such a thing as an assistant boy-actor I was that. Of course, my main effort was to become a cameraman.

LM: Had photography always been an interest of yours?

ROSSON: At that time, yes, very definitely.

LM: So you watched other cameramen at work . . .

ROSSON: Outside of the cameraman that I worked with personally, there was only one other cameraman present there. So there weren't too many cameramen to watch. I cannot recall the name of the first picture I worked on, offhand.

LM: At what point did you graduate to becoming a cameraman?

ROSSON: Well, Metro was here in California a short while, and within a year they returned east, to New York, and they offered me a job as a cameraman, if I could come east. But going east, all expenses incurred there would be on my own, so I had to make arrangements to do that, in order to take advantage of their offer. This I did, I returned east; it was a little prior to the First World War, and the Metro Pictures Corporation had arranged for studio facilities at Sixty-first Street and Broadway. That's where they set up their studio operations, and that's where I started to work. It was formerly a huge garage, on the top of a building, where cars had been stored. It had a huge glass roof, which they thought would be ideal for photographing; I was not much of an authority on that in those days. However, we made several very good pictures there. That was where I started to actually photograph.

LM: There was so much yet to be learned in the silent film era, and most of the cameramen, like yourself, started with the business. Was it learning by doing, for you? Was there a lot of experimentation on your part?

ROSSON: In thinking back, I would say a great deal. I had had quite a bit of experience—not quite a bit, but *some* experience—in photography, "still" work, but it was a great deal of experimentation . . . and watching, observing.

LM: Did you work in the lab as well?

ROSSON: Oh yes.

LM: Were most of your effects done in the camera or in the lab?

ROSSON: I would say that practically all the effects in those days were done within the camera. Very little was done as it is now, practically all in the laboratory.

LM: Which do you think achieved the better results?

ROSSON: I would prefer naturally to do them outside of the camera, because you can correct the mistakes. If the mistakes are made within the camera, you don't know how much you're spoiling. I would think it is simpler, and the results are much better, by doing them the way they are done today, with mostly lab work.

LM: One of the first films I have credited for you is THE CINEMA MURDER.

ROSSON: With Marion Davies, yes. That was after the war, after the period we were talking about. Like four million others, I got mixed up in the First World War, and upon my return from the service, I went to work with Miss Davies. That kept me in New York for a couple of years. Then I came to the Coast.

LM: How independent was the cameraman at that time? Was your job a collaborative one with the director?

ROSSON: The business was so new then that the cameraman, as I recall it, had nobody to consult with. I'm not sure that that's a correct statement, I don't know who in the world you would have consulted with. You were more or less completely on your own.

LM: What relation are you to Arthur Rosson, the director?

ROSSON: He is my brother.

LM: I see that you worked with him, first on a picture called POLLY OF THE STORM COUNTRY.

ROSSON: Yes, that was done here on the West Coast.

LM: What precipitated your move back west?

ROSSON: In those days I was following a picture; if they wanted to do it on the East Coast, I went to the East Coast, if they were shooting it on the West Coast, I went to the West Coast.

LM: Was POLLY shot in a studio, or on location?

ROSSON: It was shot in a studio, a group of buildings at the old Selig Zoo. Pictures had been made there prior to our going there. That was with a girl by the name of Mildred Harris.

LM: At the time, did you prefer shooting in a studio or outside?

ROSSON: I wish I could answer that intelligently. Practically everything I did was difficult. The problems were so varied. In those days we worked with orthochromatic film, and with orthochromatic film the ability to photograph various colors was problematic. This was greatly simplified when panchromatic film came in.

LM: How did you compensate for orthochromatic film's limitations?

ROSSON: By learning the usages of the film, what it permitted you to do, and what you were able to obtain. That was arrived at by experimentation—not solely, but greatly by experimentation.

LM: When you came out here, were you under contract?

ROSSON: Yes, I was, but in those days there were so few cameramen that any studio that had set up a routine of pictures to be made, if they came across such an individual, they were quickly chosen and put under some sort of a contract. As I recall, I was put under contract almost immediately after I started in the business.

LM: Did you have any choice as to which pictures you would shoot?

ROSSON: I would say that I had no choice, except that the picture was offered to me, and if I had chosen not to do it I'm sure I would have had that privilege, but if I did not accept a picture, I can assure you it was a very small number.

LM: Did cameramen become "typecast" with a certain type of picture?

ROSSON: I'm sure that did exist, but in all the years I worked in the motion picture business, I knew but one or two cameramen who were referred to along those lines. I was not. But many cameramen made a certain liaison with a certain director or a certain star, wherein they worked more or less exclusively with that director or star. That happened many times.

LM: I see that you worked quite a bit with director Frank O'Connor and his star, May McAvoy. Was that advantageous?

ROSSON: Oh yes, it was more congenial, more pleasant, a happier environment.

LM: You worked with a great many outstanding directors in the 1920s . . . Allan Dwan, for example.

ROSSON: A charming man, great director.

LM: At this point, what was your working relationship with the director, and at what point in production did you become involved?

ROSSON: A great many individuals, directors and producers, realized the importance of each and every person on a motion picture. It varied—why it varied, there are a thousand answers—but on some pictures a cameraman would be called in very early in production. Then again, he might not be called in until the first day he was going on the stage to work. I can recall numerous pictures where I as a cameraman was called in extremely early.

LM: I notice that you worked with Gloria Swanson quite often; was that a case of her liking the way you photographed her and requesting you as cameraman?

ROSSON: I cannot speak for Miss Swanson, but I had the great pleasure of photographing numbers of her pictures, and if she had not been agreeable to the results that she could see, I probably would not have worked with her. I do believe that the reason I photographed her on so many occasions was that the director who worked with her, Allan Dwan, had a very happy arrangement of working with me. He was assigned to direct her pictures, so he would assign me to photograph them.

LM: Obviously you are a perfectionist. Were you able to be a perfectionist in those days? If something dissatisfied you, were you allowed to shoot it again?

ROSSON: Yes and no. Many times one would see something you'd like to have done again; if it was agreeable to all concerned, and it was possible, it would be done. But often the question of money came up, and time, and could we get everyone together again to do it, and it was not done.

LM: Was there a special technique to glamour photography, in shooting someone like Miss Swanson?

ROSSON: Well, the first thing that comes to my mind when you say that is "What is glamour?" And I'm sure that if you ask ten persons you'll get ten different answers. So I might have seen something in Miss Swanson's makeup that would be desirable either to emphasize or decrease in visual importance. If that happened, I'm sure that I, with my sense of beauty, would have either covered it up or emphasized it.

Hal Rosson (right) with director Jack Conway at MGM (ca. 1932).

LM: How much could a cameraman do with a person's face? Could you take someone who was plain and make her look glamorous?

ROSSON: I don't think there's any question about that, and it's been proven a thousand and one times.

LM: How would you compare the cameraman of the silent days, who did everything, with the director of photography today, who has so many assistants helping him?

ROSSON: The same ideals are present today as they were when I began. In the early days, the cameraman had to do practically everything himself, with his own hands. Now, he has many assistants who do the actual work, but under his direction. So I would still be called upon to exercise all the various things I formerly did, but directing other people to do my work physically.

LM: One film of yours that's still shown frequently is MANHANDLED. Do you remember the subway sequence?

ROSSON: How could one forget?

LM: What problems did you have to tackle in setting that up?

ROSSON: Oh, they varied greatly. After all, when you get into a subway car—and that was a comedy, so you had to have the comedy aspects—the results on the screen had to be crowded, but people also had to be seen, Miss Swanson had to look good, so there were many many problems you wouldn't encounter on an ordinary scene. We had a lot of fun on that picture; it was so delightful to work on, and you were so happy to be on it that the troublesome shots didn't seem so troublesome.

LM: Many people have criticized the studio system, saying that it hampered creativity. Did you feel this way as a cameraman?

ROSSON: I am a product of the studio system, star system, and I thought it was a very good way to make pictures. I'm sure it hampered some, but when I think of the great help it gave to so many many more than it hampered, I think it helped a great deal more than it hampered.

LM: We're getting into the mid- and late 1920s now, chronologically; did knowing more, with more advancements being made in your field, make it less challenging for you?

ROSSON: No; the challenges were always there, and I presume that they are there as much today as they were then. When I worked in the picture business, I had great fun. I loved my work, I loved doing my work. I have to believe that the man today does not have as much fun making pictures as I did. I used to get to the studio at the crack of dawn sometimes, in order to see what I had done a day or two before. I was so happy with my work, I wanted to see it on the screen. I had the best time in the world, and for that I was paid.

LM: Let me ask you about some people you worked with: Gregory LaCava.

ROSSON: He was a charming man, a nice man.

LM: I read that he felt the best way to make a picture was to keep a partylike atmosphere on the set.

ROSSON: That's a very good description of Gregory La-Cava and his working methods. All of his pictures, as I recall them, were very humorous, and just one big laugh on the stage. If you weren't enjoying yourself, and Greg was on the stage, he would have known it, and he would have asked you to leave ... he only wanted humor around.

LM: Were some directors more visually oriented than others?

ROSSON: Yes and no—because you're taking in such a huge number of individuals, I don't know how to pin it down to yes or no.

LM: Let's get specific, then. How about Josef von Sternberg?

ROSSON: Joe von Sternberg was an individual, and working for him one had to learn a lot—you would wind up with the knowledge of a lot of things you hadn't known before. But he was a great inspiration; he always wanted you to do what you wanted to do, even if it was at variance with what he had in mind. "Well, let's do it your way and see. If by chance it's what we want, we'll keep it; if not, we'll change it." He was always prodding you—try it, try it, never mind about the front office or the back office. I enjoyed working with him. There were times when he would be a little difficult—I don't know who isn't—and there were times when he would drive you out of your mind. But he got you to try to do it the way you wanted to. Plus the fact that he was a nice person.

LM: Victor Fleming?

ROSSON: Ah! Victor Fleming was my pal, so there was a great deal of personal influence working with Vic. I always believed he was a master showman as far as the mechanics of the making of films were concerned. Victor always knew what he wanted, and if by chance you didn't quite know how to do it, he would come up with a solution. Victor Fleming knew as much about the making of pictures as any man I've ever known—all departments. He was a craftsman of the first order, he was a machinist, he did the mechanics. I doubt very much if he lacked the knowledge to answer any solution mechanically.

LM: Did he deliberately strive for challenges, then?

ROSSON: I don't think he strove for them, but they were always there.

LM: Mal St. Clair?

ROSSON: Mal St. Clair had formerly been a cartoonist, and he carried into his picture-making the background of a cartoonist. Everything always was a lark for him. He made that picture GENTLEMEN PREFER BLONDES, and nobody made it quite like St. Clair.

LM: Did he ever try to get effects in the camera that would be cartoonlike?

ROSSON: I never got that impression, but if there was a laugh connected with it, you did it with that in mind. He was an enjoyable man to be around.

LM: Harry D'Arrast?

ROSSON: Harry D'Arrast was an interesting man, and I don't think he had any theatrical background in any way, shape, or form. He came to this country, got mixed up with Chaplin and a group that was around here. He had a very happy liaison with Adolphe Menjou, and they became terribly friendly, because they had an awful lot in common. So Harry D'Arrast directed pictures with Menjou, and it was a very enjoyable association. He was very gifted in the making of pictures with the so-called French touch.

LM: Now we're coming to the transition period into talkies; it's been said that visual creativity stopped when sound came in. Do you think so?

ROSSON: The use of sound completely revolutionized the business. I recall when THE JAZZ SINGER opened, it was a bombshell. I was working on a very important picture, terribly important, which had been a fantastically successful Broadway show, ABIE'S IRISH ROSE. It was a terribly costly picture. We'd gone into production on that picture long before THE JAZZ SINGER; so, as we all know, THE JAZZ SINGER opened, and it was such a success. We were practically finishing ABIE'S IRISH ROSE when that opened. Long before the next morning arrived, I was notified by telephone that we were re-opening ABIE'S IRISH ROSE the next morning. We went back to work on the film with sound, and that was a tremendously exciting moment, a big moment in my life of making pictures. One of the things that we had was a death scene, and the Jewish boy's father was a cantor (I hope I'm not mixing this up) and he sang the Kol Nidre. [Ed. Note: Rosson is probably thinking of *The Jazz Singer*.] And when that hymn came from the loudspeaker in the projection room, it was a fantastic moment.

LM: What kind of problems did you face with sound?

ROSSON: So many varied problems ... I thought at the time, if all these things are necessary to put sound on the screen, no one will ever make a sound picture, it was so fantastically overwhelming.

LM: At the time did you think they were going to eliminate silent films?

ROSSON: I personally did not. I felt there was a very definite place for sound, but I never thought that the silent picture would be eliminated one hundred percent. Because in looking at a picture, in my experience, the individual added to what was on the screen. For instance, there was no sound originally, as we know it, and I don't recall ever missing the sound, because I think the individual put up on the screen the sound he wanted. I thought the silents gave out a universal sound that the individual expressed for himself. Therefore, I don't think that I was ever conscious of the loss of sound. I never did think that sound would eliminate the silent picture.

LM: Could you still be the cameraman you were in the early talkies?

ROSSON: Yes, because there was another avenue for me to pursue; it must have helped me. It certainly excited me, and if it excited me it had to help me.

LM: Do you remember the first time you worked with color?

ROSSON: Yes I do. Permit me if I go around this a bit: I was under contract to the MGM studio, and Mr. Eddie Mannix called me in one day, and said, "We're loaning you out to David Selznick. I want you to go over to his studio tomorrow morning and get ready to photograph his picture." I asked what was the picture, and he said GARDEN OF ALLAH. I said, "I'd love to do it, but who's going to direct it?" He told me Richard Boleslavsky. So the next day we started to work on the picture; I went back to the studio that night, I called up Mr. Mannix and said, "I want to see you." I walked in and I must have looked perturbed or something, because he said, "What's the matter?" I said, "Eddie, I'm not so sure I'm the man for this picture." He said, "Why?" I said, "It's in color!" I had

never photographed a film in color in my life. I said, "I don't know anything about color . . . I'm not the man." He said, "Oh, forget about it—you're the man. Mr. Selznick wants you to do it, and we want you to do it." So I'd spoken my piece, I certainly wasn't going to argue with my boss. So I went back the next day, photographed it, and won the Academy Award that year for color, on the first piece of color film I'd ever photographed.

LM: Perhaps it was precisely because you had never worked with it before . . .

ROSSON: I don't know that it was *because* . . .

LM: . . . I meant that being inexperienced, perhaps you brought a fresh approach to the use of color.

ROSSON: Well, that could be; I know it was a lot of guesswork on my part.

LM: Did you have a Technicolor consultant on the film?

ROSSON: Oh yes. A man by the name of Duke Green. He was there to make sure we didn't get color that clashed, and to help all he could, and I assure you there was lots of room for his help. But that was an interesting picture. Looking back, not having had any experience with color, I do believe that my thoughts were to try to *control* color.

Rosson shoots a scene with Jean Harlow and Mary Astor for RED DUST *(1932); Victor Fleming is in the director's chair.*

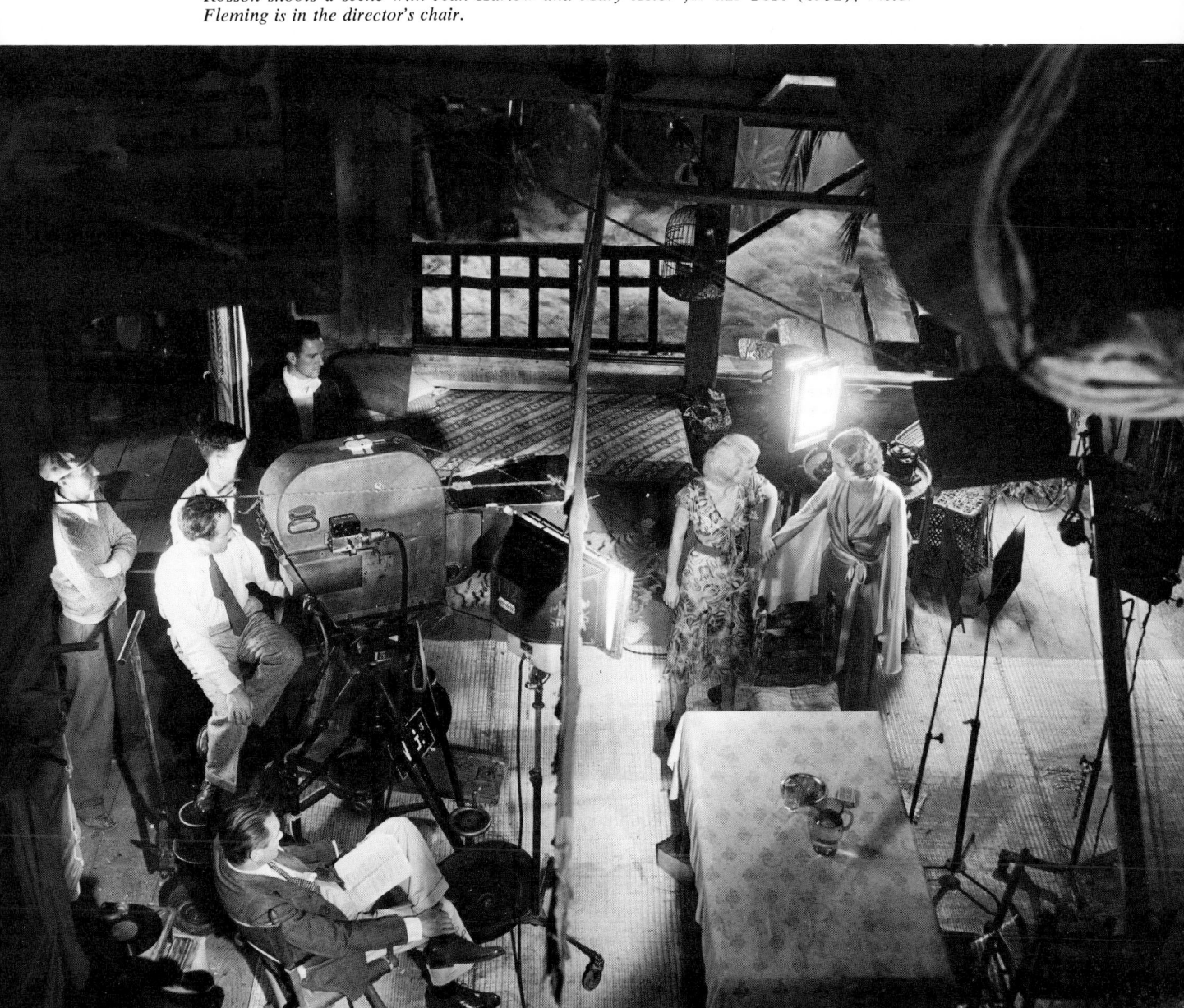

Rosson is nonchalant about set-ups like this! Munchkinland in THE WIZARD OF OZ (1939).

The good Lord, when he goes to paint the exterior, has the most lavish palette of color in the world. So my thinking was an attempt to control color, to eliminate color unless it could be used dramatically. I didn't want the color to control me. I recall one of the earliest scenes in the picture, there was a luncheon table spread, a table covered with a white cloth, and on that cloth was a bowl of fruit. The bowl of fruit consisted of every kind of fruit one could think of, a complete conglomeration of color. As I recall, it dazzled me when I looked at it. So first I emptied the bowl and put back fruit until it almost looked as if there was no color there, then I mounted a red apple in a very important position there where you could not help but see it. So as I recall, this bowl of fruit consisted of a red apple—it was almost the only color there—and it was startling on the screen. That was my idea of the control of color, and I'm very proud of the results.

LM: Which did you like better, the three-strip Technicolor of those days, or the later color?

ROSSON: Oh, the latter. At that time the three-strip had just come into its own, because the color was so gorgeous. I think all pictures should be in color.

LM: Don't you think there are some subjects that lend themselves better to black and white?

ROSSON: There are subjects that may lend themselves to black and white, but put them in color, and see if they're not better, or equally as good. I think they will be better. In this day and age—in this very room we're sitting in—there's nothing but color. Everything is color, therefore you don't even think about it. *Life* is color.

LM: Some people feel that the old three-strip color was unnatural, however, and that it was too vivid, and therefore not realistic.

ROSSON: Certain processes would amplify color out of all degrees of naturalness. But there again, I'll go back to the phrase I used earlier—I tried to control color. I looked upon color as another actor. When an actor walks on the stage, the director doesn't let him run roughshod all over the place. I think the cameraman who uses color can control it.

LM: Could you make adjustments for color when you timed the different color separations in the lab?

ROSSON: The Technicolor people controlled their end of the business, the developing of the film, one hundred percent. But if by chance I had attempted to do something that would enter into their developing of the film, that was against what they were doing, I'm sure they would have argued it.

LM: Then you weren't involved in the processing of the film?

ROSSON: Not at all, not after it left the stage.

LM: Let's go back to another picture of yours, MADAM SATAN, an unusual picture, to say the least.

ROSSON: What a fantastic picture. Mr. DeMille did that; I went to MGM studio at the request of Mr. DeMille. I did the remake of his first picture, THE SQUAW MAN.

LM: Do you remember anything about photographing the zeppelin?

ROSSON: That was a fantastic thing; originally, the floor was going to be a sheet of glass. We were going to photograph inside the zeppelin, and because the floor was glass, you would see the lights of the city below. But that's one of the joys of the picture business—the dream pictures you encounter.

LM: What were your feelings about DeMille?

ROSSON: I learned more from Mr. DeMille than from any other human being I've known. I boast of the fact that we were very close friends.

LM: Having started in the film business when everything was as you saw it on the screen, more or less, what were your feelings about rear projection and other devices that came into widespread use in the 30s?

ROSSON: I think process screening, the art of process screening, is one of the great things that has come to the motion picture business. Speaking of process work as applied to camerawork, I think it is a fantastic aid to the cameraman.

LM: Don't you think, though, that you sometimes sacrifice atmosphere when you use process work?

ROSSON: I would be inclined to say no, because, for instance, I've never been to the North Pole, but I can put the North Pole on the motion picture screen. I think that what you can do with that greatly overcomes the non-usage of it. I think you can get fantastic results with back projection.

LM: You worked with W. S. Van Dyke at this time; was his reputation as a rapid-fire director accurate?

ROSSON: Woody Van Dyke was a very interesting person; I had the great pleasure of working on numerous pictures with him. He had a style that he exercised practically all the time. His thinking, as I recall it, was to emphasize certain things in a picture. In other words, the girl in his picture had to look beautiful. So Van would permit you as a cameraman as much time as needed, within reason, to get a good result of the girl. If I was going to make a photograph of a piece of newspaper that had to be lying on that table, he wanted me to photograph that newspaper in one second, or half a second if possible, but I could

Rosson (left) and director King Vidor (right) prepare to shoot a scene for DUEL IN THE SUN *(1946).*

take hours with the girl. So I would say that all these stories you heard about Van Dyke as a one-take, hurry-up man—granted he wanted you to hurry up, *on that newspaper,* but he never hurried me up on the girl. "Let me know when you're ready."

LM: One of the first pictures you did with him was TARZAN THE APE MAN, which was quite an elaborate picture.

ROSSON: Oh yes. They had that wonderful trio, the Flying Cadonas, and they built trapezes which became part of the set. We did a lot of the flying stuff out near Lake Sherwood.

LM: Do you think that there was a "studio look" to certain films? Was there an MGM look?

ROSSON: All studios prided themselves on their work, and I was fortunate enough to be at the MGM studio when they had an unbelievable number of actors and actresses; they had half a dozen cameramen who were considered the finest in their profession—patting myself on the back a little bit with that statement. And nothing was released until it was right. So there was a great esprit de corps in the work at the MGM studios; we all stood half an inch taller than our normal height due to the fact that we were a little swell-headed about our work. I know I was, very definitely. Maybe the MGM pictures did have a look that other studios did not have, maybe it was due to the photography. I'm not privileged to say that is so, but I do know that the spirit was such that we were proud to be at MGM.

LM: You certainly worked on the top pictures at MGM during your stay there. How did you handle the color in THE WIZARD OF OZ?

ROSSON: It was just a matter of controlling color, again.

LM: But it was such a tremendous color-oriented production; it must have made things more difficult for you.

ROSSON: No, not really.

LM: Was it your idea to start the picture in black and white, and switch to color when the setting moved to Oz?

ROSSON: I don't really recall whose idea that was.

LM: It was certainly copied enough times in later fantasy films. What about shooting a B picture at MGM like the DR. KILDARE films: could you still provide the traditional studio polish working on a lower-budget picture?

ROSSON: Naturally, you didn't have as much time to spend on one of the DR. KILDARE films, but I remember Mr. Mayer saying to me, "If it's an MGM film, it has to look like an MGM film," regardless of the fact that it was officially a B picture.

LM: When you went to England to film THE GHOST GOES WEST, did you find any great difference in filmmaking technique?

ROSSON: No, I would say that it was essentially the same as here.

LM: What about working with René Clair?

ROSSON: He was a marvelous man, a wonderful man to be around.

LM: When you went to work on DUEL IN THE SUN, did you work with William Dieterle or King Vidor?

ROSSON: I worked with King Vidor ... I don't remember working at all with William Dieterle.

LM: Were you subject to any of David Selznick's memos as to how you should photograph Jennifer Jones?

ROSSON: No comment (laughing) ...

LM: When you got into CinemaScope in the 1950s, did you have to reorient your way of thinking for shooting a film?

ROSSON: When you are working in CinemaScope you have to think in CinemaScope terms, because the whole idea of the size of the screen is foreign to my entire world ... look around at any painting here, you won't see that size. But I did enjoy working in it, because if you have a Western, you automatically think in terms of the Grand Tetons, the great American desert—well, CinemaScope was half again as big as what we had been using.

LM: What about the problems, though, like faces distorting when you did close-ups, and horizons tending to curve upward?

ROSSON: CinemaScope had so many bastardized things in it, you resented it at first. I like honesty, I believe in the truth, and CinemaScope was anti-truth. But I loved the areas you could work in.

LM: The first CinemaScope lenses weren't supposed to be too good on definition ...

ROSSON: They weren't too good on *anything.* You had to overcome an awful lot of things.

LM: Did you ever work in Panavision? It's supposed to be better for a lot of these problems.

ROSSON: Yes, I think Panavision is very fine.

LM: What about VistaVision?

ROSSON: They all had so many things in them that were both honest and dishonest; in talking about them you're trying to explain the honesty against the dishonesty.

LM: Did you ever want to direct?

ROSSON: Yes.

LM: Did you?

ROSSON: No.

LM: Any particular reason?

ROSSON: Yes, I wasn't given the opportunity. I asked for it, and Eddie Mannix, of whom I spoke before, gave me a very flattering answer. He said, "You're too good a cameraman; you'll never direct. Not here, anyway."

LM: What was the most recent film you've done?

ROSSON: I didn't work for ten or twelve years, and then I went back and did a picture for Paramount, with John Wayne, called EL DORADO, with Howard Hawks. Howard's an old pal of mine, and he said, "Oh come on, come back," and I said, "You don't want me," and he said, "Yes I do." So I went back, and I was out of my mind I ever quit.

LM: Why did you stop?

Rosson at the Los Angeles County Museum in 1970.

ROSSON: Well, I'm pretty old—I'm seventy-five years old now.

LM: Do you think you'll be doing more work in the future?

ROSSON: No, I don't honestly believe so.

LM: How about television? Have you ever done any TV work?

ROSSON: Yes, but I don't choose to do television. I'm very grateful and thankful that television came in, because it's put so many of my pals to work, but I do not like it. Please don't get the wrong idea about me—I'm very proud of my work. And I've found very few cameramen who have made television pictures who say they are proud of their work. I do not choose to work—and I don't have any misconception about how "great" I was—where I wouldn't feel that way. I've been very fortunate, I made some very good investments, so I don't think anyone will ever have to throw a benefit for me.

LM: But if the right opportunity would come along . . .

ROSSON: If the opportunity comes, I honestly don't think I would work, unless it was like EL DORADO. I photographed that because Wayne and Hawks did that . . . I would do anything for Howard Hawks, and I enjoyed doing it. It was fun.

LM: Do you think that was the secret of the great films we've been talking about?

ROSSON: Yes, a group falling together and thinking together and praying together, and you wanted one result—a good picture. And you wanted to be mixed up in it.

THE FILMS OF HAL ROSSON

Once more, this is an attempt at a complete filmography from the starting point of 1920. Rosson had been photographing films for several years prior to this, but research as to titles has been fruitless. It is hoped that all of his feature films since this date are included below, however.

1. THE CINEMA MURDER—Paramount 1920—George D. Baker
2. POLLY OF THE STORM COUNTRY—First National 1920—Arthur Rosson
3. HELIOTROPE—Paramount 1920—George D. Baker
4. BURIED TREASURE—Paramount 1921—George D. Baker
5. EVERYTHING FOR SALE—Paramount 1921—Frank O'Connor
6. A VIRGINIA COURTSHIP—Paramount 1921—Frank O'Connor
7. THE CRADLE—Paramount 1922—Paul Powell
8. FOR THE DEFENSE—Paramount 1922—Paul Powell
9. A HOMESPUN VAMP—Paramount 1922—Frank O'Connor
10. THROUGH A GLASS WINDOW—Paramount 1922—Maurice Campbell
11. DARK SECRETS—Paramount 1923—Victor Fleming
12. GLIMPSES OF THE MOON—Paramount 1923—Allan Dwan
13. GARRISON'S FINISH—Paramount 1923—Arthur Rosson
14. LAWFUL LARCENY—Paramount 1923—Allan Dwan
15. ZAZA—Paramount 1923—Allan Dwan
16. A SOCIETY SCANDAL—Paramount 1924—Allan Dwan
17. MANHANDLED—Paramount 1924—Allan Dwan
18. STORY WITHOUT A NAME—Paramount 1924—Irving Willat
19. MANHATTAN—Paramount 1924—R. H. Burnside
20. A MAN MUST LIVE—Paramount 1925—Paul Sloane
21. TOO MANY KISSES—Paramount 1925—Paul Sloane
22. THE LITTLE FRENCH GIRL—Paramount 1925—Herbert Brenon
23. THE STREET OF FORGOTTEN MEN—Paramount 1925—Herbert Brenon
24. CLASSIFIED—First National 1925—Alfred Santell
25. INFATUATION—First National 1926—Irving Cummings
26. UP IN MABEL'S ROOM—Producer's Distributing Corportation (PDC) 1926—E. Mason Hopper—Collaboration with Alex Phillips
27. ALMOST A LADY—PDC 1926—E. Mason Hopper
28. FOR WIVES ONLY—PDC 1926—Victor Heerman
29. MAN BAIT—PDC 1926—Donald Crisp
30. JIM THE CONQUEROR—PDC 1927—George B. Seitz
31. GETTING GERTIE'S GARTER—PDC 1927—E. Mason Hopper
32. ROUGH HOUSE ROSIE—Paramount 1927—Frank Strayer—Collaboration with James Murray
33. EVENING CLOTHES—Paramount 1927—Luther Reed

34. SERVICE FOR LADIES—Paramount 1927—Harry D'Arrast
35. A GENTLEMAN OF PARIS—Paramount 1927—Harry D'Arrast
36. OPEN RANGE—Paramount 1927—Clifford S. Smith
37. QUICKSANDS—Paramount 1927—Jack Conway—Independently made in 1923 and supposedly released then, this film, produced and written by Howard Hawks, reappeared in 1927 as a Paramount film—Collaboration with Glen MacWilliams
38. GENTLEMEN PREFER BLONDES—Paramount 1928—Mal St. Clair
39. DRAG NET—Paramount 1928—Josef von Sternberg
40. SAWDUST PARADISE—Paramount 1928—Luther Reed
41. THE DOCKS OF NEW YORK—Paramount 1928—Josef von Sternberg
42. THREE WEEKENDS—Paramount 1928—Clarence Badger
43. ABIE'S IRISH ROSE—Paramount 1929—Victor Fleming
44. THE CASE OF LENA SMITH—Paramount 1929—Josef von Sternberg
45. FAR CALL—Fox 1929—Allan Dwan
46. TRENT'S LAST CASE—Fox 1929—Howard Hawks
47. FROZEN JUSTICE—Fox 1929—Allan Dwan
48. SOUTH SEA ROSE—Fox 1929—Allan Dwan
49. HELLO, SISTER—Sono Art 1930—Walter Lang
50. THIS MAD WORLD—MGM 1930—William DeMille
51. MADAM SATAN—MGM 1930—Cecil B. DeMille
52. PASSION FLOWER—MGM 1930—William DeMille
53. MEN CALL IT LOVE—MGM 1931—Edgar Selwyn
54. PRODIGAL—MGM 1931—Harry Pollard
55. THE SQUAW MAN—MGM 1931—Cecil B. DeMille
56. SON OF INDIA—MGM 1931—Jacques Feyder
57. SPORTING BLOOD—MGM 1931—Charles Brabin
58. CUBAN LOVE SONG—MGM 1931—W. S. Van Dyke
59. TARZAN THE APE MAN—MGM 1932—W. S. Van Dyke
60. ARE YOU LISTENING—MGM 1932—Harry Beaumont
61. WHEN A FELLER NEEDS A FRIEND—MGM 1932—Harry Pollard
62. DOWNSTAIRS—MGM 1932—Monta Bell
63. RED-HEADED WOMAN—MGM 1932—Jack Conway
64. KONGO—MGM 1932—William Cowan
65. RED DUST—MGM 1932—Victor Fleming
66. HELL BELOW—MGM 1933—Jack Conway
67. THE BARBARIAN—MGM 1933—Sam Wood
68. HOLD YOUR MAN—MGM 1933—Sam Wood
69. TURN BACK THE CLOCK—MGM 1933—Edgar Selwyn
70. PENTHOUSE—MGM 1933—W. S. Van Dyke
71. BOMBSHELL—MGM 1933—Victor Fleming—Collaboration with Chester Lyons
72. THE CAT AND THE FIDDLE—MGM 1934—William K. Howard—Sequence filmed in Technicolor
73. THIS SIDE OF HEAVEN—MGM 1934—William K. Howard
74. TREASURE ISLAND—MGM 1934—Victor Fleming
75. THE SCARLET PIMPERNEL—UA 1935—Harold Young
76. THE GHOST GOES WEST—UA 1936—René Clair
77. THE DEVIL IS A SISSY—MGM 1936—W. S. Van Dyke
78. THE GARDEN OF ALLAH—UA 1936—Richard Boleslavsky—Color—Won Rosson and W. Howard Greene a special Academy Award
79. AS YOU LIKE IT—20th Century Fox 1937—Paul Czinner—Collaboration with Jack Cardiff
80. THE MAN WHO COULD WORK MIRACLES—UA-Korda 1937—Lothar Mendes
81. CAPTAINS COURAGEOUS—MGM 1937—Victor Fleming
82. THEY GAVE HIM A GUN—MGM 1937—W. S. Van Dyke
83. THE EMPEROR'S CANDLESTICKS—MGM 1937—George Fitzmaurice
84. TOO HOT TO HANDLE—MGM 1938—Jack Conway
85. THE WIZARD OF OZ—MGM 1939—Victor Fleming—Color
86. I TAKE THIS WOMAN—MGM 1940—W. S. Van Dyke
87. EDISON THE MAN—MGM 1940—Clarence Brown
88. DR. KILDARE GOES HOME—MGM 1940—Harold S. Bucquet
89. FLIGHT COMMAND—MGM 1940—Frank Borzage
90. THE PENALTY—MGM 1941—Harold S. Bucquet
91. MEN OF BOYS TOWN—MGM 1941—Norman Taurog
92. WASHINGTON MELODRAMA—MGM 1941—S. Sylvan Simon
93. HONKY-TONK—MGM 1941—Jack Conway
94. JOHNNY EAGER—MGM 1941—Mervyn LeRoy
95. SOMEWHERE I'LL FIND YOU—MGM 1942—Wesley Ruggles
96. TENNESSEE JOHNSON—MGM 1942—William Dieterle
97. SLIGHTLY DANGEROUS—MGM 1943—Wesley Ruggles
98. MARRIAGE IS A PRIVATE AFFAIR—MGM 1944—Robert Z. Leonard
99. AN AMERICAN ROMANCE—MGM 1944—King Vidor—Color
100. 30 SECONDS OVER TOKYO—MGM 1944—Mervyn LeRoy
101. BETWEEN TWO WOMEN—MGM 1944—Willis Goldbeck
102. THREE WISE FOOLS—MGM 1946—Edward Buzzell
103. NO LEAVE, NO LOVE—MGM 1946—Charles Martin
104. MY BROTHER TALKS TO HORSES—MGM 1946—Fred Zinnemann
105. DUEL IN THE SUN—Selznick 1946—King Vidor—Color—Rosson worked on this film along with Lee Garmes and Ray Rennahan.
106. LIVING IN A BIG WAY—MGM 1947—Gregory LaCava
107. THE HUCKSTERS—MGM 1947—Jack Conway
108. HOMECOMING—MGM 1948—Mervyn LeRoy
109. COMMAND DECISION—MGM 1948—Sam Wood
110. THE STRATTON STORY—MGM 1949—Sam Wood
111. ANY NUMBER CAN PLAY—MGM 1949—Mervyn LeRoy
112. ON THE TOWN—MGM 1949—Gene Kelly and Stanley Donen—Color
113. KEY TO THE CITY—MGM 1950—George Sidney
114. THE ASPHALT JUNGLE—MGM 1950—John Huston
115. TO PLEASE A LADY—MGM 1950—Clarence Brown
116. THE RED BADGE OF COURAGE—MGM 1951—John Huston
117. SINGIN' IN THE RAIN—MGM 1952—Gene Kelly and Stanley Donen—Color

118. LONE STAR—MGM 1952—Vincent Sherman
119. LOVE IS BETTER THAN EVER—MGM 1952—Stanley Donen
120. I LOVE MELVYN—MGM 1953—Don Weis—Color
121. THE STORY OF THREE LOVES—MGM 1953—Vincente Minnelli and Gottfried Reinhardt—Color—Collaboration with Charles Rosher
122. DANGEROUS WHEN WET—MGM 1953—Charles Walters—Color
123. THE ACTRESS—MGM 1953—George Cukor—Color
124. STRANGE LADY IN TOWN—Warner Brothers 1955—Mervyn LeRoy—Color, CinemaScope
125. MAMBO—Paramount 1955—Robert Rossen
126. ULYSSES—Paramount 1955—Mario Camerini—Color—Mario Parapetti billed as "cameraman," Rosson as "cinematographer" on this Italian production
127. PETE KELLY'S BLUES—Warner Brothers 1955—Jack Webb—Color, CinemaScope
128. THE BAD SEED—Warner Brothers 1956—Mervyn LeRoy
129. TOWARD THE UNKNOWN—Warner Brothers 1956—Mervyn LeRoy
130. THE ENEMY BELOW—20th Century Fox 1957—Dick Powell—Color, CinemaScope
131. NO TIME FOR SERGEANTS—Warner Brothers 1958—Mervyn LeRoy
132. ONIONHEAD—Warner Brothers 1958—Norman Taurog
133. EL DORADO—Paramount 1967—Howard Hawks—Color

Interview with LUCIEN BALLARD

Lucien Ballard's recent popularity, through his collaborations with Sam Peckinpah and Budd Boetticher, obscures the fact that he has been in the movie business since 1930. Trained with an artist (von Sternberg), he went on to operate under less than ideal conditions at Columbia, shooting a host of forgettable B pictures. In the 1940s, his fortunes improved, as Ballard received some better assignments at 20th Century Fox, and then moved into the realm of glamour photography while shooting starring vehicles for his then-wife, Merle Oberon. But Ballard is most highly regarded for the films he has done since the mid-1950s, with such directors as Stanley Kubrick, Boetticher, Henry Hathaway, and Peckinpah. His belated fame is well-deserved, as Ballard takes his place among the finest cinematographers of our time.

A vigorous man who likes to be in control of a situation, Ballard pulls no punches in discussing his career, and like most of his colleagues, has the utmost respect for a quality that is becoming increasingly rare: professionalism.

LM: How did you get into cinematography in the first place?

BALLARD: Well, I was doing a little bit of everything at the time. I'd been kicked out of three or four universities in the Midwest, and I ended up in China. Then I came back and started working in sawmills, out in the woods, surveying. I was in L.A. in 1929, and a girl I knew was a script girl at Paramount. They'd had a fire which destroyed their sound stages, so they were working at night a lot. I went over to see her, and I would be on the lot while they were shooting; someone asked me to give him a hand, and I started helping out some of the cameramen, loading cameras onto trucks and things. Pretty soon they asked me to work there, but they were only paying $18 to $22 a week, and that didn't appeal to me. Finally they offered me a job working at night for $35 a week, which enabled me to still work for the lumber company if I wanted to during the day. I applied to the union, and by the time they got done with it I was making $75 a week, which was more than most of the others were getting. They told me I could work myself up from being a helper to eventually being first cameraman, over a period of a couple of years. I remember the first picture I was on was a circus picture with Clara Bow, and after we finished, Clara Bow invited me to a party at her home; I came home three days later, and I said, "Boy, this is the business for me!"

Opposite: Lucien Ballard keeps a straight face while director Charley Chase goes over a scene with The Three Stooges (ca. 1938).

LM: So you stayed on doing what?

BALLARD: I was an assistant cameraman mainly; I worked in a lot of pictures at Paramount, the Lubitsch films with Jeanette MacDonald . . .

LM: And then you were on MOROCCO with Josef von Sternberg.

BALLARD: Yes . . . the first time that Sternberg noticed me was on that picture.

LM: How did you learn, mainly by doing?

BALLARD: By watching others, doing what the director told me to do. I remember I used to work with a cameraman named Victor Milner quite a bit, and I'd be his camera operator. He'd have a light set up so that it was burning my arm—it was set up right next to the camera, but I couldn't do anything about it. Then I worked on a picture with Charlie Rosher, and he did the same thing. I said, "Mr. Rosher, this light is too hot for me," and he said, "Well, push it ahead and put a silk over it." Now, I could never say such a thing to Milner, but Rosher said, "Go on, push it ahead." So then I noticed that by pushing it forward and using a silk, you got the same intensity as when it was sitting back by the camera. You learn this kind of thing as you go along. And one thing you find out is that everything has been done already. Everything that's been done in pictures Billy Bitzer probably did long before I was in pictures. You always try to invent something new—I remember I was trying to light a set with just a candle, and things like that—but then you find out it's already been done. Of course, you can refine a technique. Another thing you learn is that a cameraman cannot do a picture the way he wants to, because he's not the boss. It's a collaboration of the director, the art director, and the cameraman.

LM: Sternberg was known as a director with a great visual sense.

BALLARD: He liked to try for certain things, like in THE DEVIL IS A WOMAN he had one set where everything was painted white. And we saw the rushes, went back to the set the next day and everything was painted black. Other people were frightened of him, but I wasn't, and that's why we got along. I could never sit on a fence, I was always honest and would speak my piece, and he appreciated that. I remember that during a lot of shots, he would want to look through the camera himself, and you just can't do that, because the camera operator has to see what's going on all the time. So we set up a range-finder that gave him the exact same results, and he would look through that on every shot. There was one scene where we had a 180-degree pan, and it was very awkward, so during the shot I pulled him by the seat of the pants and swung him around with the camera. Afterward I just sort of disappeared, and when he came over to me I said, "You can't fire me, I quit." He said, "What do you mean?" I said, "I knew you'd be angry about pulling you by the seat of the pants," and he said, "What do you mean, we got the shot, didn't we?"

LM: Dietrich was very aware of lighting, wasn't she?

BALLARD: Well, he'd taught her a lot, and she got to know that there was supposed to be a shadow coming over her nose, and things like that. It got so she could lick her finger and feel the intensity of the heat, and she'd know whether it was right or not.

LM: So Sternberg liked you, and had you on all of his films?

BALLARD: Yes, he'd always try to get me, and in fact, after a while, he'd be working with me and circumventing the actual first cameraman. I remember we did that with Bert Glennon, who was director of photography on one film; he was bewildered, because Sternberg and I would be working everything out—and then Glennon went to Fox on the strength of that film!

LM: Sternberg took you with him to Columbia, didn't he?

BALLARD: That's right, and then we had a falling out, and I stayed there.

LM: Was there any difference shooting a film with him at Paramount and doing it at Columbia?

BALLARD: No; when you're a professional, you know what you're doing, and it shouldn't make a difference whether it's at Paramount or Fox or Warners. But after Sternberg left, I was under contract to Columbia, and you know, the biggest pictures there were eighteen-day pictures!

LM: You did CRAIG'S WIFE, though, which was excellent and a beautifully lit film.

BALLARD: Yes, that was with Dorothy Arzner. But you know, Columbia didn't have many lights when I was there; they assigned just so many to each picture, and then if you needed more you had to go through all sorts of permissions. So on CRAIG'S WIFE I bought some baby spots myself, and got the producer to OK them. Oddly enough, even though they didn't have many lights, I was assigned a standby painter, who was always on the set for last-minute jobs and touch-ups. After a while I realized the value of this and I had it in my contract that I would always have a standby painter—even on Saturdays, when the rest of the department was closed. Pretty soon the word got around, and people were always calling to borrow this guy—I let him go out for a while, but they would keep him too long, so I had to cut it down and just say yes when it would be for ten or fifteen minutes.

LM: Doing quickies at Columbia, did you have time to be creative, and work out special ideas?

BALLARD: Oh yes. In black and white, I always liked to use low-key effects, and have the film very contrasty, so I used Agfa film, which at that time had no halftones, so everything was either black or white. Of course, the photography has to suit the individual picture you're doing. If you had perfection in every shot, you'd lose the story, and besides, the photography wouldn't mean anything—but if you had one or two great shots, say one at the beginning, a highpoint in the middle, and one at the end, those shots would stay in people's minds. But the photography always has to be appropriate for the story.

LM: You don't mean that it should be invisible . . .

BALLARD: Oh no, but for instance, I remember I always used to love French pictures, early French pictures. Did you ever see Sacha Guitry's THE STORY OF THE CHEAT? It's a great film, about this family that's planning a picnic; there are 13 kids, and one of them misbehaves before they go, so his punishment is that he can't go along. The family goes on the picnic, but they eat poisoned mushrooms and they all die. Then at the funeral you have all these coffins, from the biggest ranging down to the smallest, with a priest running behind them to catch up with the procession. Now, in those days, the French pictures we got here were dupes off of dupes, so the photographic quality was terrible. But you didn't care, because these films had substance instead of photography. I'd sacrifice photography anytime for the sake of the story.

LM: Were you able to do anything with any of the pictures you made at Columbia?

BALLARD: I remember one called SUBMARINE. Columbia had had a great hit in the early days with a picture called DIRIGIBLE, so every year they remade it with a different setting. This one was SUBMARINE, and there was a scene where the ship is sinking, and you see this inside the cabin. The lights go out, and of course there's one guy who's frightened, before they can get the emergency lights on again. So when the lights went out, I just had one broad on with about a dozen silks, and out of this blackness you heard the one frightened sailor—I remember it was played by John Gallaudet—screaming, and I thought it was a great effect, very frightening to hear a scream come out of the darkness. Then I counted 1, 2, 3, 4, 5, before I put the lights back on again, and when they came on, the sailor was praying, and there was a shadow of a crucifix over him. So that night, Harry Cohn saw the rushes, and he called me on the phone to fire me. Fortunately, I was out that night and couldn't be reached, but I saw him the next day and he told me that if he'd gotten through to me I would have been fired. "I pay all those actors," he said. "What's the idea of having them in total blackness for ten minutes?" I said, "It was only for the count of five." He said, "I want to see my actors at all times!" I remember once I wanted to do some special camerawork on one film, and we went a little over schedule. Cohn said to me, "This picture was supposed to cost $50,000 (let's say) and I'm going to sell it for $100,000. You cost $2,000 over-budget. That means I'm only going to make $48,000 on this film!" That was the way he thought—that was the way they all thought. You know, everybody talks about how little EASY RIDER cost, and how much money it made. They should be upset that it cost as much as it did. I could have made it in five days, and done it twice as good. You had amateurs doing it, and that's why it took four or five weeks. Anybody who'd schedule a film like that for more

Ballard and Hayley Mills relax on the set of THE PARENT TRAP *(1961).*

than five days ought to have his head examined. But that's what determines a professional. I know right after I'd made NEVADA SMITH, they wanted me for this little picture AN EYE FOR AN EYE; Joseph E. Levine was producing it, but Henry Hathaway had put up half the money for it. They didn't want to pay my salary at first, but I said, "Look, if I can't save you my salary, then you shouldn't hire me." It was scheduled as an eighteen-day picture, and we did it in sixteen days. And that was despite it snowing and raining, because I knew how to compensate for such things. When the picture was over, one of Joseph E. Levine's executives said to Hathaway—they'd had some casting problems with the picture—"You know, the best casting job we did was hiring Lucien Ballard."

LM: How did it happen that you left Columbia?

BALLARD: I'd been there for three years. I had a yearly contract which was renewable for another year with a raise in salary. So after three years they wanted to renew it again, only without the raise. So I said no, and I left and immediately found work elsewhere for more money. I did THE VILLAIN STILL PURSUED HER, which was a fun picture, with Eddie Cline, who was a very good comedy director.

LM: You'd done a number of two-reel comedies at Columbia, hadn't you?

BALLARD: Yes. You see, I had a forty-week contract, with a twelve-week layoff, so as soon as my forty weeks were up, I'd go across the street and shoot comedies with the short-subject unit. And it was great experience. I worked with Del Lord, Charley Chase—who was the greatest of all, I thought—and the Three Stooges.

LM: The shorts often had camera trickery in them, didn't they?

BALLARD: Yes, but everything was done on the set. Like, if you wanted to show the Stooges driving a car into a garage, and then the car exploding, you'd put a trough filled with flash powder underneath the camera, and then set it off. You'd cut and your next shot would show the car with the fenders blown off, and the Stooges would be blown to various parts of the room. Charley Chase did a more sophisticated kind of comedy—he would direct some of them, and produce too.

LM: What other films did you work on after the Columbia period?

BALLARD: Well, I worked with Howard Hawks shooting tests for THE OUTLAW for Howard Hughes. We filmed these tests on 16mm in Hughes' basement. They were testing a hundred boys and a hundred girls for the leads, as a publicity stunt—of course, Hughes had already picked the two he wanted, but we went ahead anyway. So after a while I told Howard I wanted to do some tests of my own, and I took Jane Russell, because she'd been hanging around me for a while, always asking why I did that and why I did this—she was just a kid at the time. So Howard said OK, and asked me to use Jack Buetel, who he liked quite a bit for the role. Anyway, I made these tests in the haystack, used cross-lights so her tits show big, and Hughes went wild for it. I didn't know it then, but he had a thing for tits; he had the scene made into a loop, and he'd run it over and over again. So anyway, he cancelled the two people he'd signed for the leads, and decided to use Jane Russell and Jack Buetel. Then Howard and I went out looking for locations, and finally we started filming in Flagstaff, in and around that area of Arizona. But every night Hawks would be on the phone with Hughes, and they started fighting. Finally one day we were told that we were to pack up and leave—very suddenly. So Howard and I were taken off the picture, Hughes started to direct it himself, and he hired Gregg Toland to shoot it. So Gregg came to me—I thought he was one of the best in the business—and he said, "I've seen the footage you did, and there's not a thing in this film that I could do as well as you did." Gregg wanted me to stay on the film and get him started, so I did, and I stayed on shooting the second unit. And Hughes, I found out, was very interested in effects. Every day he'd call up and say, "How did you do so-and-so?" So from then on I used a lot of filters and things to keep him happy.

LM: Then you went over to Fox and did a lot of pictures there. The first I have is WILD GEESE CALLING. Was that with Rouben Mamoulian?

BALLARD: No, no, but I did work with Mamoulian on LAURA. We shot 75 percent of that together, and it was going so well that everyone wanted to take credit for it—and it was all Mamoulian. Finally he was taken off the film, and Otto Preminger came in with another cameraman—but even there he had it easy, because Mamoulian had set every scene. Preminger used his basics, and refilmed just a little. But pretty soon I got out of that, I didn't want to be under contract. They couldn't understand it at Fox; they said, "We're paying you more than we've ever paid anyone else," but I didn't have any choice of films and I was getting tired of having to answer to so many people.

LM: But you did THE LODGER at Fox, which was quite impressive.

BALLARD: Yes, that was top black and white photography. But you know, when you're under contract to a studio like Fox, you're trying to please the studio, then you're trying to please the producer, and the director, and maybe the star. And some guys can sit on the fence, say one thing to one person and another thing to another. I can't do that, I always have to speak my piece. That was why Toland was so great—he only had to account to Goldwyn, and Goldwyn would give him anything he wanted. Anyway, I'd always wanted to do fog the way I did it in THE LODGER. Before then it was always a gray haze. I did it with the fog in spots, with black and white definition still coming through. And when they ran the rushes I got hell for it; the producer said, "I've lived in London, and the fog doesn't look like that." I said, "You may have lived in London, and the fog doesn't look like that—but that's how it *should* look."

LM: What about ORCHESTRA WIVES?

BALLARD: There again, you were able to do something with it because you had preparation. Every number was shot with a particular style. I prepared with orchestrations, and I had a musician label them for me so I knew just when it was loud, and soft, and when the trumpets were coming in. John Brahm started that picture, and worked very closely with me on it. I think the numbers are done as well as any musical numbers I've seen. Archie Mayo finished it, and brought nothing to the picture—he *couldn't* bring anything to it because he wasn't prepared.

LM: Did you start working in color at this time?

BALLARD: I turned down color, because I didn't want to work with the color men. You know, you always had to have one or two consultants with you, and all they wanted was plenty of exposure for their negative. You couldn't control the photography with them around. Finally I *had* to do color, a few years later, but I also got 3D at the same time. That was on INFERNO. But we did straight 3D, no tricks, we just shot it normally, and I lit it the same way I would light any picture. It was released flat here, because by that time the fad had died out, but in England it was 3D and it went over great. One of the men over there said that if it had been the first 3D picture, they might still be making them. When it was done Zanuck looked at it and added a few gimmicks, like a roof falling in, and someone throwing a lantern at the camera, but there were only two or three, and the rest of the picture was straight.

LM: What happened when you left Fox?

BALLARD: I free-lanced.

LM: You did a lot of pictures with Merle Oberon that were considered quite lavish at the time . . .

BALLARD: Well, you know, it was wartime, when no matter what they shot they filled the theaters, and so they made this stuff, and it was big, and beautiful, but it was crap. But one of them we did was quite good.

LM: BERLIN EXPRESS?

BALLARD: Yes, that was the first film we made in Europe after the war. Everything was in ruins, and we shot it all on location, for real. You know, everyone thinks all these techniques with hand-held camera are something new. We used hand-held camera in that, and it was a German camera that had just come out; I bought one, and the results with it were excellent.

LM: Pictures are always so much better using real locations, but some cameraman seem to favor process screens. How do you feel?

BALLARD: Oh, I hated process screens, I always tried to avoid them. Even on MAGNIFICENT MATADOR I used as little as possible, and it turned out quite well.

LM: I have no credits for you in 1949 and 1950; why is that?

BALLARD: Well, I was living in Europe at that time and I didn't work. I skied a lot, and lived all over. I guess some of it has rubbed off, because my son is now at Aspen.

LM: Then you came back to Fox, just around the time that CinemaScope was coming into use.

BALLARD: I didn't shoot in Scope for a while. Fox formed a separate company, called Panoramic Productions, and had all these people they had under contract making pictures flat. One of the films I did at that time was very fine, THE RAID, a really excellent picture, then we did another called WHITE FEATHER. Eventually I did Scope.

LM: Did it bother you?

BALLARD: No, not really, although Scope certainly isn't composition size—you'd never see a painting worked out that way; you'd like to have more top and bottom. But a good picture is a good picture, it doesn't matter if it's in 8mm.

LM: Was there any ratio you particularly favored?

BALLARD: I like 1-7.5, 1-8, almost the old screen ratio, best. I have no objection to Panavision, but it requires you to carry around so much equipment. We used Panavision on THE WILD BUNCH and we were lugging around a roomful of different lenses and things.

LM: You did PRINCE VALIANT in Scope with Henry Hathaway; I read that doing the picture in CinemaScope bothered him a lot.

BALLARD: I don't think anything ever bothered Henry a day in his life.

LM: Was there an advantage to working with a director as much as you did with him?

BALLARD: Well, it's difficult to work with Henry Hathaway and get good photography. It's all set up 1-2-3-kick with him. I like Henry a lot, but . . .

LM: Did you have to circumvent him to get what you would want?

BALLARD: Yes, you know, I'd say, "Say, Henry, I like your idea of doing so-and-so," and things like that. But I seemed to get along with all these guys who had tough reputations, because I was honest with them. I remember once Henry started shouting at me—which he does all the time, and you can't beat him because his voice is always the loudest—and he finished up saying ". . . and I don't want you fooling around like that again." Then, as he was turning away, he muttered, "Even though it did make a better shot." I remember everyone told me how tough John Farrow was. The first day on a picture I did with him I came onto the set and he had the camera all rigged up. I moved the camera twenty feet, and said, "Take a look at this, John, I think you might like it better." And he did. It was just that no one had ever had the nerve to do anything like that before. He turned out to have an excellent visual sense—he liked anything a camera would like.

LM: Should an actor be conscious of the photography in a film?

BALLARD: No, an actor shouldn't be concerned with that. An actress should care about how she looks—I mean, I would be the first to say, "God, she looks lousy" if that were the case. They should only be conscious of their own work.

LM: Do you remember A KISS BEFORE DYING?

BALLARD: I'd like to forget it. That was in the second group of pictures made under that independent Fox banner. I went out location-hunting with the director, and we found a small town that had everything we wanted. There was a library that was just perfect, the light was just great as it naturally was. So I asked the production manager, "Have you tied up all these places so we can shoot there?" and he said, "Don't worry about it." So when we got there we found that none of the buildings we'd wanted would let us shoot—after all, it was about a killing in a university, they'd all read the script. So there we were, day after day with no place to shoot. We'd use a patch of space near the library one day, part of a public park the next.

LM: Did free-lancing provide you with the kind of pictures you wanted to do?

BALLARD: No, but it let me work half the time for double the money. Plus I had more time to myself. When you'd be under contract, you were supposed to work forty weeks with twelve weeks off. But you'd be on call all the time. I remember I checked with the studio and said I wanted to go to Palm Springs. They said fine, go ahead. No sooner did I get there than they were on the phone saying, "Come back, you've got to do a test." I said, "I just got here!" They said, "You've got to come back." And then on top of that the guy who sent for me didn't realize I was in Palm Springs or he wouldn't have asked for me. So free-lancing was a lot better.

LM: This was around the time you started working with Budd Boetticher, wasn't it?

BALLARD: No, I'd done something with him before, but at this time he called me to do BUCHANAN RIDES ALONE, which originally had been a Batjac property which he'd bought from John Wayne without his knowing it. And everyone thought it was great, Wayne said it was the best story he'd had in years and he was angry at having let it go. So one night I took a plane out to the location, and Budd handed me the script. I read it before I went to sleep, and the next morning I went to him and said, "Have you read the script?" He said, "No, I only read the original treatment and I assumed . . ." I said, "You'd better read it, it's the worst piece of crap I've seen in years." He went away and read it, came back and said, "You're right." So he started rewriting it at night, during lunch breaks, all during shooting. He was still working on it during lunch hour on the last day we were shooting it.

LM: Wasn't LEGS DIAMOND the film where you deliberately made the film grainy?

BALLARD: Yes, we wanted to go for an authentic atmosphere for the 1920s where the film was showing. So after seeing some of the rushes, the producer went to Boetticher and said, "I thought you said Ballard was a great cameraman—this looks like it was shot in 1920!" And Budd said, "It's *supposed* to look like it was shot in 1920!"

LM: How would you describe the atmosphere working for Walt Disney on THE PARENT TRAP?

BALLARD: Well, the head of the photography department sent for me. I'd known Disney before, had him out to the

Ballard (with scarf) and Sam Peckinpah check a shot for RIDE THE HIGH COUNTRY
(1962).

house for dinner several times. Going out there, I met this fellow who took me on a bicycle all around the studio and introduced me to all the various people—always on a first-name basis. It was like being accepted for a country club, and after a week I guess I'd passed the test, and they were taking me to see the Big Man. On the way down the hall, Walt stepped out of a projection room and said, "Oh hello, Lucien," and the other guys nearly died. They never dreamed I already knew him. Anyway, Walt always had his films done first on a storyboard, and they'd worked out this whole film using an English process, much like the old blue-backing process, to get the twins into various scenes. It involved double-exposure with the backgrounds and it was very complicated. Plus, when you were shooting, you could never tell the girl which light to look into or anything. I told them it was too complex, and asked instead for a double. Usually they sent relatives out for assignments like that, but I told them this time I wanted a *real* double who really looked like Hayley. Finally I found a girl who was the same height, had the same features—everything was the same except her eyes were a different color, but I was able to compensate for that. And at several figures away, you couldn't tell the difference between the girl and Hayley. So I did a lot of over-the-shoulder shots, and threw out most of the vapor shots; I think we only had two double-exposures in the film. Then in the one party scene they were throwing things and with

the pie in the face you couldn't tell the difference anyway. But Walt made me put some of the trick shots back, because he, just like Hughes, liked technical things.

LM: You also did some TV work for Disney; was that much different from shooting a feature for him?

BALLARD: Well, the budget and time is a lot less, even at Disney, but I always tried to do TV as I would a feature—of course you're shooting in bad light, with a tight schedule, but often I would wait for light, and they would die, but I'd say, "Don't worry, we'll get it on schedule." Disney wanted to put me under contract, but I wouldn't go, and after I did a lot of TV over at Four Star, Dick Powell wanted to sign me. I told him that whenever I'm free I'd be happy to shoot something for them, but I wouldn't sign a contract. I did two segments of THE WESTERNER there with Sam Peckinpah; they were the first things he'd directed.

LM: And then of course you did RIDE THE HIGH COUNTRY with him; that's a beautiful film.

BALLARD: It would have been prettier still, but we only had twenty days, and it snowed. But I was with Sam on every aspect of that, preparing the film—from the costumes to the locations—that's always the best way to do a film.

LM: There was a very striking close-up in that, one of the first shots of McCrea, shot straight up into the sky.

BALLARD: Well, that might have been because we couldn't show the water towers and other things in the background at the Metro lot. You know, you can't always do what you want to do—everything in this business is a compromise. I'd have to see the film again and look at the shot, but chances are we had to do it because of necessity.

LM: Did you try for a documentary look on THE KILLING?

BALLARD: It was just my own style of contrasty black and white. I didn't think Kubrick was much of a director at that time, but I was impressed with his screen treatment.

LM: That was a quickly made picture, wasn't it?

BALLARD: Yes, and like so many other films these days I was called in very late. Today they want to wait as long as possible, they don't want to put you on salary. But I feel that I can save them money by being in on a picture from the beginning; I think I contribute a lot more than photography to a picture.

LM: I think THE SONS OF KATIE ELDER is a much underrated Western; it's really quite well-done.

BALLARD: It was a good picture. Hal Wallis' pictures are always well-prepared. He's a commercial producer, but he knows what he's doing. I remember the first picture I worked on for him, the production manager took me around and showed me one of the sets, and I said, "Well, you'll have to get rid of those curtains, and I want a different color chair . . ." and the man said, "But Mr. Wallis has okayed this set," as if he were saying, "But God has okayed this set." So I said, "He may have okayed it, but you can still tell him that I want to get rid of those curtains . . ." And sure enough, he did. And after a few days, after seeing the rushes, Wallis came to me and said, "Ballard, I like your work very much." On TRUE GRIT he came right to me and planned out certain photographic shots; every once in a while Henry Hathaway would stop and say, "Well, this is Lucien's shot," because it had been ordered by Wallis. We had big lenses, zooms, hand-held camera in that film, and you hardly ever have that with Henry—he never even dollies.

LM: After doing all those Westerns you filmed THE PARTY; if I recall, there were TV monitors on the set so you could have an instant playback of your shots. Did you find that a help?

BALLARD: Well, it was good because the film depended so much on gags. We only had a forty-page script to begin with. But it meant nothing to me photographically; if I don't know what I'm shooting, I shouldn't be shooting. I don't always go to rushes; I may go the first day, or to see certain things. But first off, it's not a corrected print, it's all been run through on one light, and it's the end of the day—my eyes are tired, and then you have to get into these long discussions with everyone who's there. They say things like, "What's wrong with the color?" and you're looking at an uncorrected print!

LM: Do you prefer working on interiors or exteriors?

BALLARD: I prefer working where I can control things, and you can't outdoors. Then they want you to do night

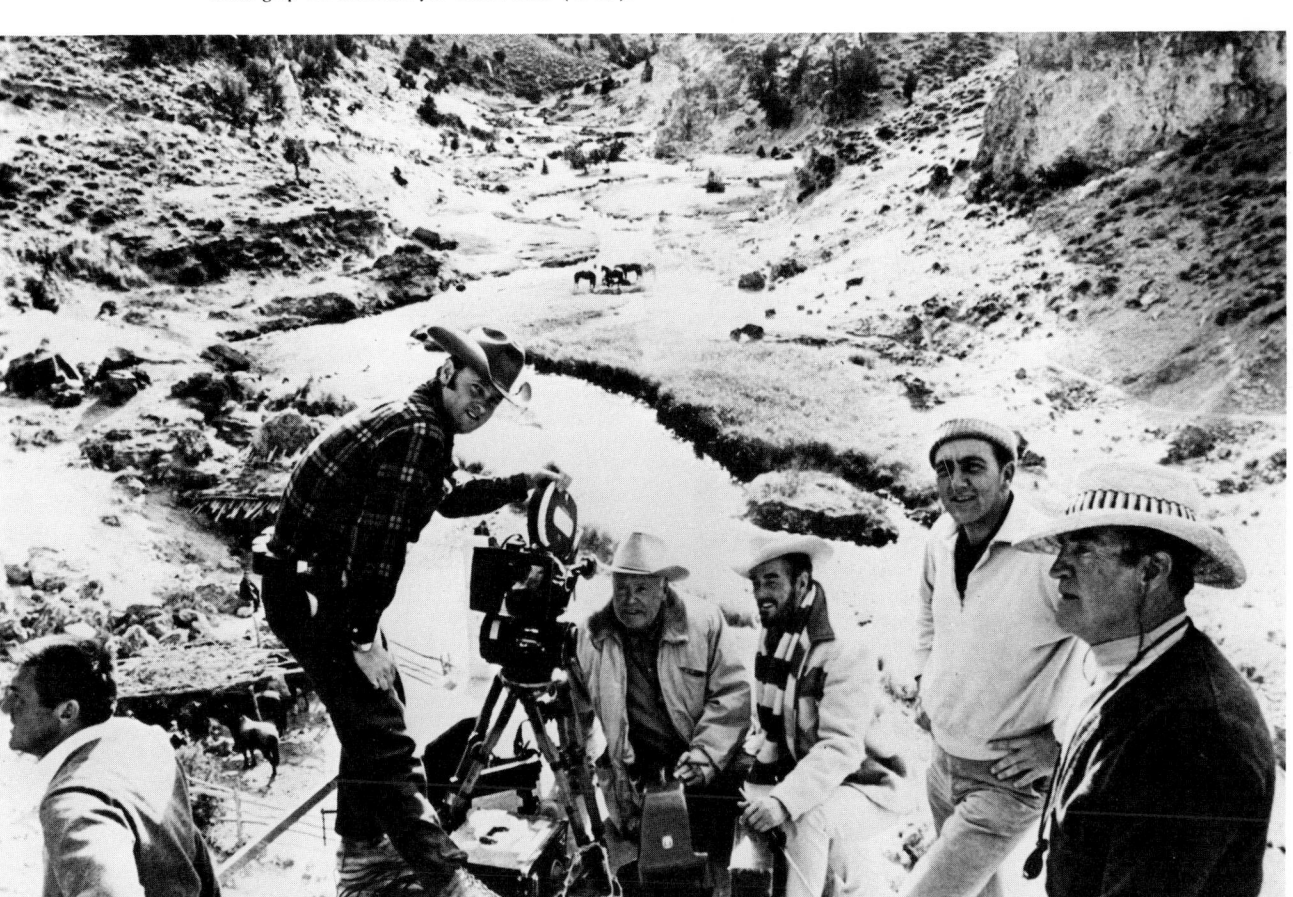

Gaffer, assistant cameraman, director Henry Hathaway, Ballard, camera operator, and head grip on location for TRUE GRIT (1969).

shots during the daytime while the sun is still moving around; those shots always look bad unless they're done carefully. But we had great locations on TRUE GRIT, those beautiful aspen trees, with the natural back-lighting. But we got snowed out of Colorado, snowed out of Lone Pine, and ended up working all over. We were lucky in getting the snow we wanted for the last scene, though—we'd tried to time it that way, and sure enough it snowed the night before we were to shoot it. We had luck, but it was all planned out that way.

LM: What about the locations for THE WILD BUNCH?

BALLARD: Sam and I had run everything we could find on Mexico around 1913; we wanted a yellow, dusty feeling. We went down there and everything was green! I was making tests with filters for a week, and finally we got pretty much what we wanted. We had some great stuff in the desert that was cut out. There was a sandstorm where you could hardly see anything—when we cut we had to shout to the actors to find their way back. At the end we had a long dolly shot as they leave the desert. It had rained, and you could see their tracks. I don't know how much of that is in the final print. Sam and I work very well together. I would go to and from work with him, so we would have that extra time to talk with each other—that kind of thing is very unusual, but I think something comes of that close proximity.

LM: What was your most recent picture?

BALLARD: Well, I started shooting THE HAWAIIANS, but I got sick and was only on it about five weeks. Apparently they've given me full credit anyway, which is very nice.

LM: What about television?

BALLARD: I haven't done any in a while, although I can always do it when I want to. But I don't want to do a series, I don't like to get tied down that way. I have to pay for the rest of this house, though, so I may yet be working on one.

LM: Is there one film you've done that has given you the most satisfaction?

BALLARD: No, not really. I get certain satisfaction out of all of them, even the bad ones. THE LODGER, AL CAPONE, and THE KILLING were all well-photographed black and white pictures. I liked this little film AN EYE FOR AN EYE; we shot on the same location we'd used for NEVADA SMITH, only NEVADA was shot in the summertime and this was during the winter. I also thought NEVADA SMITH was well-photographed. I just like to work with nice people, pleasant people; I want to contribute to a picture, not just work on it. I'm their man if they want more than a cameraman.

THE FILMS OF LUCIEN BALLARD

Ballard's first film job was on DANGEROUS CURVES (Paramount, 1929) as a general assistant. For the next four years, he worked his way up the ladder, to become an assistant cameraman, collaborating with such cinematographers as Lee Garmes (on MOROCCO) and Victor Milner. Unfortunately, a complete list of his credits during this period is unavailable, as is a thorough index of the two-reel comedies he filmed for Columbia in the late 1930s,

with Charley Chase, the Three Stooges, and others.

1. THE DEVIL IS A WOMAN—Paramount 1934—Josef von Sternberg
2. CRIME AND PUNISHMENT—Columbia 1935—Josef von Sternberg
3. THE KING STEPS OUT—Columbia 1936—Josef von Sternberg
4. CRAIG'S WIFE—Columbia 1937—Dorothy Arzner
5. THE DEVIL'S PLAYGROUND—Columbia 1937—Erle C. Kenton
6. RACKETEERS IN EXILE—Columbia 1937—Erle C. Kenton
7. I PROMISE TO PAY—Columbia 1937—D. Ross Lederman
8. VENUS MAKES TROUBLE—Columbia 1937—Gordon Wiles
9. GIRLS CAN PLAY—Columbia 1937—Lambert Hillyer
10. LIFE BEGINS WITH LOVE—Columbia 1937—Raymond McCarey
11. THE SHADOW—Columbia 1938—C. C. Coleman, Jr.
12. PENITENTIARY—Columbia 1938—John Brahm
13. THE LONE WOLF IN PARIS—Columbia 1938—Albert S. Rogell
14. FLIGHT TO FAME—Columbia 1938—C. C. Coleman, Jr.
15. SQUADRON OF HONOR—Columbia 1938—C. C. Coleman, Jr.
16. HIGHWAY PATROL—Columbia 1938—C. C. Coleman, Jr.
17. THUNDERING WEST—Columbia 1939—Sam Nelson
18. TEXAS STAMPEDE—Columbia 1939—Sam Nelson
19. LET US LIVE—Columbia 1939—John Brahm
20. BLIND ALIBI—Columbia 1939—Charles Vidor
21. COAST GUARD—Columbia 1939—Edward Ludwig
22. THE VILLAIN STILL PURSUED HER—RKO 1940—Edward F. Cline
23. THE OUTLAW—RKO 1940—Howard Hawks—Ballard was uncredited for his work on this film, with Gregg Toland; it was not shown until 1943, and not generally released until 1946.
24. WILD GEESE CALLING—20th Century Fox 1941—John Brahm
25. WHISPERING GHOSTS—20th Century Fox 1942—Alfred Werker
26. ORCHESTRA WIVES—20th Century Fox 1942—Archie Mayo and (uncredited) John Brahm
27. THE UNDYING MONSTER—20th Century Fox 1942—John Brahm
28. TONIGHT WE RAID CALAIS—20th Century Fox 1943—John Brahm
29. BOMBER'S MOON—20th Century Fox 1943—Charles Fuhr
30. HOLY MATRIMONY—20th Century Fox 1943—John Stahl
31. THE LODGER—20th Century Fox 1944—John Brahm
32. SWEET AND LOWDOWN—20th Century Fox 1944—Archie Mayo
33. LAURA—20th Century Fox 1944—Ballard and director Rouben Mamoulian started the film, and were replaced well into shooting by Joseph LaShelle and Otto Preminger.
34. THIS LOVE OF OURS—Universal 1945—William Dieterle
35. TEMPTATION—Universal 1946—Irving Pichel
36. NIGHT SONG—RKO 1947—John Cromwell
37. BERLIN EXPRESS—RKO 1948—Jacques Tourneur

38. THE HOUSE ON TELEGRAPH HILL—20th Century Fox 1951—Robert Wise

39. LET'S MAKE IT LEGAL—20th Century Fox 1951—Richard Sale

40. FIXED BAYONETS—20th Century Fox 1951—Samuel Fuller

41. RETURN OF THE TEXAN—20th Century Fox 1952—Delmer Daves

42. DIPLOMATIC COURIER—20th Century Fox 1952—Henry Hathaway

43. O. HENRY'S FULL HOUSE—20th Century Fox 1952—Ballard shot the sequence entitled "The Clarion Call," directed by Henry Hathaway.

44. DON'T BOTHER TO KNOCK—20th Century Fox 1952—Roy Baker

45. NIGHT WITHOUT SLEEP—20th Century Fox 1952—Roy Baker

46. THE DESERT RATS—20th Century Fox 1953—Robert Wise

47. THE GLORY BRIGADE—20th Century Fox 1953—Robert D. Webb

48. INFERNO—20th Century Fox 1953—Roy Baker—Color and 3D

49. NEW FACES—20th Century Fox 1954—Harry Horner—Color, CinemaScope

50. PRINCE VALIANT—20th Century Fox 1954—Henry Hathaway—Color, CinemaScope

51. THE RAID—20th Century Fox 1954—Hugo Fregonese—Color

52. WHITE FEATHER—20th Century Fox 1955—Robert D. Webb—Color, CinemaScope

53. THE MAGNIFICENT MATADOR—20th Century Fox 1955—Budd Boetticher—Color, CinemaScope

54. SEVEN CITIES OF GOLD—20th Century Fox 1955—Robert D. Webb—Color, CinemaScope

55. THE KILLER IS LOOSE—UA 1956—Budd Boetticher

56. THE PROUD ONES—20th Century Fox 1956—Robert D. Webb—Color, CinemaScope

57. A KISS BEFORE DYING—UA 1956—Gerd Oswald—Color, CinemaScope

58. THE KING AND FOUR QUEENS—UA 1957—Raoul Walsh—Color, CinemaScope

59. BAND OF ANGELS—Warner Brothers 1957—Raoul Walsh—Color

60. THE UNHOLY WIFE—Universal 1957—John Farrow—Color

61. I MARRIED A WOMAN—Universal 1958—Hal Kanter

62. BUCHANAN RIDES ALONE—Columbia 1958—Budd Boetticher—Color

63. ANNA LUCASTA—Columbia 1958—Arnold Laven

64. MURDER BY CONTRACT—Columbia 1958—Irving Lerner

65. CITY OF FEAR—Columbia 1959—Irving Lerner

66. AL CAPONE—Allied Artists 1959—Richard Wilson

67. ARRUZA—Ballard worked without billing on Budd Boetticher's yet unreleased documentary at this time, and over the next few years

68. THE BRAMBLE BUSH—Warner Brothers 1960—Daniel Petrie—Color

69. THE RISE AND FALL OF LEGS DIAMOND—Warner Brothers 1960—Budd Boetticher

70. PAY OR DIE—Allied Artists 1960—Richard Wilson

71. THE PARENT TRAP—Buena Vista 1961—David Swift—Color

72. MARINES, LET'S GO—20th Century Fox 1961—Raoul Walsh—Color, CinemaScope

73. SUSAN SLADE—Warner Brothers 1961—Delmer Daves—Color

74. RIDE THE HIGH COUNTRY—MGM 1962—Sam Peckinpah—Color, CinemaScope

75. SIX GUN LAW—Buena Vista 1962—This multi-episode segment of the Walt Disney TV show was released as a feature overseas

76. WIVES AND LOVERS—MGM 1963—John Rich—Color

77. THE CARETAKERS—UA 1963—Hall Bartlett

78. WALL OF NOISE—Warner Brothers 1963—Richard Wilson

79. TAKE HER—SHE'S MINE—20th Century Fox 1963—Henry Koster—Color, CinemaScope

80. THE NEW INTERNS—Columbia 1964—John Rich

81. ROUSTABOUT—Paramount 1964—John Rich—Color, Techniscope

82. DEAR BRIGITTE—20th Century Fox 1965—Henry Koster—Color, CinemaScope

83. THE SONS OF KATIE ELDER—Paramount 1965—Henry Hathaway—Color, Panavision

84. BOEING BOEING—Paramount 1965—John Rich

85. AN EYE FOR AN EYE—Embassy 1966—Michael Moore—Color

86. NEVADA SMITH—Paramount 1966—Henry Hathaway—Color, Panavision

87. HOUR OF THE GUN—UA 1967—John Sturges—Color, Panavision

88. WILL PENNY—Paramount 1968—Tom Gries—Color, Panavision

89. THE PARTY—UA 1968—Blake Edwards—Color, Panavision

90. HOW SWEET IT IS—National General 1968—Jerry Paris—Color, Panavision

91. THE WILD BUNCH—Warner Brothers 1969—Sam Peckinpah—Color, Panavision

92. TRUE GRIT—Paramount 1969—Henry Hathaway—Color, Panavision

93. THE BALLAD OF CABLE HOGUE—Warner Brothers 1970—Sam Peckinpah—Color, Panavision

94. THE HAWAIIANS—UA 1970—Tom Gries—Ballard had to bow out of production after several weeks; he was replaced by Philip Lathrop; both received billing for their work—Color, Panavision

95. THAT'S THE WAY IT IS—MGM 1970—Denis Sanders—Color, Panavision

96. WHAT'S THE MATTER WITH HELEN?—UA 1971—Curtis Harrington—Color

97. A TIME FOR DYING—Etoile 1971 (made in 1969)—Budd Boetticher—Color

98. JUNIOR BONNER—Cinerama 1972—Sam Peckinpah—Color, Todd AO-35

99. THE GETAWAY—National General 1972—Sam Peckinpah—Color

100. ARRUZA—Avco Embassy 1972 (filmed over a period of many years)—Budd Boetticher—Color

101. LADY ICE—National General 1973—Tom Gries—Color

102. THOMASINE AND BUSHROD—Columbia 1974—Gordon Parks, Jr.—Color

103. THREE THE HARD WAY—Allied Artists 1974—Gordon Parks, Jr.—Color

104. BREAKOUT—Columbia 1975—Tom Gries—Color

105. BREAKHEART PASS—UA 1976—Tom Gries—Color

106. FROM NOON TILL THREE—UA 1976—Frank D. Gilroy—Color

107. DRUM—UA 1976—Steve Carver—Color

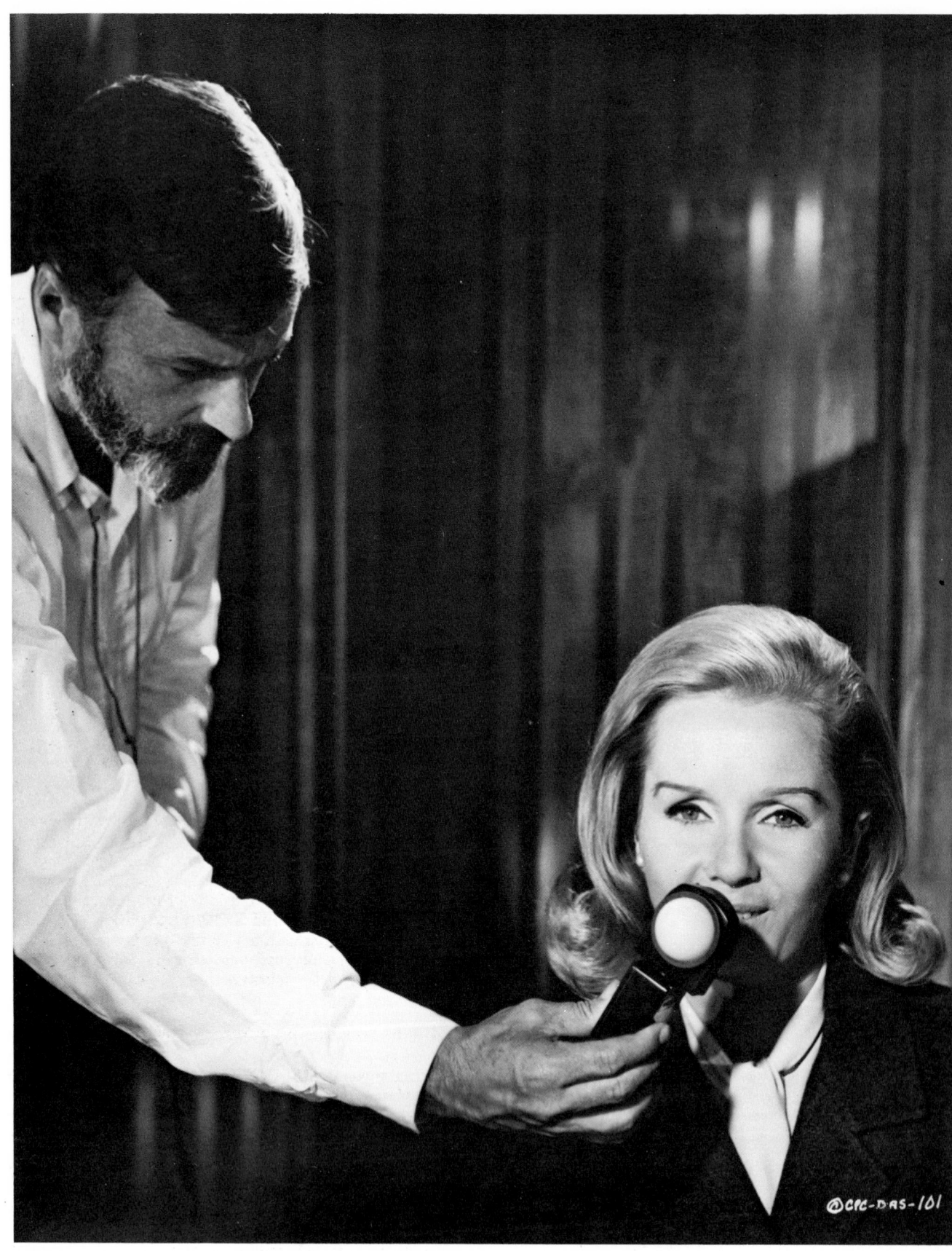

Conrad Hall lighting Debbie Reynolds for DIVORCE AMERICAN STYLE (1967).

Interview with *CONRAD HALL*

In a field dominated by men who have been practicing their craft for decades, forty-year-old Conrad Hall has distinguished himself in a comparatively short span of time, becoming one of the most respected contemporary cinematographers.

After achieving success as an independent filmmaker, Hall (the son of *Mutiny on the Bounty* author James Norman Hall) was forced to start again at the beginning when he wanted to join the trade union. His reward was the opportunity of working with most of the great cameramen in the business. His first solo work was shooting several TV series, where he says he fooled around a lot and got that urge out of his system. By the time he graduated to feature films, he had unusual skill and artistry, which immediately put him in demand. Since that time, he has amassed an impressive list of credits.

Having won an Academy Award for photographing BUTCH CASSIDY AND THE SUNDANCE KID, Hall would now like to turn to directing, if he can clear the necessary obstacles. Until that time, he must be content with his reputation as one of the finest cameramen in the business. He discusses his career articulately, with a keen awareness of exactly what is happening in all departments, and like most of his colleagues, he is candid and forthright.

LM: When did your interest in cinematography develop?

HALL: I'd have to say that the beginning was when I was in college. It came about by accident, and then quickly caught fire. I was a journalism major at the University of Southern California, and I got a D in a course called Creative Writing, and you must get a C to get credit for a course in your major; however, D is a passing grade, and I didn't feel like taking the course over again, so I changed my major. I picked up the liberal arts and science manual and it says A, Astronomy, B, Biology, C, Cinema ... Well, I got no further than that. I picked a major, and it said Cinema. I picked it because I felt that it was something new, that had only existed for fifty years, at that time, and if I became interested in it, it would be something that you were on the ground floor of, at the beginning. I had no interest in photography, or anything else; my father was a writer, and I don't know if I was interested in storytelling or not. But as soon as I took some courses in cinema, I was consumed with doing it, and here I am.

LM: I assume you took film history courses; do you recall being especially impressed with any films you saw?

HALL: Well, we looked at them all. I was very fortunate to be at the cinema department when a man named Slavko Vorkapich was the head of it. He was a very inspirational fellow, insofar as he wasn't interested in whether you made a living at it, or didn't make a living at it or anything else like that. He spoke of it as an art, and he imbued that quality in us. He didn't care about culture, or anything else; he was just interested in film as an art form, and not as a method of recording what he called photoplays. However, we didn't all agree with that, and we viewed all of the old great filmmakers' work.

LM: But did any specific ones inspire you to say "I'd like to do that"?

HALL: Not really . . . just the ones that inspire everybody, like CITIZEN KANE; that inspired me, just as it does everybody. There were quite a number of inspirational films, but I don't remember just which those are. Some of his own pictures inspired me ... Slavko Vorkapich made MOODS OF THE SEA and FOREST MURMURS, and these visualizations of pieces of music appealed to me very much.

LM: How did you gravitate to photography within the realm of cinema?

HALL: After two years, I graduated from USC, and two classmates and myself had made a picture called SEA THEME, which won first prize in cinematography at the USC international amateur contest, in which they choose ten pictures; we were one of the ten. When we graduated, we thought about making a living at cinema, and so we formed a company, the three of us, and the first thing we did was to cut our class project down to fifteen minutes, and put canned, licensed music (rather than canned *unlicensed* music) on it, and sold it to television. The man who bought it from us hired us to do other projects, and we started being productive in cinema, doing documentaries, commercials, industrial films, whatever we could do.

LM: What was the name of your company?

HALL: Canyon Films. Finally, after a number of years—there were many months when there was nothing doing, and we'd just sit around the office, which was a one-room shack, and throw around ideas for stories. We'd write stories when there was nothing to do; jot down ideas, try to develop them, try to interest people in them, and that kind of thing. And one day we found a short story called "My Brother Down There," in 1954, and we bought the rights, wrote a script, raised the money, and started production on a feature motion picture. We had all written the script; now it came time to divide the jobs into director, producer, cameraman. So we wrote three names on pieces of paper and threw them in a hat, and I picked cameraman. It meant a lot of money, to get into the union and stuff like that—$1,200 for myself, and I think it was $1,200 for the director, who had to join the Directors Guild. As a result of that picture I got into the union, and it was easier to just follow along as a cameraman than to switch all of a sudden and do something else. That's how I became involved in this.

LM: How did the film turn out?

HALL: I don't know . . . it had very lofty ideals, but it didn't work out financially, and it didn't work out artistically. It was less than we all wanted. But at the beginning, you're running a little bit scared, for one thing because you've got all this money responsibility—it cost $150,000. We didn't have enough money to finish it, because actually it was going to be $115,000, and we had to raise another $35,000 to finish it. That put pressures on it that I'm sure hurt the film. We disagreed completely about how to do it, and it broke our company up. But when a guy picks a thing called "Director," you've got to let him do it, you can't direct by committee. I don't know . . . I can't look at it any more. I could at one time. There are pieces of it that I like, little pieces that I like very much. We sold it for $150,000—it cost $150,000—it broke up our company, and it gave us a lot of experience. But I'm sure it would have done better had not the small picture been on the way out at that time. It was released in 1957, and about that time, pictures like BEN HUR were coming in, and the little picture was lost—and television was coming on strong.

LM: Then you went into your first picture, as cameraman, cold?

HALL: No, no, I had been a cameraman from the time I was at USC. All students are; I was always a cameraman, I was never an assistant cameraman or anything else. I had a camera, I bought a camera. I used to be associated with another present cameraman named Dick Moore. Dick Moore had been in Europe when the war closed, and had gone to Arnold and Richter in Germany, and asked for the Western Hemisphere distribution rights to the German combat camera, called the Arriflex. Arnold and Richter gave it to him; Dick didn't have any money, and I had $900, which paid for the demonstrator, and we set up a company called Arriflex Imports. Well, everybody here at MGM, Columbia, and people like that, said, "What is this Mickey Mouse camera?" when we brought it around. "It's a German camera—we've got our own. It's terrific; it's called a Bell and Howell." And I said, "Yeah, but it's not reflex. This is reflex—you can see right through it, and it's got a lot of advantages that the American cameras don't have." Nobody would even talk to us about it. And after a year we didn't sell any cameras. Arnold and Richter wrote us a letter and said, "Hey, boys, enough's enough, you've been in business a year and haven't sold any cameras, so we have taken away your franchise . . ." The only reason I'd gotten into this was that I wanted to own a camera. Because when you're not in the union, it's easier to have your own equipment, and go out as a package. A producer who needs some pickup shots to finish a feature, and doesn't have to pay the union rates, he wants to contract for five or six shots. You make him a contract price.

LM: What about the art of cinematography; how do you think this developed in you—when you were a student, or from the experience you got subsequently?

HALL: That's a very difficult question. I mean, pick some other area—how does Picasso develop what he developed? It just happens.

LM: But there are so many technical things you have to know . . .

HALL: I disagree with you. I personally think—everybody is in great awe of the technical aspects of cinematography; I, on the contrary, am not in awe of it at all. I think it's much more difficult to be a mechanic than it is to be a cinematographer, as far as technical things are concerned. When I look at an engine taken apart, or an automatic transmission, I'm in great awe of the man who knows how to take it apart, and put it together again, and make it work. A camera is nothing. First off, you don't have to take it apart and put it back together again; all you have to do is to be able to use it. There's a thing called a lens, a little thing called an f. stop, and a couple of minor kinds of laws that govern what happens on the film, and I learned all these things from a guy named Slavko Vorkapich. I knew how to make a camera work like a mechanic knows how to make a motor work. I knew what happens when you take the film and turn it upside down, and backwards, and inside out; when you stop it down, and open it up. I learned it in two years, and I didn't need that long to learn it—I could have learned it in six months easily, or less time, for that matter. The *rest* of it, there's no way to explain; how the artistry comes out of you is part of you, part of your experience in life, the way you see things.

LM: One of the first films I have credited for you is one of the Disney true-life films.

HALL: That's right. One of my partners was a naturalist, his name was Jack Couffer; he's a director now. He deals with animals, mostly; he did RING OF BRIGHT WATER, that sort of thing. A very talented man. At that time Disney was going into their program of animal films, and Jack said, "What the hell, why don't we do that? We've got some ideas; let's approach him. So Jack had some ideas, and he approached Disney, and Disney said, "Why not?" Jack came back and said, "We've got a contract to do this and that," and we started to work making pieces of his animal films. Then Jack and I had a chance to go to the Galapagos in 1954, for eight months, to do a film down there for Disney, and we did work for him, on and off, for quite a number of years.

LM: You were not making entire films, then, only sections?

HALL: The Galapagos film was an entire film, although there was other people's work in it, but the lump of it was ours. It was called ISLANDS OF THE SEA. We did quite a bit of work for Disney over the years, in 16mm color.

LM: It was blown up to 35mm?

HALL: Yes.

LM: You'd never know it; the optical work must have been outstanding.

HALL: Well, I'll tell you, the eye accustoms itself to what is offered it, very quickly. If you were to intercut 35mm with 16mm blowup, you would immediately think something was wrong. You would see the difference. If you dissolved it, you might not see it at all. But if you juxtapose it quickly, then you're going to see that there's a different quality. But if you start right out on 16, you might say at the beginning, "Isn't it a little bit fuzzy?" and then forget about it.

LM: How long were you doing that type of work?

HALL: We made the feature in 1956—I'd graduated in 1949, and we were a company from that moment on, until we dissolved in 1957, after making this one feature. Then I formed my own company, and I did commercials, which I'd been doing all along anyway. We were film bums to begin with; we had been doing anything to make a living at cinema. We edited, photographed, directed, did educational films, industrial films, commercials, TV things, pieces of features—*lots* of feature work with producers who would run out of money and not want to use a union crew. They'd come to us, and we'd moonlight for them.

LM: Any interesting films?

HALL: I don't remember. Things like MAN CRAZY, a lot of Benedict Bogeaus films.

LM: How did you get away with that?

HALL: Well, first of all, the producers felt they were getting away with it by contracting with you, instead of paying you a wage. They would be saying, "We don't want to know how you do this, but we're contracting for you to deliver this." Well, then you'd go out with the director and work just like you would normally. Legally, I guess that's the way they did it. *We* didn't care. I wanted to join the union; the fact that they wouldn't let me wasn't my fault. I was perfectly willing to join the union. I believe in unions that anybody can get into, providing he passes whatever requirements of excellence the union requires. I was willing to take tests, if there were something like that, but there wasn't, and I was refused entry into the union. So when we became harassed by the union on our independent work, a bunch of us got together and formed our own union. Four or five of us started a union called the Association of Film Craftsmen . . . and we were still harassed by the IATSE. So we started thinking of how to get some power, and we analyzed that the way they controlled the industry was to control the projectionists. They could say, "We won't show your picture unless it's union made." We said, "Is there anybody else that we can affiliate with?" and we found out that in television there was a union called NABET, and they were basically projectionists for television. We made overtures to NABET, and asked them if they would be interested; so we affiliated with them. We had a little more leverage then; we could say, "If you won't project our films, we won't project your films." Slowly, the legitimacy of the union developed, and now it is quite a legitimate working union, and certainly a thorn in the side of the IATSE.

LM: Are there jurisdictional disputes between the two?

HALL: I don't know any more. Either you fight those battles all your life, or you fight them when you need them. I needed to work, I wanted to be allowed to work, and people were preventing me from it. I took whatever measures I had to in order to be able to work. Once having done that, I'm not going to do that for the next guy—that's his problem. He has to do it for himself. I did it, it helped a lot of people in the future, but I'm not a union man—I want to make films. I just got into it long enough for myself to be able to work in the industry. I subsequently had a falling out with NABET, and tried to get into the IA again, as a result of my feature film, and forced the Taft-Hartley law on them: the owner of a company is allowed to do any one thing in that company that he chooses. And they said, "Yeah, but you can't. If you try to photograph your own picture, we'll pull the crew." I said, "If you pull the crew, you'll cause me to lose money, and I'll take you to court and sue you." He hung up the phone—this was my friend Herb Aller. I talked to my lawyer, and my lawyer said, "You're right; you could probably win, but you neither have the inclination nor the funds to do it, and it might take ten years." And I didn't want to do that. About that time Herb called again and said, "What do you want to make trouble for?" I said, "I don't want to make trouble, I just want to photograph my own film." He said, "Do you always want to just photograph your own film, or do you want to become a cameraman?" I said, "No, I'd like to be a cameraman." He said, "OK, I'll tell you what I'll do. If you'll hire somebody to photograph your picture, he can sit in the bus, he doesn't have to actually do it, if you give him credit for doing it. And when you get back from location I'll see what I can do about getting you into the union." I was very young at the time, and I said, "Ahh, I might as well join them," so I joined them. I worked my way up; I was an assistant cameraman for a year, an operator for a year, and then became a first cameraman—again. I worked with a lot of the top cameramen in the industry like Ted McCord, Ernie Haller, Robert Surtees, Hal Mohr, Burnie Guffey, lots of them. At one time or another I must have worked with twenty-five or thirty really top cameramen. I paid a lot of attention.

LM: Does the camera operator have a chance to be creative on his own?

HALL: Yes, absolutely. I believe in creative focus, and creative operating, and there's a difference between a mechanical focus and a creative focus. I mean, how do you tell somebody when to change focus? That's what he feels. He's telling the story when he's changing focus; he's in charge of telling that story, because he's shifting the story from over there to over here, and it's a good feeling when you're doing it—very creative.

LM: Does anything stand out in your mind from that period when you were assisting other cameramen?

HALL: Working with Ted McCord was such an inspirational thing for me, because here was a man who started when the industry started. He started when he was nineteen, and had been a cameraman for many many years. I saw that this man was not set in his ways; he was as open as any young man that I've ever known in my life—ready to experiment, ready to change his ideas. Working with somebody like that was very inspirational, to see that you could grow, and not just stay in one place, being good at one thing in your whole life, and age really has nothing to do with it.

LM: You had a lopsided progression, being first cameraman twice, as you say, but do you feel it was helpful to work your way up, so to speak, in the business?

HALL: No. I consider it an honor to have been part of a continuity of films from the beginning to now, because I worked with all the guys who began it. Jimmy Wong Howe was in it at the beginning, here in Los Angeles. I liked that, I liked picking their brains. I liked having that connection with the beginning very much.

LM: Your first solo credits then were two TV series, STONEY BURKE and THE OUTER LIMITS.

HALL: Yes; when I finally became a cameraman again, Leslie Stevens hired me. He is a writer-producer-director, a very talented man that I had worked for as an operator with Ted McCord on a picture called PRIVATE PROPERTY. Leslie Stevens and I formed a friendship and admiration for each other that made him make me a cameraman when he started a series called STONEY BURKE. In PRIVATE PROPERTY his wife played the lead; we shot it at his home, and it was fun, really fun. One of those things, cost $60,000. It was much before its time, and a very interesting film. Anyway, I did STONEY BURKE, and then OUTER LIMITS, then I left after a year of OUTER LIMITS.

LM: Having worked on features, it must have been a challenge to work under the restrictions of TV shooting.

HALL: Yes it was. You keep fighting the feeling that you're in a sausage factory. And when somebody doesn't appreciate something, there's not much sense in doing it, although I never took that attitude, really. It always counted, it always mattered to me whether I did good work or not, and I never ever threw it in. That meant that I was always sort of a bad guy, because it took a little more time, budgets would go over slightly, that sort of thing.

LM: So often, people who do TV just don't care.

HALL: But enough people cared to make it worthwhile for me; the producer cared, the directors cared, the people I was photographing cared, and some of the audience cared. There were people who would say, "Gee, that's a well-photographed show." There were other shows that were done by other cameramen that were really good too. I remember HONG KONG being a very good one, and the one that Phil Lathrop did was beautiful—PETER GUNN. PETER GUNN was exquisitely done. There were quite a number where the people cared about what they did.

LM: THE OUTER LIMITS was a show that lent itself to imaginative photography.

HALL: Yes, you had a lot of opportunities in that show to be gimmicky, and I'm glad I had it, because I sort of got it out of my system there, rather than on a big screen. I hate gimmicks now.

LM: How did you progress to your first feature film?

HALL: After a year I had an opportunity to photograph a feature at Universal called THE WILD SEED, with Michael Parks, directed by Brian Hutton and produced by Al Ruddy. We made a feature for $285,000, with twenty-four shooting days, black and white, a film I like very much—a very good film, much ahead of its time. Univer-

sal didn't know what to do with it, they just slipped it on the lower half of double bills. It had some good things in it. I've made maybe four or five great shots in my life—I mean really great—and one of them is in that picture. What I mean by a great shot is one that tells the story so perfectly that you want to cry, because it does its job so well. It's not noticed, nobody pays attention to it, but it is so right, with what has been said, with what has been going on. Everything has to be right for a shot to be great—the acting, the whole thing. And this is a shot in which the girl is reading a letter from her father, left her by her mother—which turned out not to be from him at all, but one she had written to make it seem like she had a father. She starts to read that, and the camera starts to pan off of her, but it moves so slowly that you don't notice it; it's just moving and pretty soon she's on the edge of the frame, but you don't think about it. Soon she's in half, and then she's out of the frame, and there's some sort of out-of-focus pepper trees in the background; the voice is still going on. This shot has got the power of the San Andreas fault; it moves that slowly. But when it breaks apart, it's really something. What happens is all of a sudden you come onto him, and when you come onto him the focus changes, so he will be in focus just at the right time, and an eye comes on quite big. Because the story is really happening in him; her reading doesn't make any difference at all. He's trying to get involved in her. It comes into a close-up of him, she finishes reading the letter, and then they cut to something else. But it's one of the most cinematic shots I've ever seen in my life, because it tells the story so well.

LM: It must be difficult to reach a happy medium as cameraman; I mean, you want to tell the story in a pictorial way, in a beautiful way, perhaps, and yet you don't want people to start watching your camerawork instead of the story. It must be frustrating at times for you . . .

HALL: It is frustrating not being involved in the whole picture; it's having a concept about how something is done, then going to see the picture, and the film that had a different concept at one time is now used to tell a different story entirely—because of what has happened in editing, the decisions that one goes through in the editing process that cause you to change your mind. And you're not benefit of those changes. So you can't ever enjoy your own pictures, unless you forget about it completely, and just be an audience.

LM: What about the compromise between storytelling and photography?

HALL: There's tons of ways of doing things, and what I try to do is what the director wants to do. When you work for somebody like Richard Brooks, he tells you just exactly where to put the camera; that's the way he wants it, it's his picture, if you don't want to do it that way, you can work for somebody else. The first thing he said to me when I stepped on THE PROFESSIONALS was, "Look, kid, do you want to be a director?" I said, "No, not really." He said, "Well, you probably will, you'll probably want to be a director someday. I'm all for it. I'm all for everybody being a director, for directing one picture anyway, because they might not like it—they might find it's too hard work, and they might like doing something else. But direct your own picture, don't direct mine." That's the way he wants it, and that's the way I do it. I do what *any* director wants to do, but a lot of directors don't know what they want to do, and they say to you, "What'll we do?" and then you naturally have to come ahead and tell them what you feel. I always tell anybody what I feel anyway. But if you're a good cameraman, you do what the director wants to do, because he's the one who's telling the story. If you're fighting the director, you're hurting the picture. Because then *you* should be directing it. If a director wants me to help him direct it, I'll help him direct it; if he doesn't want me to help him direct it, I don't help him direct it.

LM: Have you encountered directors who have ignored the visual aspect of the film entirely, leaving it all in your hands?

HALL: I would say that on WILD SEED, the way we worked on that was that Brian Hutton had some specific ideas about how he wanted certain things done, but basically he would rehearse the scene with his actors, block it out, then he'd come to me and say, "What do you think about how to shoot it?" and I would tell him, and he would agree with me, or if he didn't agree with me, we'd talk it out, and come to an agreement. But because he had never directed before, and because he didn't have a background in visuals, he left it basically up to me.

LM: That must give you great satisfaction.

HALL: No. If I'm going to be in charge of it, I want to be the director then. All or nothing at all. I don't want somebody to say, "Here's sixty pages of a chase, go out and set it up any way you want to; pretend you're the producer and director, and I'll abide with what you say," and then when you come in, the actors have a different idea, but I can't tell the actors what my idea was—all of a sudden you're in the background, and your concept is down the drain. If I want to direct it, I want to direct it for real. Otherwise, I want to do what somebody else wants to do. And I can be good at what I do, and that gives me plenty of satisfaction.

LM: The next film I have credited for you is INCUBUS.

HALL: INCUBUS—ah, I love it. Shot in Esperanto, ten days' shooting, great fun. Leslie Stevens is a madman, a lovable one, and has a compulsion about putting his wives in pictures. We went off and had a great ten days making INCUBUS. I don't know what ever came of it, except I saw Francis Coppola recently in San Francisco and he said, "Hey, I saw a picture you did years ago called INCUBUS." I said, "Oh, how'd you like it?" He said, "Well, I think they cut in a lot of new stuff—were there any nudes in it?" I said no. He said, "Well, it's a nudie now." I don't think that Leslie had anything to do with that. His was a black magic film. I don't know what the reason was for shooting it in Esperanto.

LM: That sort of limits its appeal.

HALL: It really does, because visually I'm proud of everything I did in it. We had not only camera trickery but every kind of skullduggery. We had people emerging from the ground, you know, the earth shaking and somebody coming up with horns, and in the background are mists swirling, and there's a kind of gallowslike structure in the background, on which are standing three nuns in habits, and a giant bat with eighteen-foot wing span is folding and unfolding, flapping its wings in the background. If you don't call that trickery, I don't know. I don't know what it means, but I loved it.

LM: On the subject of trickery, do you prefer doing things with your camera, or having them done by optical effects?

HALL: I don't mind opticals, they're all very necessary tools to use in telling the story. But how can I like that when I'm not doing it?

LM: So you would prefer to have the chance to do it yourself?

HALL: If it's something that's easier for me to do, or better; there are some things that are better for the optical printer to do, and I'm all for it.

LM: Next we come to MORITURI, or SABOTEUR: CODE NAME MORITURI . . . that went through several title changes.

HALL: Right . . . MORITURI is the title I remember. It was a good-bad film experience. They hired a director named Bernhard Wicki, who was a very talented man—he made a picture called THE BRIDGE, which I liked very very much. But he's used to working under the influence of a small group of people, with an Arriflex camera; loop the stuff, shoot the sound later, you know, not worry about microphones and all that kind of thing. And he was suddenly thrown into the Hollywood system, with an actor who gave him a lot of heat, and a producer who gave him a lot of heat, and a production department that gave him a lot of heat. It was a mismatch. We had all sorts of problems. They were very unrealistic; going into it, the people wanted us to make a picture in sixty days that even the people who laid it out said would take ninety. Then they said, "Well, it can't take ninety—do it in sixty." So you go into it knowing that it's not going to be done in sixty. Then problems arise, and all kinds of stuff. I enjoyed working with him very much, I admire him greatly. I loved working on a freighter, no sets or anything else like that.

LM: Do you like working exteriors? Some cinematographers have said they only like to work when they can control the situation.

HALL: I can control it outside, and inside. You've got all the control in the world in that lens. You can overexpose it, underexpose it, filter it, do anything you want.

LM: Next comes HARPER.

HALL: HARPER was my first color picture, and it was a can of corn. I did it just like black and white pictures, and it turned out terrific. I enjoyed working with Jack Smight, Paul Newman, and all the other people. Working with big studios you become sort of detached from everything except your own job. I remember one time, people looked at the schedule and saw what we were going to shoot, and the electrical department decided we would need forty electricians for the job. Right away, I know that forty electricians and eight generators is going to mean twenty miles of cable, and headaches galore. And I say, "How can we have this, we won't be able to get anything done."

So I cut it down from forty to twenty, and we still didn't get much done. But working in studios, the more people you have, the slower you go, the more cumbersome it becomes, the less fun it is. I like INCUBUS, where you've got two or three people, and you go out and shoot.

LM: Is there a danger on a picture with a long shooting schedule of becoming stagnant?

HALL: Not if it's something you believe in. I never got tired of IN COLD BLOOD, or THE PROFESSIONALS. Pictures like HARPER are entertainments, and you don't have the same involvement in them that you do in pictures that you feel are saying something, or trying to say something, while entertaining too.

LM: Have you experienced outside interference about how you should be photographing various pictures, from the studios themselves, for instance?

HALL: Yes, I've had a lot of harassment, because I probably don't do it the way they like it. On WILLIE BOY, for instance, most recently, I was called into a projection room one day, and there were about eight or ten people in black suits sitting there, all with a dour look on their faces, and the lab man was there. I said, "What's up?" They said, "There's a shot here that they say won't pick up on TV." I said, "So what? I'm not shooting a thing for TV, I'm shooting a feature. I don't give a shit about TV!" Well, they do, because they want to sell it to TV, and if there's a shot that somebody thinks won't register well on TV, they come and tell you, and try to make you feel bad, and probably would fire you if they could. But I just had nothing to do with them, I just turned around and walked out of the room.

LM: They could always keep protection takes and out-takes and use them later.

HALL: They don't know anything! All they know is, they have a job, and unless they make a crisis and bring the importance of their job to the fore, their job is liable to be overlooked; people are liable to say, "What do we need him for?" and fire him. They have to justify themselves, and they justify themselves for really the stupidest reasons of all. This was a *beautiful* shot—and it will look great on TV. One of the greatest compliments I've ever had was when Philip Scheuer, who used to review for L.A. *Times*, said about MORITURI, "I hope I never have to see this on TV, because it was so dark." I hope he doesn't have to see it on TV either, because I don't want him to see it on TV—I want him to see it in a theater.

LM: You received your first Academy Award nomination for MORITURI, didn't you?

HALL: The strangest thing that ever happened to me. It's hard to believe that all of a sudden you can get nominated for something. Very strange. I didn't belong to the ASC, or anything else at that time.

LM: Going on to THE PROFESSIONALS, one thing that stays in my mind is the very fine use of the wide screen, in a creative way, not just because it was there.

HALL: I liked my work on THE PROFESSIONALS. I don't any more, but I did then. I've since come to detest saturated colors, except for story-telling purposes.

LM: You had a lot of that in HARPER, in the kitchen scenes and others . . .

HALL: All very saturated stuff, and now I've done a complete flip-flop from that, so I don't like my work on those pictures any more. But that's just a matter of evolving into another area of creativity.

LM: You've worked in widescreen on virtually all of your films, right?

HALL: For the most part. DIVORCE AMERICAN STYLE was not, that was 1.85.

LM: Do you have to reorient yourself to something like that?

HALL: No. It's just a frame, just like paintings, in all different frames.

LM: When you're shooting widescreen, there are so many problems in the way it will ultimately be projected, the fact that many theaters cut off part of the sides, and on TV they cut off even more . . .

HALL: I prefer to have them cut off the sides than to have them cut off the top and bottom. The problem with shooting in 1.85 is that many studios won't let you hard-matte it, and the reason I recommend Panavision is that there's no way to change it. The top and bottom are there. If you're just one inch off, you see the frame-line, and the projectionist can do nothing but frame it exactly. True, he might not have a wide enough screen, and some of the picture might fall into black, but then that makes it better because it's not quite so wide.

LM: What is hard-matteing?

HALL: The Academy aperture is 1 by 1.33 in proportion, and if they cut the top of the top and the bottom of the picture off slightly, you get the proportion 1 by 1.85, which gives you a wider screen. When CinemaScope came in, the people with regular lenses had no other way to do but narrow the top and the bottom. People do things to make money, not for any artistic reasons. I love Panavision's equipment because it's the best equipment in the business; the greatest lenses, the greatest cameras. They are a modern company, they keep on top of the business. They keep changing and improving their things.

LM: I was very surprised by your comments about Richard Brooks, because one doesn't think of him being visually oriented; he's a writer-director and that's probably his most dominant image in most people's minds.

HALL: Listen, he's an original talent, like Bergman, Fellini, Kurosawa, and people like that. He's a storyteller all the way. He can do any job, as I imagine most storytellers can. He knows photography as well as you do, maybe better; he's a complete filmmaker. I don't always agree with him, but I respect him greatly.

LM: On DIVORCE AMERICAN STYLE the big news was the deglamorization of a star like Debbie Reynolds.

HALL: Of the pictures I've done, I like that least, primarily because I was scared when I was making it. I had been ill, and I was scared, afraid of dying. It's hard to do good work when you're scared. And I was breaking in a new operator, which is tough on a feature, because there are a

Hall checks a light reading while director Richard Brooks (in light jacket), assistant cameraman Jordan Cronenwerth (with beard), Claudia Cardinale, and others wait on location for THE PROFESSIONALS in Nevada (1966).

lot of pressures. There are a lot of reasons that it was not a good experience. Debbie Reynolds always wanted to be glamorized; she always wanted me to put the key light over the camera; I didn't want to put the key light there, because she was supposed to be a mother of a sixteen-year-old, and the producer and director were always telling me to make her look that way, and she wanted to look glamorous. She looks fourteen or fifteen herself anyway, she's got one of those faces; I don't try to make anybody ugly, I try to make them real. There was no reason why she should be ugly in the story, she could be attractive, as long as she looked more her age, and that's what I tried to do. I paid probably less attention to lighting her than other cameramen had, and it bothered her.

LM: Are there actors who are particularly conscious of their lighting and photography?

HALL: Yes.

LM: Do you find that good or bad?

HALL: I find that bad for them. How can you act and think about the key light at the same time? One day Debbie had the producer show me a picture, and I didn't know what it was all about until we were a third of the

way through it. I said, "What the hell am I looking at this for?" He said, "Well, Debbie wanted you to see it." I said, "What for? Why don't you get Harry Stradling to photograph this picture? I can't do what Harry Stradling does. It's wonderful, I love what he does, but I can't do it. I'm Conrad Hall and I do it the way Conrad Hall does it. And if she wants to look the way she did in that picture, she ought to get Harry Stradling." And I walked out.

LM: Then it was a decided step up for you to do COOL HAND LUKE.

HALL: Yes. I went in to talk to Gordon Carroll and Stu Rosenberg about it, and Gordon said, "I think we have the possibility of something good here." I read it, and I liked it, and we did it. And Richard Schickel said I made it look too good—I probably did. I wish we'd been able to shoot it in black and white. I hadn't seen I AM A FUGITIVE FROM A CHAIN GANG, but I saw it about six months ago— Jesus Christ, what a film! It's ten times better than COOL HAND LUKE, and it's so right in black and white—you know what I mean. Really terrific. I didn't realize how much we had stolen from that picture.

LM: Then you feel that certain subjects lend themselves to black and white.

s. Absolutely. I think you work with all the [...] at your hand to tell the story as well as you [...], and I think black and white is a tool. It's [...] ything's changing; black and white was one [...] time, now it's another thing. Now it can [...] ings to you artistically. It can mean some-body saying, "This is old-fashioned" subconsciously. If you're doing a period piece that might be a good subconscious thing to achieve. I don't think anybody's going to say—if you pull them into the story—"Aw, this is black and white" and walk out.

LM: It seems sometimes that certain color pictures are so desaturated as to be almost black and white.

HALL: Yeah.

LM: I didn't get that feeling in COOL HAND LUKE.

HALL: No, I hadn't gotten into that yet. What I usually do is make tests for my next picture, or tests about anything, on the picture I'm on, on the slates. The slates are mine, I can do anything I want to with them. It's before the scene begins, and I can overexpose it, underexpose it, throw filters on it, throw filters off it, and I can see what happens in the projection room. It doesn't cost anybody any money, and I've learned a lot, on ten or fifteen feet of film, while you get up to speed.

LM: You've worked with several directors who are just starting out; does that kind of relationship encourage you?

HALL: I like working with new directors, because they involve you more. They're running scared a little bit, and they involve you more creatively.

LM: Do you find them to be more daring in what they do?

HALL: Yes, I think so. I think new directors don't know what the mistakes can be, so they're willing to try just about anything. They demand a lot from you, and want a lot from you. Filmmakers like Richard Brooks have been through it all, they've seen it all; they've got a style that they like, and that's right for the picture.

LM: Here's the perfect example of appropriate use of black and white: IN COLD BLOOD.

HALL: Well, don't think the studio didn't try to get that in color. We were even starting to shoot, and Technicolor had desaturated a film for John Huston, REFLECTIONS IN A GOLDEN EYE. They had a reel of this film that they brought back to us, and they said, "You've got to shoot it this way." We tried it out, but it looked purple, and it wasn't very pleasing, so we just continued on. Richard Brooks felt that it was a black and white subject, and I felt that it was best done in black and white also. We got a lot of heat from the studio, but because Richard is a very strong man, he was able to overcome it, and do it in black and white. The reason we did it in Panavision was that first we were going to do it in 1.85. I said, "OK, I want it hard-matted," and the studio said no, and they spent a lot of money doing a paper on why: how other theaters will be showing it, and your film will be screwed up anyway. So Richard said, "Let's shoot it in Panavision and be done with it."

LM: But the *prints* were by Technicolor.

HALL: Well, that's because we prefer Technicolor to any other lab, although other people do very good work. It just depends on finding a group of people that know what you're after, and try for it, and I liked the way they handled things at Technicolor best.

LM: What about the lighting on a film like that? It was supposed to achieve a documentary look, wasn't it?

HALL: Yes. It was supposed to; it didn't always—some of it is slicker than it should be. We'd do it differently nowadays probably.

LM: How?

HALL: I don't know, maybe shoot the whole thing hand-held; not balancing so well . . .

LM: Deliberately not do such a good picture?

HALL: Yeah. It's pretty good, actually. I'd screw it up more now.

LM: Toward the goal of the picture, saying what it was trying to say.

HALL: Yeah, to make it—I don't know if that would make it more real or not.

LM: But is it supposed to be real, or merely giving that impression?

HALL: Well, it's not really real, is it? It's supposed to give you the impression. But you can certainly get caught up with the drama, and it should be fairly real to you. The photography should help the drama.

LM: Do you think the locations were a big asset to that film?

HALL: Yes . . . don't ask me why. They made us feel spooky. They should make *you* feel spooky, when you know that this is really the house . . . I don't know. But it sure made us feel spooky, and it seemed right to do it that way.

LM: Do you watch your own films?

HALL: Yes.

LM: Because you want to see the finished product, or because you want to learn from them?

HALL: I want to see the finished product. I want to see how it turned out.

LM: Do you learn from watching your own films?

HALL: Yeah; mostly what not to do. Usually *always* what not to do.

LM: Did you use a different approach to color than you had before on HELL IN THE PACIFIC?

HALL: I was experimenting for a picture that I hadn't agreed to do yet; I was experimenting with overexposure. I didn't do it on that picture, but I was experimenting with it on the slates, and on my next picture, which was WILLIE BOY, I started overexposing, and I wish I'd begun a long time before.

LM: It probably would have been effective in HELL IN THE PACIFIC.

HALL: Yes, it would have. It would have been terrific to overexpose the hell out of those jungles, and not use any lights at all. Overexposure just so you can see. It would have funked it up a lot. The trouble with overexposing is that it can look so beautiful—it's the same trouble with long lenses—it gives a beautiful quality to things. I saw a picture the other night that was overexposed, called AD-ALEN 31. It's absolutely exquisite, overexposed by two or three stops. It's *too* pretty . . . it's a little bit unreal.

LM: What kind of film would be appropriate for that, then?

HALL: A love story; it would work terrifically. I think he did the same thing with ELVIRA MADIGAN; I've never seen ELVIRA MADIGAN but I understand it's beautiful, with a lot of back-lit, overexposed stuff. I think that half of it, for one thing, is the light in Sweden; in fact, I'm certain that it is. You know, people used to talk about what English cameramen do. Hell, it's the *light*. Here we've got harsh sunlight to deal with most of the time, and it's much more difficult than dealing [in color] with soft, clouded skies. And you've got that low sun in Sweden, with cloudy conditions, and beautiful hazy soft things. It's not a matter of what you do, it's where you are, a lot of times.

LM: Just a point of interest: on HELL IN THE PACIFIC, did you shoot two endings?

HALL: No, we only shot one ending. The day before we were going to shoot the ending that we shot, we were going to shoot an ending which I had suggested to John Boorman, and he liked it. Then that night, Lee [Marvin] came to him with another ending, which he liked very much. The following day when we were shooting it, he came to me and he said, "We're not going to shoot that; we've got a terrific new ending." I said, "What? What is it?" He told it to me, and I said, "What's so terrific about that? Let's shoot a couple of them." He said no, so we shot it. This is the very end; I don't mean the part where they're getting drunk and all that—that was all planned. This was just the final denouement.

LM: Was there an ending in the original script?

HALL: Yes, but not anything like the present ending, or even leading up to the present ending. The ending in the script had them find two people there when they arrive, Japanese men, and they want to do Marvin in right away, but Mifune says no. So one day they hear gunfire on the other side of the island, and Mifune goes to see what it is; when he comes back, Marvin is lying in the compound, decapitated, and these two guys are sort of sheepishly grinning, knowing they had done something wrong, but kind of proud that they had killed the American. And Mifune, in his rage, grabs the sword and decapitates both of them. That was the ending in the script. The ending that I suggested—well, do you remember the confrontation on the beach, when each imagines the other kills him? I wanted to take the part where they get drunk, and maybe Marvin is reading *Life* magazine, or something like that, and Mifune wants to smoke, and he grabs a page from the magazine and rolls it up. Marvin says, "Hey, wait a minute. I haven't finished that page yet!" And what was a friendly thing all of a sudden ruptures into violence, and they're at each other. It's just like Mifune imagined Marvin would kill him. Marvin's knife is out, and he's got

Mifune around him, and it cuts to a close-up, and Mifune falls out of frame. Marvin is left there, and I wanted to see the change in Marvin's face to "Oh my God, what have I done?", freeze on that, and go out. That was what John liked, and we were going to shoot. Then Lee had this idea about how he's always been a guy who has to solve a problem by killing the bad guy, and that he was tired of that—could he solve it without killing? It seemed to John to be the real answer to the story, what he was trying to say: that even if we can't agree, or get along, we don't have to kill one another because of it—we can just go away and live separately. And I didn't appreciate it until after I'd shot it, and then I loved it, because it *is* the answer, as far as I'm concerned. That was what we tried to say, but because we had so little time to think about it, I think we botched it; we weren't clever enough in making that a satisfying ending. Which is just a matter of artistry. For one thing, I didn't know what I was doing; I didn't understand the concept. The last shot was Mifune walking away, and Lee putting on his tie, and getting ready to leave, or something. And nothing happens—but that's what John wanted to say.

LM: Of course, the final print that went out doesn't have that ending either.

HALL: I have no idea, because I haven't seen it.

LM: It was never released with your ending.

HALL: No? That's why—I'm into directing now—I won't direct a picture that I don't have final cut on.

LM: As I heard it, Boorman finished the picture to his satisfaction—

HALL: —I saw it that way—

LM: —and then went away on vacation. After he left, the producer decided he didn't like the ending, and tacked on footage of an explosion. So as it now stands, Marvin and Mifune are sitting in the house, and there's just the slightest indication of an argument brewing, when suddenly there is a series of explosions, and that's the end of the film.

HALL: See what I mean? See why you have to have final cut? Because what you believe in, and what you worked so hard to do . . . Imagine how Boorman feels, or Lee, who thought of it, and believed in it. It just kills you. That's why you've got to get final cut.

LM: Now we come to Richard Brooks again, with THE HAPPY ENDING, which I thought was more interesting photographically than practically any other way.

HALL: That makes me feel better than it would Richard Brooks. But I liked a lot of the things that I did in that picture photographically. It was a change of lighting style for me; I used soft light instead of hard light, mostly all umbrella lighting . . .

LM: What's that?

HALL: They're umbrellas which you shoot light into, and they reflect back. Very soft, it leaves no shadows. I used a lot of that kind of lighting. I worked very fast, didn't try to make anything look too good.

LM: The scene by the fireplace was lovely.

HALL: Well, that's sort of the old style. The only thing I didn't like about that picture, from my standpoint, was the fact that because Richard is the complete filmmaker, he doesn't always involve you in everything that I consider important for a cameraman. He didn't involve me in the art direction in that picture. He didn't have an art director; sometimes an art director will be able to help a cameraman—not always, but sometimes. If you *don't* have an art director, I feel the cameraman should certainly be involved in picking things that visually might obstruct the story somehow or other. Things like busy wallpaper, that kind of thing. That house that we shot in I hated, because of the wallpapers.

LM: Wasn't it difficult to shoot in an actual house, like that?

HALL: It was. It's difficult, but I like it. It's a challenge, and I think it keeps you from being slick.

LM: Many cameramen today are frustrated because they aren't called in to work on a picture until very late in preparation. What has been your experience?

HALL: I'm usually—I insist, really—on being on for quite a bit beforehand. I believe that it benefits the director for me to be around him, to know what he's trying for—just to be with him when you're not under the pressure of the gun, so that I can more clearly reflect what he actually wants when it comes time to do it. And he can have the benefit of your ideas beforehand, rather than when you're actually doing it. Because if he's got too much to think about at that time, with actors, and all of that kind of thing, and suddenly you start arguing with him about something, he doesn't need it.

LM: Do you think the formula for a good picture is preparation?

HALL: Yes, I think it definitely is. All the ones that look unprepared were usually prepared the hell out of. It's very difficult to get an "unprepared" picture that works by going out unprepared.

LM: TELL THEM WILLIE BOY IS HERE is the first picture you did, then, with desaturated color.

HALL: Well, I did some desaturation for day-for-night effects in HELL IN THE PACIFIC, took the color out and made it more or less black and white. They didn't quite come up to my expectations, but that's because nobody asks you to come in and take charge of that aspect in order to follow through. If somebody would insist, "I wouldn't get a print of this picture unless the cameraman was here to give us his views on it"—that's what the producer should do, but he just wants to get you off the payroll as quickly as possible. Even if you don't want to charge anything, by that time the editor feels it's his, and that kind of thing, and so a concept you might had is not executed the way you wanted it to. Nobody ever prints a day-for-night shot correctly for me. They want to see too much, and they always wreck it. Then you have the argument about "If you can't see it, what good is it? If you can't see Paul Newman, it could be just anybody there." And I say, "No, it's not, because you *know* it's Paul Newman, you know it's not Charlie Bronson all of a sudden because it's dark." And if the darkness helps tell

the story, why does it have to be seen so well? Anyway, I did some desaturation for the day-for-night stuff there. Then on WILLIE BOY I also did desaturation for the day-for-night . . .

LM: How do you accomplish that?

HALL: They take the color out of it, in varying degrees. It's a filter process, so they can control the amount of red, yellow, and blue that goes into it, and they can make a black and white of the color print. Then they run that with it, and they can take out the various colors and bring in the black and white and control it all electronically, until you get what you think looks like night, which hopefully is something which is monochromatic.

LM: Did you use it throughout the picture?

HALL: No, just in the day-for-night sequences. The rest of the picture, the exteriors are overexposed, which I really like, and I'll probably do that for all my exteriors from now on, for a while, until I find something else to do. It gets rid of that sickly color look, which I hate. I hate color, really, because it has so many more chances to go wrong than black and white. Black and white doesn't have any chance to go wrong.

LM: What about exterior lighting, especially in a desert locale such as you had on WILLIE BOY?

HALL: Everybody's talking about going out to do a picture without any lights, and I'm going to do it too. That's what I want to do, someday.

LM: But what kind of lights are necessary in the desert?

HALL: You need to put light where there isn't light.

LM: In the desert? It seems to me that other than reflectors . . .

HALL: Well, reflectors are very tough to use on the desert. Often there is a lot of wind, and you can't use reflectors in the wind. They bounce all over the place—you need a person to hold each one, and it's not worth it. It's better to have a light. So you use lights to fill in shadows, and things like that.

LM: And now we come to your Academy Award winning endeavor . . .

HALL: That was the biggest surprise in the world. I wanted it earlier!

LM: Did you feel another picture was more deserving prior to this?

HALL: I thought I had it on IN COLD BLOOD, but they knocked me out of the box, they took the category away. It was the only black and white nominated that year. I probably would have voted for another film; I probably would have voted for BATTLE OF ALGIERS that year. Anyway . . . it's nice to have one of those things. I like it, I like the way it looks on the mantel. I don't know what it means, but it's nice.

LM: The color in BUTCH CASSIDY is very rich.

HALL: Very rich, that's the way Fox does it, and DeLuxe too. I overexposed a lot of that picture, and they just brought it back again. But I didn't think that it needed to be completely desaturated in that picture. The treatment of it was not serious, and therefore there was no need to be dramatic in your lighting and such.

LM: What about the practical as well as artistic problems in showing the tracking party?

HALL: That was done with radios. It's very simple; you take a guy, and send him to a plateau a mile away and get a long lens on.

LM: In some cases the timing was so perfect as to be incredible—one shot where Newman and Redford are coming over the rocks, just before they leap, and the posse is seen off in the distance through a little clearing at the exact split second they've left . . .

HALL: It takes good operating; I operated that one myself. I'm a good operator, and I love to do it.

LM: Was it a deliberate decision not to show the posse too clearly?

HALL: A deliberate decision.

LM: A directorial decision?

HALL: Yes.

LM: Do you often operate for yourself?

HALL: Yes. I like to do it whenever I can; whenever I want to, I do it. Whenever it's something that I feel is

going to be a hassle to describe—when there's a zoom lens, and not a specific shot in mind, because you create by opening that lens or closing that lens. Why leave it up to the operator?

LM: Which is not how you felt when you were an operator.

HALL: No, but I was doing all that stuff myself, because nobody else wanted to do it, and I was good at it, and I continued to do it afterwards.

LM: Now that you're in the other position, you know how much the operator can affect your work, so you do it yourself.

HALL: Yes. I do it myself. You see, the old-timers all started as their own operators, and then the union system came in and wanted to have more jobs—it became more complex, too—so they started having operators and assistants. Then they had the finder, and it became a guess as to what you were going to get, and I think it turned people off of operating. And then, all of a sudden, came the reflex camera. Well, you can see exactly what you're getting in there, and you can do things on the spur of the moment which you can't tell somebody to do. And you realize that if you let the operator do it, he's being the creative person.

LM: And doesn't it give you more satisfaction, knowing that you're doing it yourself?

Hall at work on TELL THEM WILLIE BOY IS HERE (1969).

HALL: Yes ... I just enjoy the job. That's just the most fun job, operating; you see the movie before anybody else does. It's a kick.

LM: I read that you were dissatisfied with the night scenes in BUTCH CASSIDY.

HALL: Oh, they're awful—so much light, shadows all over the place.

LM: Which ones in particular?

HALL: The bicycle one, where the guy is selling them, and they're up on the balcony, with people in the street.

LM: Wouldn't it be indistinguishable with much less light?

HALL: I'll tell you how you know it: when you look at somebody else's work and you see how little light he used. I'll tell you whose night stuff I loved after I'd seen it— BONNIE AND CLYDE. You remember the shots of the car driving along at night? No car—just two headlights. But people have a tendency to light up too much at night, and I'm one of the ones that has that tendency. I keep fighting it, because night is not that way to me. I don't see a lot of light at night.

LM: But you still have to see what's going on in the film, don't you?

HALL: If it were a picture all at night, you might use a little different tactic, but it's not important to see some things. The reason people want to see them is because they're paying for them, and they feel that if they don't, they've been cheated. But artistically speaking, it's not important to see them. You could even turn off the picture and just hear the sound and still get the story, for short periods of time.

LM: Now you're turning to directing, aren't you?

HALL: Yes, if I can ever get a chance to do it. I found something I want to direct. I've had many chances, but I've never found anything I wanted to say, or that it was something I just had to do. When somebody offered me the book *The Wild Palms* to read, and I read it, it was something I *had* to do. I said I'd direct it, and Katharine [Ross] said, "Why don't you write it, too?" I said, "Oh, I've never written anything really." She said, "If you think you can direct it, why can't you write it?" I said, "OK, I'll try it, if you'll help me." So we agreed to do it, and it took us a long time, and we hated every minute of it, and then missed it as soon as we'd stopped. But it's something really worthwhile, I think. We wrote a script, and then we got into a hassle with the producers, because I wanted creative control, and final cut, and they were unwilling to try to raise the money for it with those demands. So now I'm going to try to produce it myself, but I don't know if I can raise the money.

LM: Do you think as a director you'll be able to work with another cinematographer?

HALL: Yes, but I may not want to on this one. I may want to shoot it myself. It's a love story, just two people, so it's easy enough to do. When it gets complex, with logistics, and this and that to work out, I'd want a cameraman, so I wouldn't have to think about it. But in an intimate story, I might see something, and I'd want to tell a story with that camera. I still may have a cameraman there for when I don't feel like doing it.

LM: Is there one film you've made that gives you special satisfaction?

HALL: I'm proud of them all. I'm not very proud of DIVORCE AMERICAN STYLE, but I'm proud of all the rest of them. Not that I think they're very good films. I haven't done my good film yet. I think IN COLD BLOOD is a good film. THE PROFESSIONALS is a good film. HELL IN THE PACIFIC is one of the best experiences I've ever had on a film, the relationship with the director . . . I really like John Boorman, we got along well, and really worked well together. He's a really talented guy; he involves you, and I like the way he works. There was a lot of improvising on that picture. But it's preparation that gives you the opportunity to do it that way; the script is a point of departure.

LM: Finally, you represent the younger breed of cinematographers in the business. As such, do you feel that you're following the same tradition that they have carried on for the past fifty years?

HALL: I think I've contributed to the evolvement of techniques as they are now, along with everybody else who's been working in the business. I don't think I'm unique in any sense other than I fought a lot of battles that people don't have to fight any more; but there are always new battles to fight. I look for a golden age of cinema to come to pass very soon, when they have the little cassette movies that you stick into a machine which shoots it up on the wall. Films won't have any definite length; there won't be hour films or two-hour films. There will be hour films, and ten-minute films, and five-minute films, however long it takes to tell that story. It won't have to be any more that you have to make up a program of X amount of time which is worth the price you have to pay to watch it in a theater. Because you'll go down and buy a five-minute film, which may cost a dollar; CATCH-22 may cost $10 to buy. There will be all different lengths. There will be hundreds of thousands of films, just a very few good ones, and a lot of bad ones.

LM: You, of course, will be making the good ones.

HALL (laughing): I don't know about that.

THE FILMS OF CONRAD HALL

Even though Conrad Hall only started in the film business in the 1950s, it is unlikely that a complete list of his credits could be compiled. As explained in his interview, he and his partners shot footage for sundry filmmakers, professional, industrial, for theaters, television, etc. Later, Hall worked as operative cameraman and assistant cameraman on a variety of features. He shot footage for Walt Disney's true-life features THE LIVING DESERT and ISLANDS OF THE SEA, and with his filmmaking partners photographed a low-budget feature film in the 1950s, RUNNING TARGET (UA, 1956; based on "My Brother Down There"). He became an official director of photography in television, filming two series, STONEY BURKE and THE OUTER LIMITS. Following is a list of his official feature-film credits since becoming a director of photography.

1. THE WILD SEED—Universal 1965—Brian G. Hutton
2. SABOTEUR: CODE NAME MORITURI—20th Century Fox 1965—Bernhard Wicki—Color
3. INCUBUS—Leslie Stevens 1966—Leslie Stevens
4. HARPER—Warner Brothers 1966—Jack Smight—Color
5. THE PROFESSIONALS—Columbia 1966—Richard Brooks—Color, Panavision
6. DIVORCE AMERICAN STYLE—Columbia 1967—Bud Yorkin—Color
7. COOL HAND LUKE—Warner Brothers 1967—Stuart Rosenberg—Color, Panavision
8. IN COLD BLOOD—Columbia 1967—Richard Brooks—Panavision
9. HELL IN THE PACIFIC—Cinerama 1968—John Boorman—Color, Panavision
10. THE HAPPY ENDING—UA 1969—Richard Brooks—Color, Panavision
11. TELL THEM WILLIE BOY IS HERE—Universal 1969—Abraham Polonsky—Color, Panavision
12. BUTCH CASSIDY AND THE SUNDANCE KID—20th Century Fox 1969—George Roy Hill—Color, Panavision
13. FAT CITY—Columbia 1972—John Huston—Color
14. ELECTRA GLIDE IN BLUE—UA 1973—James William Guercio—Color, Panavision
15. CATCH MY SOUL—Cinerama 1974—Patrick McGoohan—Color
16. SMILE—UA 1975—Michael Ritchie—Color
17. THE DAY OF THE LOCUST—Paramount 1975—John Schlesinger—Color, Panavision
18. MARATHON MAN—Paramount 1976—John Schlesinger—Color

ACADEMY AWARDS FOR CINEMATOGRAPHY 1927-1977

Following is a listing of the nominees, and winners, of the Academy Award for Best Cinematography since the award's inception in 1927. The question of separate awards for color and black and white cinematography caused some uncomfortable variances in voting procedure in recent years, before it was decided to eliminate the black and white category entirely. Whatever arguments are to be made for or against the Academy Awards, the validity of the cinematography category is maintained by the fact that the yearly nominations have always been selected by cinematographers themselves. Thus, what follows is a valuable honor roll of achievements over the years, not merely a popularity contest. An asterisk denotes the winner each year.

1927/28
THE DEVIL DANCER (George Barnes)
DRUMS OF LOVE (Karl Struss)
MAGIC FLAME (George Barnes)
MY BEST GIRL (Charles Rosher)
SADIE THOMPSON (George Barnes)
*SUNRISE (Charles Rosher and Karl Struss)
THE TEMPEST (Charles Rosher)

1928/29
THE DIVINE LADY (John Seitz)
FOUR DEVILS (Ernest Palmer)
IN OLD ARIZONA (Arthur Edeson)
OUR DANCING DAUGHTERS (George Barnes)
STREET ANGEL (Ernest Palmer)
*WHITE SHADOWS IN THE SOUTH SEAS (Clyde DeVinna)

1929/30
ALL QUIET ON THE WESTERN FRONT (Arthur Edeson)
ANNA CHRISTIE (William Daniels)
HELL'S ANGELS (Gaetano "Tony" Gaudio and Harry Perry)
THE LOVE PARADE (Victor Milner)
*WITH BYRD AT THE SOUTH POLE (Joseph T. Rucker and Willard Van der Veer)

1930/31
CIMARRON (Edward Cronjager)
MOROCCO (Lee Garmes)
THE RIGHT TO LOVE (Charles B. Lang, Jr.)
SVENGALI (Barney McGill)
*TABU (Floyd Crosby)

1931/32
ARROWSMITH (Ray June)
DR. JEKYLL AND MR. HYDE (Karl Struss)
*SHANGHAI EXPRESS (Lee Garmes)

1932/33
*A FAREWELL TO ARMS (Charles B. Lang, Jr.)
REUNION IN VIENNA (George Folsey)
SIGN OF THE CROSS (Karl Struss)

1934
AFFAIRS OF CELLINI (Charles Rosher)
*CLEOPATRA (Victor Milner)
OPERATOR 13 (George Folsey)

1935
BARBARY COAST (Ray June)
THE CRUSADES (Victor Milner)
LES MISÉRABLES (Gregg Toland)
*A MIDSUMMER NIGHT'S DREAM (Hal Mohr)

1936
*ANTHONY ADVERSE (Tony Gaudio)
THE GENERAL DIED AT DAWN (Victor Milner)
THE GORGEOUS HUSSY (George Folsey)

1937
DEAD END (Gregg Toland)
*THE GOOD EARTH (Karl Freund)
WINGS OVER HONOLULU (Joseph Valentine)

1938
ALGIERS (James Wong Howe)
ARMY GIRL (Ernest Miller and Harry Wild)
THE BUCCANEER (Victor Milner)
*THE GREAT WALTZ (Joseph Ruttenberg)
JEZEBEL (Ernest Haller)
MAD ABOUT MUSIC (Joseph Valentine)
MERRILY WE LIVE (Norbert Brodine)
SUEZ (J. Peverell Marley)
VIVACIOUS LADY (Robert de Grasse)
YOU CAN'T TAKE IT WITH YOU (Joseph Walker)
THE YOUNG IN HEART (Leon Shamroy)

1939
Black and white:
STAGECOACH (Bert Glennon)
*WUTHERING HEIGHTS (Gregg Toland)

Color:
*GONE WITH THE WIND (Ernest Haller, Ray Rennahan)
THE PRIVATE LIVES OF ELIZABETH AND ESSEX (W. Howard Greene, Sol Polito)

1940
Black and white:
ABE LINCOLN IN ILLINOIS (James Wong Howe)
ALL THIS AND HEAVEN TOO (Ernest Haller)
ARISE MY LOVE (Charles B. Lang, Jr.)

BOOM TOWN (Harold Rosson)
FOREIGN CORRESPONDENT (Rudy Mate)
THE LETTER (Tony Gaudio)
THE LONG VOYAGE HOME (Gregg Toland)
*REBECCA (George Barnes)
SPRING PARADE (Joseph Valentine)
WATERLOO BRIDGE (Joseph Ruttenberg)

Color:
BITTERSWEET (Allen Davey, Oliver T. Marsh)
THE BLUE BIRD (Arthur Miller, Ray Rennahan)
DOWN ARGENTINE WAY (Leon Shamroy, Ray Rennahan)
NORTH WEST MOUNTED POLICE (W. Howard Greene, Victor Milner)
NORTHWEST PASSAGE (William V. Skall, Sidney Wagner)
*THE THIEF OF BAGDAD (George Perinal)

1941
Black and white:
THE CHOCOLATE SOLDIER (Karl Freund)
CITIZEN KANE (Gregg Toland)
DR. JEKYLL AND MR. HYDE (Joseph Ruttenberg)
HERE COMES MR. JORDAN (Joseph Walker)
HOLD BACK THE DAWN (Leo Tover)
*HOW GREEN WAS MY VALLEY (Arthur Miller)
SERGEANT YORK (Sol Polito)
SUN VALLEY SERENADE (Edward Cronjager)
SUNDOWN (Charles B. Lang, Jr.)
THAT HAMILTON WOMAN (Rudy Mate)

Color:
ALOMA OF THE SOUTH SEAS (Wilfred M. Cline, Karl Struss, William Snyder)
BILLY THE KID (William V. Skall, Leonard Smith)
*BLOOD AND SAND (Ernest Palmer, Ray Rennahan)
BLOSSOMS IN THE DUST (Karl Freund, W. Howard Greene)
DIVE BOMBER (Bert Glennon)
LOUISIANA PURCHASE (Harry Hallenberger, Ray Rennahan)

1942
Black and white:
KINGS ROW (James Wong Howe)
THE MAGNIFICENT AMBERSONS (Stanley Cortez)
*MRS. MINIVER (Joseph Ruttenberg)
MOONTIDE (Charles G. Clarke)
THE PIED PIPER (Edward Cronjager)
THE PRIDE OF THE YANKEES (Rudy Mate)
TAKE A LETTER, DARLING (John Mescall)
TALK OF THE TOWN (Ted Tetzlaff)
TEN GENTLEMEN FROM WEST POINT (Leon Shamroy)
THIS ABOVE ALL (Arthur Miller)

Color:
ARABIAN NIGHTS (W. Howard Greene, Milton Krasner, William V. Skall)
*THE BLACK SWAN (Leon Shamroy)
CAPTAINS OF THE CLOUDS (Sol Polito)
JUNGLE BOOK (Lee Garmes, W. Howard Greene)
REAP THE WILD WIND (Victor Milner, William V. Skall)
TO THE SHORES OF TRIPOLI (Edward Cronjager, William V. Skall)

1943
Black and white:
AIR FORCE (Elmer Dyer, James Wong Howe, Charles Marshall)

CASABLANCA (Arthur Edeson)
CORVETTE K-225 (Tony Gaudio)
FIVE GRAVES TO CAIRO (John Seitz)
THE HUMAN COMEDY (Harry Stradling)
MADAME CURIE (Joseph Ruttenberg)
THE NORTH STAR (James Wong Howe)
SAHARA (Rudy Mate)
SO PROUDLY WE HAIL (Charles B. Lang, Jr.)
*THE SONG OF BERNADETTE (Arthur Miller)

Color:
FOR WHOM THE BELL TOLLS (Ray Rennahan)
HEAVEN CAN WAIT (Edward Cronjager)
HELLO, FRISCO, HELLO (Charles G. Clarke and Allen M. Davey)
LASSIE COME HOME (Leonard Smith)
*THE PHANTOM OF THE OPERA (W. Howard Greene and Hal Mohr)
THOUSANDS CHEER (George Folsey)

1944
Black and white:
DOUBLE INDEMNITY (John Seitz)
DRAGON SEED (Sidney Wagner)
GASLIGHT (Joseph Ruttenberg)
GOING MY WAY (Lionel Lindon)
*LAURA (Joseph LaShelle)
LIFEBOAT (Glen MacWilliams)
SINCE YOU WENT AWAY (Stanley Cortez and Lee Garmes)
THIRTY SECONDS OVER TOKYO (Harold Rosson and Robert Surtees)
THE UNINVITED (Charles B. Lang, Jr.)
THE WHITE CLIFFS OF DOVER (George Folsey)

Color:
COVER GIRL (Allen M. Davey and Rudy Mate)
HOME IN INDIANA (Edward Cronjager)
KISMET (Charles Rosher)
LADY IN THE DARK (Ray Rennahan)
MEET ME IN ST. LOUIS (George Folsey)
*WILSON (Leon Shamroy)

1945
Black and white:
THE KEYS OF THE KINGDOM (Arthur Miller)
THE LOST WEEKEND (John Seitz)
MILDRED PIERCE (Ernest Haller)
*THE PICTURE OF DORIAN GRAY (Harry Stradling)
SPELLBOUND (George Barnes)

Color:
ANCHORS AWEIGH (Charles Boyle and Robert Planck)
*LEAVE HER TO HEAVEN (Leon Shamroy)
NATIONAL VELVET (Leonard Smith)
A SONG TO REMEMBER (Allen M. Davey and Tony Gaudio)
SPANISH MAIN (George Barnes)

1946
Black and white:
*ANNA AND THE KING OF SIAM (Arthur Miller)
THE GREEN YEARS (George Folsey)

Color:
THE JOLSON STORY (Joseph Walker)
*THE YEARLING (Arthur Arling, Leonard Smith, and Charles Rosher)

1947
Black and white:
THE GHOST AND MRS. MUIR (Charles B. Lang, Jr.)
*GREAT EXPECTATIONS (Guy Green)
GREEN DOLPHIN STREET (George Folsey)

Color:
*BLACK NARCISSUS (Jack Cardiff)
LIFE WITH FATHER (J. Peverell Marley and William V. Skall)
MOTHER WORE TIGHTS (Harry Jackson)

1948
Black and white:
A FOREIGN AFFAIR (Charles B. Lang, Jr.)
I REMEMBER MAMA (Nicholas Musuraca)
JOHNNY BELINDA (Ted McCord)
*THE NAKED CITY (William Daniels)
PORTRAIT OF JENNIE (Joseph August)

Color:
GREEN GRASS OF WYOMING (Charles G. Clarke)
*JOAN OF ARC (Joseph Valentine, William V. Skall, and Winton Hoch)
THE LOVES OF CARMEN (William Snyder)
THE THREE MUSKETEERS (Robert Planck)

1949
Black and white:
*BATTLEGROUND (Paul C. Vogel)
CHAMPION (Franz Planer)
COME TO THE STABLE (Joseph LaShelle)
THE HEIRESS (Leo Tover)
PRINCE OF FOXES (Leon Shamroy)

Color:
THE BARKLEYS OF BROADWAY (Harry Stradling)
JOLSON SINGS AGAIN (William Snyder)
LITTLE WOMEN (Robert Planck and Charles Schoenbaum)
SAND (Charles G. Clarke)
*SHE WORE A YELLOW RIBBON (Winton Hoch)

1950
Black and white:
ALL ABOUT EVE (Milton Krasner)
THE ASPHALT JUNGLE (Harold Rosson)
THE FURIES (Victor Milner)
SUNSET BOULEVARD (John Seitz)
*THE THIRD MAN (Robert Krasker)

Color:
ANNIE GET YOUR GUN (Charles Rosher)
BROKEN ARROW (Ernest Palmer)
THE FLAME AND THE ARROW (Ernest Haller)
*KING SOLOMON'S MINES (Robert Surtees)
SAMSON AND DELILAH (George Barnes)

1951
Black and white:
DEATH OF A SALESMAN (Franz Planer)
THE FROGMEN (Norbert Brodine)
*A PLACE IN THE SUN (William C. Mellor)
STRANGERS ON A TRAIN (Robert Burks)
A STREETCAR NAMED DESIRE (Harry Stradling)

Color:
*AN AMERICAN IN PARIS (Alfred Gilks and John Alton)
DAVID AND BATHSHEBA (Leon Shamroy)

QUO VADIS (Robert Surtees and William V. Skall)
SHOWBOAT (Charles Rosher)
WHEN WORLDS COLLIDE (John Seitz and W. Howard Greene)

1952
Black and white:
*THE BAD AND THE BEAUTIFUL (Robert Surtees)
THE BIG SKY (Russell Harlan)
MY COUSIN RACHEL (Joseph LaShelle)
NAVAJO (Virgil E. Miller)
SUDDEN FEAR (Charles B. Lang, Jr.)

Color:
HANS CHRISTIAN ANDERSEN (Harry Stradling)
IVANHOE (F. A. Young)
MILLION DOLLAR MERMAID (George Folsey)
*THE QUIET MAN (Winton Hoch and Archie Stout)
THE SNOWS OF KILIMANJARO (Leon Shamroy)

1953
Black and white:
THE FOURPOSTER (Hal Mohr)
*FROM HERE TO ETERNITY (Burnett Guffey)
JULIUS CAESAR (Joseph Ruttenberg)
MARTIN LUTHER (Joseph C. Brun)
ROMAN HOLIDAY (Frank Planer and Henry Alekan)

Color:
ALL THE BROTHERS WERE VALIANT (George Folsey)
BENEATH THE TWELVE MILE REEF (Edward Cronjager)
LILI (Robert Planck)
THE ROBE (Leon Shamroy)
*SHANE (Loyal Griggs)

1954
Black and white:
THE COUNTRY GIRL (John F. Warren)
EXECUTIVE SUITE (George Folsey)
*ON THE WATERFRONT (Boris Kaufman)
ROGUE COP (John Seitz)
SABRINA (Charles B. Lang, Jr.)

Color:
THE EGYPTIAN (Leon Shamroy)
REAR WINDOW (Robert Burks)
SEVEN BRIDES FOR SEVEN BROTHERS (George Folsey)
THE SILVER CHALICE (William V. Skall)
*THREE COINS IN THE FOUNTAIN (Milton Krasner)

1955
Black and white:
BLACKBOARD JUNGLE (Russell Harlan)
I'LL CRY TOMORROW (Arthur E. Arling)
MARTY (Joseph LaShelle)
QUEEN BEE (Charles B. Lang, Jr.)
*THE ROSE TATTOO (James Wong Howe)

Color:
GUYS AND DOLLS (Harry Stradling)
LOVE IS A MANY-SPLENDORED THING (Leon Shamroy)
A MAN CALLED PETER (Harold Lipstein)
OKLAHOMA! (Robert Surtees)
*TO CATCH A THIEF (Robert Burks)

1956
Black and white:
BABY DOLL (Boris Kaufman)
THE BAD SEED (Harold Rosson)

THE HARDER THEY FALL (Burnett Guffey)
*SOMEBODY UP THERE LIKES ME (Joseph Ruttenberg)
STAGECOACH TO FURY (Walter Strenge)

Color:
*AROUND THE WORLD IN 80 DAYS (Lionel Lindon)
THE EDDY DUCHIN STORY (Harry Stradling)
THE KING AND I (Leon Shamroy)
THE TEN COMMANDMENTS (Loyal Griggs)
WAR AND PEACE (Jack Cardiff)

1957
One award given:
AN AFFAIR TO REMEMBER (Milton Krasner)
*THE BRIDGE ON THE RIVER KWAI (Jack Hildyard)
FUNNY FACE (Ray June)
PEYTON PLACE (William C. Mellor)
SAYONARA (Ellsworth Fredericks)

1958
Black and white:
*THE DEFIANT ONES (Sam Leavitt)
DESIRE UNDER THE ELMS (Daniel L. Fapp)
I WANT TO LIVE! (Lionel Lindon)
SEPARATE TABLES (Charles B. Lang, Jr.)
THE YOUNG LIONS (Joe MacDonald)

Color:
AUNTIE MAME (Harry Stradling)
CAT ON A HOT TIN ROOF (William Daniels)
*GIGI (Joseph Ruttenberg)
THE OLD MAN AND THE SEA (James Wong Howe)
SOUTH PACIFIC (Leon Shamroy)

1959
Black and white:
ANATOMY OF A MURDER (Sam Leavitt)
CAREER (Joseph LaShelle)
*THE DIARY OF ANNE FRANK (William C. Mellor)
SOME LIKE IT HOT (Charles B. Lang, Jr.)
THE YOUNG PHILADELPHIANS (Harry Stradling)

Color:
*BEN HUR (Robert Surtees)
THE BIG FISHERMAN (Lee Garmes)
THE FIVE PENNIES (Daniel L. Fapp)
THE NUN'S STORY (Franz Planer)
PORGY AND BESS (Leon Shamroy)

1960
Black and white:
THE APARTMENT (Joseph LaShelle)
THE FACTS OF LIFE (Charles B. Lang, Jr.)
INHERIT THE WIND (Ernest Laszlo)
PSYCHO (John S. Russell)
*SONS AND LOVERS (Freddie Francis)

Color:
THE ALAMO (William H. Clothier)
BUTTERFIELD 8 (Joseph Ruttenberg and Charles Harten)
EXODUS (Sam Leavitt)
PEPE (Joe MacDonald)
*SPARTACUS (Russell Metty)

1961
Black and white:
THE ABSENT-MINDED PROFESSOR (Edward Coleman)

THE CHILDREN'S HOUR (Franz Planer)
*THE HUSTLER (Eugene Shuftan)
JUDGMENT AT NUREMBERG (Ernest Laszlo)
ONE, TWO, THREE (Daniel L. Fapp)

Color:
FANNY (Jack Cardiff)
FLOWER DRUM SONG (Russell Metty)
A MAJORITY OF ONE (Harry Stradling)
ONE-EYED JACKS (Charles B. Lang, Jr.)
*WEST SIDE STORY (Daniel L. Fapp)

1962
Black and white:
THE BIRDMAN OF ALCATRAZ (Burnett Guffey)
*THE LONGEST DAY (Jean Bourgoin, Henri Persin, Walter Wottitz)
TO KILL A MOCKINGBIRD (Russell Harlan)
TWO FOR THE SEESAW (Ted McCord)
WHATEVER HAPPENED TO BABY JANE (Ernest Haller)

Color:
GYPSY (Harry Stradling)
HATARI! (Russell Harlan)
*LAWRENCE OF ARABIA (F. A. Young)
MUTINY ON THE BOUNTY (Robert Surtees)
THE WONDERFUL WORLD OF THE BROTHERS GRIMM (Paul C. Vogel)

1963
Black and white:
THE BALCONY (George Folsey)
THE CARETAKERS (Lucien Ballard)
*HUD (James Wong Howe)
LILIES OF THE FIELD (Ernest Haller)
LOVE WITH THE PROPER STRANGER (Milton Krasner)

Color:
THE CARDINAL (Leon Shamroy)
*CLEOPATRA (Leon Shamroy)
HOW THE WEST WAS WON (William Daniels, Milton Krasner, Charles B. Lang, Jr., Joseph LaShelle)
IRMA LA DOUCE (Joseph LaShelle)
IT'S A MAD MAD MAD MAD WORLD (Ernest Laszlo)

1964
Black and white:
THE AMERICANIZATION OF EMILY (Philip H. Lathrop)
FATE IS THE HUNTER (Milton Krasner)
HUSH . . . HUSH, SWEET CHARLOTTE (Joseph Biroc)
THE NIGHT OF THE IGUANA (Gabriel Figueroa)
*ZORBA THE GREEK (Walter Lassally)

Color:
BECKET (Geoffrey Unsworth)
CHEYENNE AUTUMN (William H. Clothier)
MARY POPPINS (Edward Coleman)
*MY FAIR LADY (Harry Stradling)
THE UNSINKABLE MOLLY BROWN (Daniel L. Fapp)

1965
Black and white:
IN HARM'S WAY (Loyal Griggs)
KING RAT (Burnett Guffey)
MORITURI (Conrad Hall)
A PATCH OF BLUE (Robert Burks)
*SHIP OF FOOLS (Ernest Laszlo)

Color:
THE AGONY AND THE ECSTASY (Leon Shamroy)

*DR. ZHIVAGO (Freddie Young)
THE GREAT RACE (Russell Harlan)
THE GREATEST STORY EVER TOLD (William C. Mellor and Loyal Griggs)
THE SOUND OF MUSIC (Ted McCord)

1966
Black and white:
THE FORTUNE COOKIE (Joseph LaShelle)
GEORGY GIRL (Ken Higgins)
IS PARIS BURNING? (Marcel Grignon)
SECONDS (James Wong Howe)
*WHO'S AFRAID OF VIRGINIA WOOLF (Haskell Wexler)

Color:
FANTASTIC VOYAGE (Ernest Laszlo)
HAWAII (Russell Harlan)
*A MAN FOR ALL SEASONS (Ted Moore)
THE PROFESSIONALS (Conrad Hall)
THE SAND PEBBLES (Joseph MacDonald)

1967
*BONNIE AND CLYDE (Burnett Guffey)
CAMELOT (Richard H. Kline)
DR. DOLITTLE (Robert Surtees)
THE GRADUATE (Robert Surtees)
IN COLD BLOOD (Conrad Hall)

1968
FUNNY GIRL (Harry Stradling)
ICE STATION ZEBRA (Daniel L. Fapp)
OLIVER! (Oswald Morris)
*ROMEO AND JULIET (Pasqualino De Santis)
STAR! (Ernest Laszlo)

1969
ANNE OF THE THOUSAND DAYS (Arthur Ibbetson)
BOB AND CAROL AND TED AND ALICE (Charles B. Lang, Jr.)
*BUTCH CASSIDY AND THE SUNDANCE KID (Conrad Hall)
HELLO DOLLY! (Harry Stradling)
MAROONED (Daniel L. Fapp)

1970
AIRPORT (Ernest Laszlo)
PATTON (Fred Koenekamp)
*RYAN'S DAUGHTER (F. A. Young)
TORA TORA TORA (Charles F. Wheeler, Sinsaku Humeda, Masamichi Satoh, Osami Furuya)
WOMEN IN LOVE (Billy Williams)

1971
*FIDDLER ON THE ROOF (Oswald Morris)
THE FRENCH CONNECTION (Owen Roizman)
THE LAST PICTURE SHOW (Robert Surtees)
NICHOLAS AND ALEXANDRA (F. A. Young)
SUMMER OF '42 (Robert Surtees)

1972
BUTTERFLIES ARE FREE (Charles B. Lang)
*CABARET (Geoffrey Unsworth)
THE POSEIDON ADVENTURE (Harold E. Stine)
1776 (Harry Stradling Jr.)
TRAVELS WITH MY AUNT (Douglas Slocombe)

1973
*CRIES AND WHISPERS (Sven Nykvist)
THE EXORCIST (Owen Roizman)
JONATHAN LIVINGSTON SEAGULL (Jack Couffer)
THE STING (Robert Surtees)
THE WAY WE WERE (Harry Stradling Jr.)

1974
CHINATOWN (John A. Alonzo)
EARTHQUAKE (Philip Lathrop)
LENNY (Bruce Surtees)
MURDER ON THE ORIENT EXPRESS (Geoffrey Unsworth)
*THE TOWERING INFERNO (Fred Koenekamp and Joseph Biroc)

1975
*BARRY LYNDON (John Alcott)
THE DAY OF THE LOCUST (Conrad Hall)
FUNNY LADY (James Wong Howe)
THE HINDENBURG (Robert Surtees)
ONE FLEW OVER THE CUCKOO'S NEST (Haskell Wexler)

1976
*BOUND FOR GLORY (Haskell Wexler)
KING KONG (Richard H. Kline)
LOGAN'S RUN (Ernest Laszlo)
NETWORK (Owen Roizman)
A STAR IS BORN (Robert Surtees)

1977
*CLOSE ENCOUNTERS OF THE THIRD KIND (Vilmos Zsigmond)
ISLAND IN THE STREAM (Fred J. Koenekamp)
JULIA (Douglas Slocombe)
LOOKING FOR MR. GOODBAR (William A. Fraker)
THE TURNING POINT (Robert Surtees)

INDEX

(Numbers in italics refer to photographs)